iPod® & iTunes® For Dummies, 3rd Edition

Cheat Sheet

iTunes Keyboard Shortcuts

Function	Mac Shortcut	
Play the selected song or video from beginning	Return	
Play song or video after pausing	Space bar	
Pause playing the song or video	Space bar	
Play the next song or video	→	
Play the previous song or video	←	←
Increase the volume	⌘+↑	Ctrl+↑ or Ctrl++
Decrease the volume	⌘+↓	Ctrl+↓ or Ctrl+−
Mute the volume	⌘+Option+↓ or ⌘+Option+↑	Ctrl+Alt+↓ or Ctrl+Alt+↑
Eject the CD	⌘+E	Ctrl+E
Open the Song info window	⌘+I	Ctrl+I
Show currently playing song or video	⌘+L	Ctrl+L
Create a smart playlist	Option++	Shift++
Shrink to mini-player (Windows)	(not applicable)	Ctrl+M
Minimize to Dock (Mac)	⌘+M	(not applicable)
Display visuals full-screen	⌘+F	Ctrl+F
Go to the next page in iTunes Music Store	⌘+]	Ctrl+]
Go to the previous page in iTunes Music Store	⌘+[	Ctrl+[

D0764490

iPod Shortcuts

- ✔ **Prevent the iPod from automatically updating:** Press ⌘+Option when connecting to Mac, or press Ctrl+Alt when connecting to a Windows PC.

- ✔ **Reset first-, second-, and third-generation iPods:** Toggle the Hold switch on and off, and then press the Menu and Play/Pause buttons simultaneously for five seconds. (For first- and second-generation iPods, you don't need to toggle the Hold switch, but it doesn't hurt.)

- ✔ **Reset fourth-generation iPod, iPod mini, iPod U2 Special Edition, and color-display iPod:** Toggle the Hold switch on and off, and then press the Menu and Select buttons simultaneously for six seconds.

- ✔ **Increase the volume:** Scroll clockwise while the song is playing. On an iPod shuffle, press the plus (+) button.

- ✔ **Decrease the volume:** Scroll counterclockwise while the song is playing. On an iPod shuffle, press the minus (-) button.

- ✔ **Fast-forward a song:** Press and hold the Next/Fast-Forward button.

- ✔ **Rewind a song:** Press and hold the Previous/Rewind button.

- ✔ **Turn the iPod off:** Press and hold the Play/Pause button.

- ✔ **Turn the iPod on:** Press any button with the Hold switch off.

- ✔ **Go to the previous menu:** Press the Menu button.

For Dummies: Bestselling Book Series for Beginners

iPod® & iTunes® For Dummies, 3rd Edition

iPod Shuffle Shortcuts

- **Turn the iPod shuffle on:** Slide the position switch to either the middle or bottom position.
- **Turn the iPod shuffle off:** Slide the position switch to the top position.
- **Play songs in an iPod shuffle randomly:** Slide the position switch to the bottom position.
- **Play songs in an iPod shuffle sequentially:** Slide the position switch to the middle position.

Twelve Soundtracks for Travel Experiences

- *The Joshua Tree,* **by U2:** Cruising Death Valley. (If you start the album at the entrance, you hear "In God's Country" at an appropriate spot — no matter how fast or slow you drive.)
- *Anthem of the Sun,* **by the Grateful Dead:** As you drive over the Golden Gate Bridge into San Francisco at sunset.
- **"Across the Great Divide," by The Band:** As you reach the crest of Donner Pass in the California Sierras on I-80, or the crest of Monarch Pass on the Continental Divide on U.S. 50 in Colorado. "Just grab your hat / And take that ride."
- *Magical Mystery Tour,* **by the Beatles:** Take the Number 77 double-decker out of Liverpool to Grove Street, Dale Street, Smithdown Road, and yes, Penny Lane (where you can walk to Strawberry Fields, if you have the directions in the Notes section of your iPod).
- **"All Aboard," by Muddy Waters (from the** *Fathers and Sons* **album):** Take a train heading north to Chicago, and then follow this tune with Junior Parker's "Mystery Train" and John Lee Hooker's "Peavine."
- **"East-West," by the Butterfield Blues Band; or "Eight Miles High," by the Byrds:** On a plane heading East or West.
- **The Beach Boys, Fleetwood Mac, and Jan and Dean:** Roller-skating on the Venice, California boardwalk.
- **"Walk on the Wild Side," by Lou Reed; and** *Paul's Boutique,* **by the Beastie Boys:** Jogging in Central Park.
- **"Wooden Ships," by Crosby, Stills, and Nash; anything by Jimmy Buffett; and "Sail Away," by Randy Newman:** Sailing around the Florida keys and up the coast into Charleston Bay.
- **"Feets Don't Fail Me Now," by Little Feat; and "I've Been Everywhere," by Johnny Cash:** Driving an 18-wheeler, rolling through northern New Jersey into New York City.
- **Miles Davis, John Coltrane, Herbie Hancock, John McLaughlin, and Sonny Rollins:** Hiding backstage in the Green Room at the Village Gate.
- **Pink Floyd:** Hopping around in an astronaut suit on the dark side of the moon.

For Dummies: Bestselling Book Series for Beginners

iPod® & iTunes®
FOR
DUMMIES®
3RD EDITION

by Tony Bove and Cheryl Rhodes

WILEY

Wiley Publishing, Inc.

iPod® & iTunes® For Dummies; 3rd Edition

Published by
Wiley Publishing, Inc.
111 River Street
Hoboken, NJ 07030-5774

Copyright © 2005 by Wiley Publishing, Inc., Indianapolis, Indiana

Published by Wiley Publishing, Inc., Indianapolis, Indiana

Published simultaneously in Canada

For general information on our other products and services or to obtain technical support, please contact our Customer Care Department within the U.S. at 800-762-2974, outside the U.S. at 317-572-3993, or fax 317-572-4002.

Wiley also publishes its books in a variety of electronic formats. Some content that appears in print may not be available in electronic books.

Library of Congress Control Number: 2005927619

ISBN-13: 978-0-471-74739-0

ISBN-10: 0-471-74739-4

Manufactured in the United States of America

10 9 8 7 6 5 4 3

3O/SR/QZ/QV/IN

WILEY

About the Authors

Tony Bove and **Cheryl Rhodes** have kicked around the computer industry for decades, editing the influential *Inside Report on New Media* newsletter and writing for weekly and monthly magazines, including *Computer Currents, NeXTWORLD, The Chicago Tribune* Sunday Technology Section, and *NewMedia*. They also co-founded and edited *Desktop Publishing/Publish* magazine.

Tony and Cheryl have written over a dozen books on computing, desktop publishing, and multimedia, including *iLife All-in-One Desk Reference For Dummies* (Wiley), *The Art of Desktop Publishing* (Bantam), and a series of books about Macromedia Director, Adobe Illustrator, and PageMaker. Tony has also worked as a director of enterprise marketing for a large software company, and as a communications director and technical publications manager. Cheryl recently founded and served as director of a charter school and has worked as a professional courseware designer and an instructor in computer courses at elementary and high schools.

Tracing the personal computer revolution back to the Sixties counterculture, Tony and Cheryl produced a CD-ROM interactive documentary in 1996, *Haight-Ashbury in the Sixties* (featuring music from the Grateful Dead, Janis Joplin, and the Jefferson Airplane). They also developed the Rockument music site, www.rockument.com, with commentary and radio programs focused on rock music history. As a founding member of the Flying Other Brothers (www.flyingotherbros.com), Tony has performed with Hall-of-Fame rock musicians and uses his iPod to store extensive concert recordings.

Dedication

This book is dedicated to John Paul Bove and James Eric Bove, both of whom contributed tips and spent considerable time testing iPods while turning a vacation into a book project. They have earned their own iPods.

Authors' Acknowledgments

John Paul Bove contributed technical expertise and writing for this edition, and dedicated his Windows PC for testing versions of iTunes and iPods. He certainly earned his new laptop.

We want to thank Rich Tennant for his wonderful cartoons. We also want to thank our Wiley project editor Tonya Maddox Cupp, and Editorial Manager Carol Sheehan, for ongoing assistance that made our job so much easier. A book this timely places a considerable burden on a publisher's production team, and we thank the production crew at Wiley for diligence beyond the call of reason.

We owe thanks and a happy hour or three to Carole McLendon at Waterside, our agent. And we have acquisitions editor Bob Woerner at Wiley to thank for coming up with the idea for this book and helping us to become professional dummies — that is, dummy authors.

Finally, our heartfelt thanks to members of the Flying Other Brothers (Pete Sears, Barry Sless, Jimmy Sanchez, Bill Bennett, Bert Keely, TBone, and Roger and Ann McNamee) for the music that inspired us while writing this book.

Publisher's Acknowledgments

We're proud of this book; please send us your comments through our online registration form located at www.dummies.com/register.

Some of the people who helped bring this book to market include the following:

Acquisitions, Editorial, and Media Development

Project Editor: Tonya Maddox Cupp

Previous edition: Mark Enochs

Acquisitions Editor: Bob Woerner

Technical Editor: Dennis Cohen

Editorial Manager: Kevin Kirschner

Media Development Manager: Laura VanWinkle

Media Development Supervisor: Richard Graves

Editorial Assistant: Amanda M. Foxworth

Cartoons: Rich Tennant (www.the5thwave.com)

Production

Project Coordinator: Shannon Schiller

Layout and Graphics: Carl Byers, Andrea Dahl, Denny Hager, Joyce Haughey, Clint Lahnen, Barbara Moore, Barry Offringa, Melanee Prendergast, Ron Terry

Proofreaders: Joe Niesen, Carl William Pierce, TECHBOOKS Production Services

Indexer: TECHBOOKS Production Services

Publishing and Editorial for Technology Dummies

    Richard Swadley, Vice President and Executive Group Publisher

    Andy Cummings, Vice President and Publisher

    Mary Bednarek, Executive Acquisitions Director

    Mary C. Corder, Editorial Director

Publishing for Consumer Dummies

    Diane Graves Steele, Vice President and Publisher

    Joyce Pepple, Acquisitions Director

Composition Services

    Gerry Fahey, Vice President of Production Services

    Debbie Stailey, Director of Composition Services

Contents at a Glance

Table of Contents

Introduction

● ●

Y ou don't need much imagination to see why we're so happy with our
iPods.

Imagine no longer needing CDs. We take road trips that last for weeks, and we
never hear the same song twice. We leave our music library safe at home and
grab an iPod for a hike or jog and always listen to something different.

Imagine not waiting for hot new music. You can listen to it, purchase it, and
load it onto your iPod within minutes of discovering it on the Internet. Be the
first in your circle of friends to hear the exclusive new music available from
the iTunes Music Store.

Imagine not having to buy music more than once. You can purchase a CD or
downloadable music and import the music into a digital library that lasts forever. Imagine never again having to replace an unplayable CD.

Imagine a musician going backstage after a performance and meeting a promoter who says that he can get him ten more gigs if he can confirm the dates
right now. This musician calmly scrolls through his calendar for the entire
year (conveniently stored on his iPod), finding all the details that he needs
about gigs and recording sessions, right down to the minute, including travel
directions to each gig. "No problem," he says. And of course, he gets the gigs.

Okay, maybe you're not a rock star whose career depends on the information
on your iPod. But if rock stars can use them, so can average music lovers.

When we first encountered the iPod, it came very close to fulfilling our dreams
as road warriors — in particular, the dream of filling up our cars with music as
easily as filling it up with fuel. Now we use our iPod with the Alpine KCA-420i,
an in-vehicle interface adapter, which lets us plug any iPod, color-display iPod,
or iPod mini into a compatible 2004 Alpine Ai-NET head unit. That unit can
be installed in just about any car. (It works great in a Volkswagen Passat.)
Another car integration is available for BMW cars — you can control an iPod
or iPod mini through the BMW audio system and multifunction steering wheel.
Whether you want to be *On the Road* with Jack Kerouac (in audio book form),
or "Drivin' South" with Jimi Hendrix, just fill up your iPod and go!

About This Book

We designed *iPod & iTunes For Dummies,* 3rd Edition, as a reference. You can easily find the information you need when you need it. We organized the information so that you can read from beginning to end to find out how to use iTunes and your iPod from scratch. But this book is also designed so that you can dive in anywhere and begin reading because you find all the info you need to know for each task.

We don't cover every detail of every function of the software, and we intentionally leave out some detail so that we don't befuddle you with techno-speak when it's not necessary. (Really, engineers can sometimes provide too many obscure choices that no one ever uses.) We write brief but comprehensive descriptions and include lots of cool tips on how to get the best results from using iTunes and your iPod.

If your PC is on the trailing edge rather than the leading edge, don't worry — you won't miss out on the iPod revolution. True, if you don't use Windows 2000 or Windows XP on your PC, you can't use iTunes for Windows. However, if you use Windows Me (Millennium Edition), you can use MusicMatch Jukebox. Please note that if you're using MusicMatch, you can find that content online. A companion Web site is available for you at www.dummies.com/go/ipod.

Conventions Used in This Book

Like any book that covers computers and information technology, this book uses certain conventions:

- **Choosing from a menu:** In iTunes, when you see "Choose iTunes⇨ Preferences in iTunes," you click iTunes on the toolbar and then click Preferences from the iTunes menu.

  With the iPod, when you see "Choose Extras⇨Calendars from the iPod main menu," you highlight Extras in the main menu with the scroll wheel, press the Select button to select Extras, and then highlight and select Calendars from the Extras menu.

- **Clicking and dragging:** When you see "Drag the song over the name of the playlist," we mean click the song name, hold the mouse button down, and drag the song with the mouse over to the name of the playlist before lifting your finger off the mouse button.

✓ **Keyboard shortcuts:** When you see ⌘-I, press the ⌘ key on a Mac keyboard, along with the appropriate shortcut key. (In this case, press I, which opens the Song Information window in iTunes.) On a Windows PC, the same keyboard shortcut is Ctrl+I (which means press the Ctrl key along with the I key).

✓ **Step lists:** When you come across steps you need to do in iTunes or on the iPod, the action is in bold, and the explanatory part is underneath. If you know what to do, read the action and skip the explanation. But if you need a little help along the way, check out the explanation.

And Just Who Are You?

You don't need to know anything about music or audio technology to discover how to make the most of your iPod and the iTunes software that comes with it. Although a course in music appreciation can't hurt, the iPod is designed to be useful even for air-guitar players who barely know the difference between downloadable music and System of a Down. You don't need any specialized knowledge to have a lot of fun with your iPod and the iTunes software while building up your digital music library.

However, we do make some honest assumptions about your computer skills:

✓ **You know how to use the Mac Finder or Windows Explorer:** We assume that you already know how to locate files and folders and that you can copy files and folders from one hard drive to another on the computer of your choice: a Mac or a Windows PC.

✓ **You know how to select menus and applications on a Mac or a Windows PC:** We assume that you already know how to choose an option from a menu, how to find the Dock on a Mac to launch a Dock application (or use the Start menu in Windows to launch an application), and how to launch an application directly by double-clicking its icon.

For more information on these topics, see that excellent book by Mark L. Chambers, *Mac OS X All-in-One Desk Reference For Dummies,* or the massive tome *Windows XP GigaBook For Dummies,* by Peter Weverka and company (both from Wiley).

A Quick Peek Ahead

This book is organized into six parts, with each part covering a different aspect of using your iPod. Here's a quick preview of what you can find in each part.

Part 1: Setting Up and Acquiring Music

This part gets you started with your iPod, powering it up, recharging its battery, using its menus, and connecting it to your computer. You install and set up the iPod and iTunes software on your Mac or Windows PC. We show you what you can do with iTunes. To acquire music, you can buy music from the iTunes Music Store, or you can rip audio CDs. You also find out how to share your iTunes music.

Part II: Managing Your Music

This part shows you how to sort the music in your iTunes library by artist, album, duration, date, and other items. You can add and edit iTunes song information. You discover how to arrange songs and albums into iTunes playlists that you can transfer to your iPod. When you have your music organized efficiently, transfer it to the iPod. And, for your peace of mind, we cover backing up your music and burning it to a CD, including printing CD jewel case inserts with the song information.

Part III: Playing Music

We show you how to locate and play songs on your iPod and then we move on to various accessories for connecting your iPod to your home stereo and using your iPod on the road with car stereos and portable speakers. You discover how to play music on your iPod through any computer by using advanced DJ techniques, such as cross-fading song playback and using the iTunes Party Shuffle. You also discover how to acquire and play videos in iTunes.

Part IV: Using Advanced Techniques

In this part, you discover digital music encoding and how to change your importing preferences. You can also fine-tune the sound playback with the iTunes equalizer and on your iPod with the iPod equalizer. We describe what you need to record sound and music into your computer from old records and tapes, and how to modify songs in iTunes for playback on your iPod. We cover how to enhance your iTunes library with alternate music sources and Web radio. We also describe how to acquire and play podcasts — radio broadcasts that you can automatically transfer to iTunes and your iPod.

Part V: Have iPod, Will Travel

In this part, use your iPod as a road warrior would: setting your alarm clock, sorting your contacts, recording voice memos, entering personal information into your computer (such as calendar appointments, To-Do lists, and contacts), and synchronizing your iPod with all your personal information. Use a digital camera link to temporarily store photos on the road on your iPod and reclaim the camera's memory card space to take more photos. Use the color-display iPod to show photos and slideshows on televisions. We also provide trouble-shooting first steps and details about updating and restoring your iPod.

Part VI: The Part of Tens

In this book's Part of Tens chapters, we outline common problems and solutions that happen to most iPods and provide tips about the iPod equalizer.

Icons Used in This Book

The icons in this book are important visual cues for information you need.

Remember icons highlight important things you need to remember.

Technical Stuff icons highlight technical details you can skip unless you want to bring out the technical geek in you.

Tip icons highlight tips and techniques that save you time and energy, and maybe money.

Warning icons save your butt by preventing disasters. Don't bypass a warning without reading it. This is your only warning!

On the Web icons let you know when a topic is covered further online at www.dummies.com/go/ipod, this book's companion Web site.

Part I
Setting Up and Acquiring Music

The 5th Wave   By Rich Tennant

In this part . . .

Part I shows you how to do all the essential things with your iPod and iTunes.

- ✔ Chapter 1 gets you started with your iPod. Here you find out how to get the most from your battery, use the menus and buttons, connect your iPod to your Mac or PC, and reset your iPod.

- ✔ Chapter 2 describes how to install the iPod software and iTunes on a Mac or on a Windows PC.

- ✔ Chapter 3 gets you started with iTunes on a Mac or a Windows PC.

- ✔ Chapter 4 covers purchasing music online from the iTunes Music Store.

- ✔ Chapter 5 describes how to import music into iTunes from CDs or other sources (such as the Web).

- ✔ Chapter 6 shows how you can share music (legally) with other iTunes users on your network and copy songs to other computers (even songs purchased online).

Chapter 1

Firing Up Your iPod

Bob Dylan and Dave Van Ronk in Greenwich Village, David Bowie and Iggy Pop on the Lower East Side, and the Velvet Underground in the subway. Dire Straits on Wall Street, Steely Dan in Midtown, and Sonny Rollins on the Brooklyn Bridge. The Drifters on Broadway, Miles Davis uptown, John and Yoko on the Upper West Side. Charlie Parker in Harlem, Yo-Yo Ma on the Upper East Side, Primal Fear across Central Park. "The music must change," sang Roger Daltrey of the Who, and the only way you can conveniently carry that much music around while touring the Big Apple in one day is with an Apple iPod.

Music has changed so much during the shift from purchasing music in stores to obtaining music online that the music industry hardly recognizes it, and the Apple iPod music player is one of the major catalysts. The iPod holds so much music that no matter how large your music collection, you will seriously consider putting all your music into digital format on your computer, transferring portions of it to the iPod, and playing music from both your computer and your iPod from now on. You might never stop buying CDs, but you won't have to buy all your music that way. And you'll never again need to replace the music that you already own.

As an iPod owner, you're on the cutting edge of music player technology. This chapter introduces the iPod and tells you what to expect when you open the box. We describe how to power up your iPod and connect it to your computer, both of which are essential tasks that you need to know how to do — your iPod needs power, and your iPod needs music, which it gets from your computer.

Introducing the iPod

The iPod is, essentially, a hard drive and a digital music player in one device, but that device is such a thing of beauty and style and so highly recognizable by now that all Apple needs to do in an advertisement is show it all by itself. Even the 60GB iPod (the largest capacity as of this writing) weighs less than two CDs in standard jewel cases, and the iPod nano weighs just 1.5 ounces.

The convenience of carrying music on an iPod is phenomenal. For example, the 60GB iPod model can hold around 15,000 songs. That's about a month of nonstop music played around the clock — or about one new song a day for the next 40 years. And with the iPod's built-in skip protection in every model, you don't miss a beat as you jog through the park or your car hits a pothole.

A common misconception is that your iPod becomes your music library. Actually, your iPod is simply another *player* for your music library, which is safely stored on your computer. One considerable benefit of digital music technology is that you can use your computer to serve up your music library and make perfect-quality copies. Copy as much of it as you want onto your iPod, and take it on the road. Two decades from now those digital songs will be the same in quality — the music won't be trapped on a cassette or CD that can degrade over time (CDs can stop working after 15-20 years). The wonderfully remixed, remastered, reconstituted version of your favorite album can be copied over and over forever, just like the rest of your information, and it never loses its sound fidelity. If you save your music in digital format, you will never lose a song and have to buy it again.

The iPod experience includes iTunes (or, in older-generation models, MusicMatch Jukebox), which lets you organize your music in digital form, make copies, burn CDs, and play disc jockey without discs. Suddenly your music world includes online music stores and free music downloads. Without iTunes (or MusicMatch Jukebox), your iPod is merely an external hard drive. As a result of using iTunes (or MusicMatch Jukebox), your music library is more permanent than it ever was before because you can make backup copies that are absolutely the same in quality. We introduce iTunes in Chapter 2. If you're using MusicMatch, visit the companion Web site at www.dummies.com/go/ipod.

You'll spend only about ten seconds copying an entire CD's worth of music from iTunes on your computer to your iPod. Any iPod can play any song in the most popular digital audio formats, including MP3, AIFF, WAV, and Apple's AAC format, which features CD-quality audio in smaller file sizes than MP3. The iPod also supports the Audible AA spoken word file format.

The iPod is also a *data player,* perhaps the first of its kind. As an external hard drive, the iPod serves as a portable backup device for important data files. You can transfer your calendar and address book to help manage your affairs on the road, and you can even use calendar event alarms to supplement your iPod's alarm and sleep timer. Although the iPod isn't as fully functional as a personal digital assistance (PDA) — for example, you can't add information directly to the device — you can view the information. You can keep your calendar and address book automatically synchronized to your computer, where you normally add and edit information. We cover using the iPod as a data player in detail in Chapter 22 and as a general-purpose hard drive in Chapter 23.

Comparing iPod Models

Introduced way back in the Stone Age of digital music (2001), the iPod family has grown by four generations as of this writing, and spawned at least 20 different models, including a private-label version (the HPod from Hewlett-Packard) and a custom version (iPod U2 Special Edition, featuring all of U2's songs).

Today's iPod works with iTunes on either Windows computers or Macs, but that wasn't always the case. The first-generation iPods work only with Macs. In 2002, Apple introduced the second generation — one version for Windows and another for the Mac, using the same design for both. For the third generation (2003), Apple changed the design once again.

Third-generation and fourth-generation iPods, and offshoots such as iPod mini, iPod shuffle, and color-display iPod, work with either Windows or Mac and come in a variety of hard-drive sizes. One way to tell what kind of iPod you have is by its navigational controls. By design, you can hold an iPod in your hand while you thumb the *scroll wheel* (our generic term for scroll wheel, scroll pad, touch wheel, or click wheel). The LCD screen on full-size models offers backlighting so that you can see it in the dark.

For a nifty chart that shows the differences between iPod models, see the "Identifying iPod different models" page on the Apple iPod Web site (http://docs.info.apple.com/article.html?artnum=61688).

First-generation iPods

Apple doesn't sell first-generation iPods anymore, but you might see a few on eBay. More likely, their proud owners are Mac users who still find them useful. Despite its high price tag ($399) compared with other MP3 players, the first 5GB iPod (offering 5GB of storage space) was an unqualified success when it was introduced in October 2001. Apple sold more than 125,000 units within 60 days. "Listening to music will never be the same again," Apple CEO Steve Jobs told the press at the introduction of the first iPod, and he was right. Months later, Apple introduced the 10GB model.

First-generation iPods work only with Macs, connecting to a Mac with a standard FireWire cable. The first generation offers a distinctive scroll wheel that physically turns with your finger as you use it. These early iPods are hefty at 6.5 ounces and have a stainless-steel back and dual-plastic top casing.

FireWire is called *IEEE 1394* by the engineers who designed it and *DV terminal* by camcorder manufacturers that use it, except Sony, which calls it *i.Link*.

These models don't offer all the features of newer generations and can't be used with accessories that are designed for newer generations. For example, you can't expect these older models to use extensions such as voice recorders and memory card readers. First-generation models can't be updated to version 2 or newer versions of the iPod software, so they also lack support for features such as adding notes to the iPod and setting up an on-the-go playlist. However, battery life is comparable to newer models, offering up to eight hours before requiring a recharge. (For more about battery life, see "Facing Charges of Battery," later in this chapter.)

Second-generation iPods

Just as enterprising Linux and Windows developers were trying to cobble together ways to make the iPod work with their systems, Apple introduced a second-generation design in the form of two models: the 20GB iPod for the Mac and the 10GB for Windows, which was supplied preformatted for Windows. The Windows model of the second generation shipped with MusicMatch Jukebox.

Second-generation models use an innovative solid-state touch wheel that doesn't physically turn as you use it but instead responds to finger pressure. These models use a standard FireWire connection to connect to the computer with a six-pin FireWire cable.

Second-generation models can't be updated to version 2 or 3 of the iPod software, so they don't offer all the features of the third and fourth generation and can't be used with dock-connector and voice recorder accessories designed for third-generation and fourth-generation models. Although standard FireWire accessories (such as power adapters for automobiles) are available for these models, digital camera accessories such as memory card readers are not (as of this writing).

Third-generation iPods

The third-generation models, many of which are still sold in stores as of this writing, include the 10GB, 15GB, and 30GB models introduced in 2003, and the 20GB and 40GB models introduced later in that same year. All third-generation models share the same basic features and work with the Mac or Windows, and Apple continually provides software updates for these models.

Models of the third generation are thinner than the second generation and use touch-sensitive buttons with audible feedback (replacing the pressure-sensitive buttons of the second generation that offer tactile feedback). Third-generation models also use a *dock connector* to connect to a computer or power supply; see Figure 1-1. The dock keeps your iPod in an upright position while connected and lets you connect a home stereo or headphones through the dock, which makes it convenient as a base station when you're not traveling with your iPod — you can slip the iPod into the dock without connecting cables.

The dock doesn't come standard with the 15GB model, but you can order it as an extra from the Apple Store.

Figure 1-1:
The third-generation iPod in its dock connected to the power adapter.

The supplied cables connect to the dock on one end (or to the iPod itself, if you don't use a dock) and connect to a computer or power supply on the other end, using standard FireWire or USB 2.0 (some models may not include the USB cable, but you can order it from the Apple Store for about $20). (PC users crave choice — you can read about USB in the sidebar "FireWire or USB: That is the question" in this chapter.)

iPod mini

The iPod mini, an offshoot of the third generation, is small enough to fit in a shirt pocket; see Figure 1-2. Its smooth, ultra-thin, anodized aluminum case comes in five different colors. The original model houses a 4GB drive that can hold about 1,000 songs — as much as the original 5GB model; newer models sport a 6GB drive that holds about 1,500 songs. (An iPod mini can fit more songs in the same amount of space because Apple introduced a better compression format called AAC in second-generation models, as described in Chapter 17. The AAC format can also be used in older models, so in effect when Apple introduced AAC the capacity of all models increased.)

Figure 1-2:
iPod mini
fits in a shirt
pocket.

Besides its smaller size (and therefore, smaller dock), another of iPod mini's distinguishing characteristic is the click wheel, which offers the same functions as the third-generation iPod touch wheel but is more suitable for such a small device. The click wheel combines the scroll wheel and buttons, with pressure-sensitive buttons underneath the top, bottom, left, and right areas of the circular pad of the wheel.

iPod mini has the same features as full-size third-generation iPods except that it uses a different set of accessories because of its size, and it offers up to 18 hours of battery time between charges. We describe both types of iPods and their accessories throughout this book.

Fourth-generation and color-display iPods

In 2004 Apple introduced a fourth-generation iPod that uses the same click wheel and buttons that iPod mini uses. Fourth-generation iPod software includes the ability to randomly shuffle song playback with the press of a button, and to charge up the iPod through the USB connection to your computer. (Previously only FireWire connections to the computer provided power.) The fourth-generation iPods were at first available in 40GB and 20GB models with black-and-white displays. Currently, Apple offers 20GB and 60GB models with color displays that can store photos and display slideshows.

The fourth-generation units with black-and-white displays offer up to 12 hours of battery time between charges. You can play up to 15 hours of continuous music on a color-display iPod between charges, or up to five hours of continuous slideshows with music. The battery is the same type as used in other models — the improvement is in how the software manages power in the iPod. Like third-generation iPods, the fourth generation also uses a dock connector to connect the iPod to a computer or power supply, and the dock itself is available separately from the Apple Store. The fourth-generation iPods connect to computers using either FireWire or USB connections.

The fourth-generation iPod models differ from earlier models by offering a top-level Music choice in the main menu and the ability to create multiple on-the-go playlists. You can also play audio books at slower or faster speeds while maintaining natural-sounding pitch.

Considered a "fifth generation" by some, the iPod color display models, including the earliest model known as *iPod photo,* let you store and view color digital photos as well as store and play sound; it also does everything a fourth-generation iPod can do and uses the same accessories. As of this writing, Apple provides a 20GB model and a whopping 60GB model that can hold up to 15,000 songs and full-color album cover art — or as many as 25,000 photos.

The 60GB iPod with color display, shown in Figure 1-3, uses the same click wheel and buttons iPod mini uses. The color display provides crisp definition for the iPod's menus, making them easier to read, even in sunlight.

Figure 1-3: The iPods with color displays let you store photos and present slideshows in color.

The iPod color display, at 220×176-pixel resolution and over 65,000 colors, offers excellent viewing with built-in backlighting. With the optional AV cable, you can connect the iPod to a television monitor or video projector for a video-quality slideshow. It even optimizes your photos to fit on a standard (4:3 ratio) or widescreen (16:9 ratio) TV.

To get photos onto your color-display iPod, you can transfer them directly from iPhoto on a Mac or Adobe Photoshop Elements or Adobe Album on a Windows PC — it even synchronizes with photo albums to grab your latest shots. And with the optional iPod Camera Connector, you can copy photos directly from a digital camera to the iPod hard drive, saving memory card space in your camera as you continually take more photos. iTunes also automatically copies album cover art supplied with the music you buy from the iTunes Music Store, so you can enjoy the art while playing the music.

iPod nano

Apple's new iPod nano model is thinner than a pencil — only 0.27 inches — but it packs a powerful color backlit display, the fourth-generation click wheel and dock connection, and full support for fourth-generation iPod features. Apple achieved this design by using *flash memory*, which are chips that hold their contents without power, rather than a hard drive. The iPod nano, shown in Figure 1-4, is meticulously designed to feel good in your hand. While as small as a business card and feather light, it is not flimsy or delicate — the stainless steel back and polymer front don't flex.

Figure 1-4:
The iPod nano is the smallest fully featured color-display model (photo courtesy of Apple).

Apple offers 2GB and 4GB models in stylish black or white. The 2GB model holds about 500 songs, while the 4GB model holds about 1,000 songs. Both provide up to 14 hours of playback time between battery charges, or four hours of a photo slideshow.

The iPod nano color display improves the readability of the iPod's menus even in sunlight, and lets you view album art as well as photos downloaded from your computer. However, one major difference between an iPod nano and a full-size color-display iPod is that you can't use an iPod nano to display photos and slideshows on a television or with video equipment.

While the iPod nano offers a dock connection that works with most accessories that connect via the dock, it supports only USB and USB 2.0 — although you can use a FireWire cable to connect to the FireWire AC Adapter to charge its battery. (You can read about USB in the sidebar "FireWire or USB: That is the question.")

The iPod nano offers a headphone minijack and dock connection, but not a remote controller connection, so you can't use some accessories designed for full-sized iPods such as voice recorders and remote controllers. However, you can use most of the accessories that can connect to the iPod mini dock connection, such as speaker systems and car stereo adapters, though the iPod nano's dock connection is off-center. Power-related accessories that use the dock connection, such as car chargers, external batteries, and Apple's USB charger, also work fine, but some wireless transmitter accessories that rely on the remote controller connection don't work. Many new accessories are designed specifically for the iPod nano and are available at www.apple.com/ipodnano/accessories.html.

You can't get a new iPod model without new features, and the iPod nano is no exception. The new Stopwatch feature, which includes a lap counter, is a natural for a model that is designed for sport and exercise. The Clock can tell you the time in other parts of the world. It also offers a Screen Lock to protect access with a password. The iPod nano is also the first to display a podcast indicator (a small blue dot) that indicates podcasts you haven't heard yet. And the new Lyrics screen shows any lyrics you've added to the iTunes song information window for a track.

Doing the iPod shuffle

If the regular iPod models are not small enough to fit into your lifestyle, try the iPod shuffle, which is as much a fashion statement as a state-of-the-art music player — this one you can wear! The iPod shuffle, shown in Figure 1-5, is 3.3 inches long, less than 1 inch wide, and about a third of 1 inch thick — so tiny it weighs only 0.78 of an ounce, which is little more than a car key or pack of gum. You can hang it from your ears using the supplied earbuds and wear it around your neck like a necklace.

The 512MB iPod shuffle can hold 120 songs, and the 1GB model can hold 240 songs — assuming an average of 4 minutes per song, using the AAC format at the High Quality setting (as described in Chapter 17). Remember, the iPod shuffle is not for storing music permanently — you use it just to play selections from your iTunes library on your computer. It has no display, but that's actually a good thing, because it keeps the size and weight down to a minimum — and you don't need a display to play a couple of hundred songs in random or sequential order. You can also use your iPod shuffle to hold data files, just like an external flash memory drive.

Figure 1-5:
The iPod
shuffle
weighs
less than
an ounce
and offers
skip-free
playback.

With skip-free playback, lightweight design, and no need for a display, you can easily use it while skiing, snowboarding, or even skydiving (and if you're at a high altitude, try "Expecting to Fly" by Buffalo Springfield, or "Astral Traveling" by Pharoah Sanders). That's because it uses flash memory rather than a hard drive — you can shake it as hard as you want without a glitch. The iPod shuffle's battery, similar to those used in other fourth-generation iPods, offers up to 12 hours of power between charges.

Unlike other iPods, the iPod shuffle can't play tunes in the AIFF or Apple Lossless formats, which consume a lot of storage space but are higher in sonic quality. You can play songs in the AAC format (including songs from the online iTunes Music Store) or the MP3 format. These formats compress the music to use much less space. You can also use the Audible book format and the uncompressed WAV format. See Chapter 17 for more details on encoding formats.

To turn on the iPod shuffle, use the three-position toggle switch on the back; a green stripe below the switch helps you see what position the switch is in. The top position turns the iPod shuffle off; the middle position starts playing the list of songs from beginning to end in sequential order; and the bottom position shuffles through songs randomly — you don't know what song will come next, and that's its appeal. You may want a little randomness in your life.

Using the buttons on the front side that look like standard CD-player buttons, you can skip forward to the next song or skip back to the previous one. The center button either starts or pauses playback. The plus (+) button turns the volume up, and the minus (-) button turns it down.

The iPod shuffle shines a yellow LED on the front side to show when the player is charging, and a green LED when the shuffle is completely charged. A blinking green LED indicates that the player is on pause. On the back side just below the toggle switch is a Battery Status button that, when pressed, flashes an LED that indicates how much battery juice remains: Green is a good charge, yellow a low charge, and red a very low charge. No glow means no power remains.

Underneath the cap on the tip of the iPod shuffle is a convenient USB 2.0 connector that links the iPod shuffle to a computer or to an optional power supply and supplies power for recharging its battery. You don't need a separate cable. The iPod shuffle charges its battery from your computer, so you don't need the optional power supply. You can also get the optional $29 iPod shuffle External Battery Pack, which provides 20 additional hours of playtime with two AAA batteries.

Thinking Inside the Box

Don't destroy the elegantly designed box while opening it; you might want to place it prominently in your collection of Equipment That Ushered in the 21st Century. Before going any further, check the box and make sure that all the correct parts came with your iPod.

Things you have and things you need

The iPod box includes a CD-ROM with the iTunes software for the Mac and PC and the FireWire or USB cable you can use to connect your iPod to a computer. All models (except the iPod shuffle and iPod nano) come with an AC power adapter for connecting either the older iPod (using FireWire) or the newer iPod-in-dock to an AC power source.

With most models, you also get a set of earbud headphones and a remote controller that connects to the iPod by wire. The accessories don't stop there — you might also have a carrying case and some other goodies. Optional accessories, many of which we describe in this book, are available at the online Apple Store (www.apple.com/store).

You also need a few things that don't come with the iPod:

- **A PC or Mac to run iTunes:** On a PC, iTunes requires Windows 2000 or XP, a 500-MHz Pentium-class processor or faster, and a minimum of 128MB (256MB or more recommended). With a Mac, iTunes requires Mac OS X 10.2.8 or newer for connecting with FireWire (OS X 10.3.4 or newer for connecting via USB or for using AirPort Express), a 400-MHz G3 processor or better and at least 256MB of RAM. The iTunes installer for the PC also installs the newest version of QuickTime, replacing any older version you may have. Macs have QuickTime preinstalled; however, you may need to upgrade your version of QuickTime to 6.5.2 (current as of this writing) or newer to use purchased music from the iTunes Music Store in other iLife applications on a Mac.

- **A PC to run MusicMatch Jukebox** *(alternative to iTunes):* You can alternatively use the iPod with MusicMatch Jukebox and a 300 MHz or faster PC with at least 96MB of RAM running Windows Me, 2000, or XP (with at least 128MB of RAM). If you're using MusicMatch, visit the companion Web site at www.dummies.com/go/ipod.

- **FireWire or USB connection on a PC:** PCs running Windows must have either FireWire (also called IEEE 1394) or USB 2.0. All Macs provide USB and most provide FireWire — it's your choice. See the sidebar "FireWire or USB: That is the question" in this chapter for more information about FireWire and USB 2.0 connections on PCs.

- **FireWire cable** *(alternative to USB):* While older iPod models came with a FireWire cable, current color-display iPods are supplied with just a USB cable for connecting to either a Mac or a PC. You can use a FireWire connection on either a Mac or PC by using a FireWire cable, available from the Apple Store.

- **iTunes 4.9 or newer:** You can download Mac or Windows versions for free from the Apple Web site (www.apple.com/itunes). The CD-ROM supplied with current-model iPods should have both versions of iTunes as well. Older models, still available in stores and online, may include versions of iTunes as old as version 4.5 — which is fine, because version 4.5 works. (It just doesn't have all the features of 4.9.) You can download version 4.9 or newer versions at any time to replace it.

- **MusicMatch Jukebox for PCs** *(alternative to iTunes):* CD-ROMs supplied with some older iPod models provided MusicMatch Jukebox instead. You can use MusicMatch Jukebox if you don't meet the requirements to run iTunes.

- **Applications for managing contacts and calendars** *(Optional):* Mac users can install Address Book (for managing contacts) and iCal (for managing calendars), both of which can synchronize your iPod with contacts and calendars. Both are available for free from www.apple.com. Windows users can use Outlook or Outlook Express for creating a contacts list and calendars for an iPod.

Using FireWire or USB cables with a Mac

If you have a Mac and a full-size iPod, the choice is easy: FireWire has been a part of every Mac since at least 2000. (To find out about FireWire, see the sidebar "FireWire or USB: That is the question" in this chapter.) However, differences exist between iPod generations.

Current (third-generation and fourth-generation) models, including iPod mini and color-display models, offer a special cable with a flat dock connector to connect the dock — or the iPod itself — to the Mac's FireWire or USB port. The dock includes a cable with a flat dock connector on one end and a FireWire or USB connector on the other (some cables have both FireWire and USB). You can connect the FireWire or USB end of the cable to the computer (to synchronize with iTunes and play iPod music in iTunes) or to the power adapter.

The connection on the bottom of the iPod is the same as the connection on back of the dock. Plug the flat connector of the cable into the iPod or dock, and then plug the six-pin FireWire connector on the other end to the FireWire port on your Mac (marked by the Y symbol that resembles a radiation symbol), or plug the USB connector to the USB port on your Mac.

 The full-size third-generation iPods don't support USB 2.0 on the Mac, but iPod mini, iPod nano, and fourth-generation models support it if your Mac offers USB 2.0, and a USB cable is provided. You need OS X 10.3.4 for connecting via USB 2.0 to a Mac.

The iPod shuffle offers only a USB connector: Remove the cap from one end and connect it directly to the USB or USB 2.0 connection on your Mac. You can also use an iPod shuffle Dock or a USB extension cable (available from Apple at www.ipod.com/store).

First-generation and second-generation models offer only a standard FireWire connection, so you can use a standard Mac-style FireWire cable to connect the iPod to the Mac's FireWire connection. Plug the six-pin connector of a standard FireWire cable into the iPod, and plug the six-pin connector on the other end to the FireWire port on your Mac. (The six-pin connector is marked by the Y symbol that resembles a radiation symbol.)

Using FireWire or USB cables with a PC

If you have a Windows PC you can use FireWire (called IEEE 1394 in PC circles), or USB 2.0 (a.k.a. *high-powered USB*), which is available on most current desktop PCs and laptops. While you can use a low-powered USB connection, it doesn't supply power to most iPod models, and performs too slowly.

FireWire or USB: That is the question

If you use a Mac, FireWire is the choice to make unless your Mac offers USB 2.0 and you're using an iPod mini, color-display iPod, or iPod shuffle — all three of which support USB 2.0. The iPod shuffle supports only USB and USB 2.0, so you have no choice but to use the USB or USB 2.0 connection.

FireWire can hustle data at rates up to 400 Mbps over its cable. That's typically fast enough — with FireWire, you can transfer an entire CD's worth of music in less than ten seconds.

USB (Universal Serial Bus) has been around for a while, connecting hundreds of nifty devices to PCs. USB version 1.1 offers a speed of only 12 Mbps. The more advanced generation of USB, Version 2.0, has a transfer rate of 480 Mbps — that's 40 times faster than the first version — but since USB in practice does not sustain that rate for the entire data transfer, as FireWire does, FireWire is still a wee bit faster.

Both FireWire and USB 2.0 connections are plug-and-play: You can plug them in at any time whether your computer is on or off. Depending on the device that you use with these connections, FireWire or USB 2.0 can provide power to the device. For example, fourth-generation iPods, the iPod shuffle, the iPod nano, and the color-display iPod can draw power from a USB 2.0 connection.

Many Mac models now sport USB 2.0 connectors, but for many older Mac users, FireWire is the only choice. Many desktop PCs and laptops offer PCI and/or CardBus slots for adding FireWire or USB 2.0 cards, and some PCs offer built-in FireWire or USB 2.0.

Have we made your choice easier yet? If you have a PC with USB 2.0 (which is more common than one with FireWire), go with it. The only drawback is that with an iPod older than the fourth generation, you might not be able to get power from the connection (depending on the PC), so you wouldn't be able to recharge its battery from your PC.

You can add FireWire to your PC with an expansion card such as the FireCard 400 CardBus card from Unibrain (`www.unibrain.com`), which plugs into a PC desktop or laptop CardBus slot. Before you buy a FireWire/IEEE 1394 card, make sure that it's compatible with your hardware and operating system. Apple offers approved FireWire expansion cards at the online Apple Store (`http://store.apple.com/1-800-MY-APPLE/WebObjects/AppleStore`).

If you have trouble installing your FireWire or USB 2.0 card or using your iPod with it, see Chapter 27 for troubleshooting tips.

FireWire/IEEE 1394 expansion cards are available in various formats: Some offer the standard six-pin port found on Macs, and some offer a four-pin port that is also used in camcorders. If your card has a six-pin port, you can plug your iPod cable directly into it.

For cards with four-pin ports, Apple provides the FireWire cable adapter, as shown in Figure 1-6, and you can hook it up to the standard six-pin connector at the end of your FireWire cable. The small four-pin connector on the adapter plugs into the four-pin port on the FireWire card. Then plug the other end of your cable to your iPod or your dock. You can purchase a special FireWire/ IEEE 1394 cable that has a six-pin plug on one end and a four-pin plug on the other — look for it in well-stocked electronics stores that sell digital camcorders, as many camcorders use such a cable.

Figure 1-6: The FireWire cable adapter for connecting to a FireWire card that has a four-pin port.

The FireWire cable adapter is supplied with full-size fourth-generation iPods but not with iPod mini or iPod nano. You can purchase one from the Apple Store.

If you use USB 2.0 with your PC, you can use the USB 2.0 cable supplied with your iPod, iPod nano, or iPod mini. The USB 2.0 cable has a flat dock connector on one end and a USB 2.0 connector on the other. Apple also offers a combination FireWire/USB 2.0 cable with a dock connector on one end and a cable that forks into two connectors — one for FireWire and one for USB 2.0 — but this cable won't work with an iPod nano for music transfer.

Don't use another USB device in a chain, or a USB 2.0 hub, to connect your iPod — unless the hub is a powered hub. Note that a USB keyboard acts like a hub, but is not powered. Therefore it wouldn't provide power to the iPod.

The iPod shuffle offers only a USB connector: Remove the cap from one end and connect it directly to the USB or USB 2.0 connection on your PC. You can also use an iPod shuffle Dock or a USB extension cable (available from Apple at www.ipod.com/store).

Powering Up Your iPod

All iPods come with essentially the same requirement: power. Fortunately, it also comes with a battery and a way of charging it — either directly from your computer, or using a cable and an AC power adapter that works with voltages in North America and many parts of Europe and Asia. (See Chapter 15 for information about plugging into power in other countries.)

First-generation and second-generation iPod models offer a Mac-style FireWire connection on the top of the iPod. The power adapter also sports a FireWire connection, so all you need is a standard six-pin FireWire cable to plug in. Third-generation and fourth-generation models, color-display iPods, and iPod minis can use a dock that offers FireWire and USB connections. The dock can also connect to your home stereo through a line-out connection. The iPod nano models come with a USB dock cable that provides power from the USB port on your computer.

A FireWire connection to a Mac provides power to the iPod and recharges the battery as long as the Mac isn't in sleep mode. A FireWire connection to a FireWire/IEEE 1394 card in a PC might not be able to provide power — check with the card manufacturer. The smaller 4-pin connections for FireWire/IEEE 1394 cards typically don't supply power to the iPod.

If your iPod shows a display but doesn't respond to your touch, don't panic — check the Hold switch on top of the unit and make sure that it's set to one side so that the orange bar disappears (the normal position). You use the Hold switch for locking the buttons, which prevents accidental activation.

You might notice that the iPod's display turns iridescent when it gets too hot or too cold, but this effect disappears when its temperature returns to normal. iPods can function in temperatures as cold as 50 degrees and as warm as 95 degrees (Fahrenheit) but work best at room temperature (closer to 68 degrees).

If you leave your iPod out in the cold all night, it might have trouble waking from sleep mode, and it might even display a low battery message. Plug the iPod into a power source, wait until it warms up, and try it again. If it still doesn't wake up or respond properly, try resetting the iPod as we describe in "Resetting Your iPod," later in this chapter.

Facing Charges of Battery

You can take a six-hour flight from New York City to California and listen to your iPod the entire time — and with some models, listen all the way back on the return flight, without recharging. All iPod models use the same type of built-in rechargeable lithium-ion battery with the following power specs:

- The first-, second-, and third-generation iPod models offer up to eight hours of battery power.

- The fourth-generation models and the iPod shuffle offer up to 12 hours.

- The iPod mini offers up to 18 hours.

- The iPod nano offers 14 hours of music playing time or 4 hours of photo display with music.

- The color-display iPod models offer 15 hours of music playing time or 5 hours of photo display with music.

However, keep in mind that playback battery time varies with the type of encoder that you use for the music files in iTunes — Chapter 17 has more information about encoders. It also varies depending on how you use your iPod controls and settings.

It takes only four hours to recharge the battery fully for all models. Need power when you're on the run? Look for a power outlet in the airport terminal or hotel lobby — the battery fast-charges to 80-percent capacity in two hours. After the first two hours, the battery receives a trickle charge for the next two hours, until fully charged.

Don't fry your iPod with some generic power adapter — use *only* the power adapter supplied with the iPod from Apple.

A battery icon in the top-right corner of the iPod display indicates with a progress bar how much power is left. When you charge the battery, the icon turns into a lightning bolt inside a battery. If the icon doesn't animate, the battery is fully charged. You can also use your iPod while the battery is charging, or disconnect it and use it before the battery is fully charged.

To check the battery status of an iPod shuffle, press the battery status button on the back (the long button above the Apple logo and below the position switch). If the battery status light is green, the iPod shuffle is fully charged; if yellow, the charge is low; if red, very little charge is left and you need to recharge it. If no light is visible, the iPod shuffle is completely out of power and you need to recharge it to use it.

Maintaining battery life

The iPod's built-in rechargeable lithium-ion battery is, essentially, a life-or-death proposition. After it's dead, it can be replaced, but the replacement may cost more than $50 (some services may charge less for older models). If your warranty is still active, you should have Apple replace it — don't do it yourself because opening the iPod invalidates the warranty.

Fortunately the battery is easy to maintain. We recommend *calibrating* the battery once soon after you get your iPod — that is, run it all the way down (a full discharge) and then charge it all the way up (which takes four hours). Although this doesn't actually change battery performance, it does improve the battery gauge so that the iPod displays a more accurate indicator.

Unlike nickel-based batteries that require you to fully discharge and then recharge in order to get a fuller capacity, the iPod lithium-ion battery prefers a partial rather than a full discharge, so avoid frequent full discharges after the initial calibration (frequent full discharges can lower battery life).

Lithium-ion batteries typically last three years or more and are vulnerable to high temperatures, which decrease their life spans considerably. Don't leave your iPod in a hot place, such as on a sunny car dashboard, for very long.

For a complete description of how Apple's lithium-ion batteries work, see the Apple — Batteries page at www.apple.com/batteries.

The bottom of the iPod warms up when it's powered on. The bottom functions as a cooling surface that transfers heat from inside the unit to the cooler air outside. The iPod's carrying case acts as an insulator, so be sure to remove the iPod from its carrying case before you recharge it.

Keeping the iPod encased in its carrying case when charging is tempting but also potentially disastrous. The iPod needs to dissipate its heat, and you could damage the unit by overheating it and frying its circuits, rendering it as useful as a paperweight. To get around this problem, you can purchase one of the heat-dissipating carrying cases available in the Apple Store. For example, Marware (www.marware.com) offers the SportSuit Convertible case ($39.95).

Even when not in use, your iPod drinks the juice. If your iPod is inactive for 14 days, you must recharge its battery — perhaps the iPod gets depressed from being left alone too long.

Saving power

Full-size iPods include a hard drive, and whatever causes the hard drive to spin causes a drain on power. Your iPod also has a *cache* — a memory chip holding the section of music to play next. The iPod uses the cache not only to eliminate skipping when something jostles the hard drive but also to conserve power because the drive doesn't have to spin as much.

If you use the AIFF or WAV formats for importing music into iTunes (or MusicMatch Jukebox), don't use these formats with your iPod — convert the music first, as we describe in Chapter 20. These formats take up way too much space on the iPod hard drive and fill up the iPod cache too quickly, causing skips when you play them and using too much battery power because the drive spins more often. (See Chapter 5 for importing with iTunes. Chapter 17 provides detailed information about these formats.)

The following are tips on power saving while using your iPod:

- **Pause:** Pause playback when you're not listening. Pausing (stopping) playback is the easiest way to conserve power.

- **Back away from the light:** Use the iPod backlight sparingly. Select Backlight from the iPod main menu to turn it on or off, or turn the Backlight Timer setting to a number of seconds, or to Off, in the iPod's Settings menu. (Choose Settings from the main menu.) Don't use the backlight in daylight if you don't need it.

- **Hold it:** Flip the Hold switch to the lock position (with the orange bar showing) to make sure that controls aren't accidentally activated. You don't want your iPod playing music in your pocket and draining the battery when you're not listening.

- **You may continue:** Play songs continuously without using the iPod controls. Selecting songs and using Previous/Rewind and Next/Fast-Forward requires precious energy. Not only that, but the hard drive has to spin more often when searching for songs, using more power than during continuous playback.

Always use the latest iPod software and update your software when updates come out. Apple is always trying to improve the way your iPod works, and many of these advancements relate to power usage.

Replacing your battery

Apple customers aren't always happy campers. Early iPods came with batteries that couldn't be replaced, but all it took were a few premature battery failures and quite a few customer complaints for Apple to institute a battery replacement service. Apple also offers a special AppleCare warranty for iPods.

You can't remove or replace the iPod internal battery yourself — you need Apple to replace it if it dies.

If your iPod isn't responding after a reset (see "Resetting Your iPod" in this chapter for how to reset your iPod), follow the troubleshooting steps in Chapter 27. If these steps don't restore your iPod to working condition, you might have a battery problem. Go to the Apple support page for the iPod (www.apple.com/support/ipod) and click the iPod service FAQ link to read frequently asked questions and answers about iPod support. Then click the iPod battery service request form link on the support page and follow the instructions to request service and return your iPod for a replacement.

The only time we had to do this (with a 30GB iPod), Apple required us to send just the iPod unit itself, without the power adapter or any other accessories, to Apple's service facility. Within a week, Apple sent back a brand new iPod (same model).

Thumbing Through the Menus

After you import music into the iPod, you're ready to play music. The design of the iPod lets you hold it in one hand and perform simple operations by thumb. The iPod's unique circular scroll wheel makes scrolling through an entire music collection quick and easy. With your finger or thumb, scroll clockwise on the wheel to scroll down a list, or counter-clockwise to scroll up. As you scroll, options on the menu are highlighted. Use the Select button at the center of the scroll wheel to select whatever is highlighted in the menu display.

In full-size third-generation models, the touch-sensitive buttons above the scroll wheel perform simple functions when you touch them. (First-generation and second-generation models aren't touch-sensitive, so you need to press them.)

iPod mini, iPod nano, and fourth-generation iPods, including color-display models, provide a click wheel that offers the same functions as the scroll wheel *and* the clickable buttons. It has pressure-sensitive buttons underneath the top, bottom, left, and right areas of the circular pad of the wheel. These areas tilt as you press them, activating the buttons.

The iPod main menu for fourth-generation, iPod nano, and color-display models, shown in Figure 1-7, offers the following selections:

- **Music:** Select music by playlist, artist, album, song, genre, or composer, or select an audio book.

- **Photos:** Select photos by photo album or select individual photos in the photo library. This selection appears only on color-display models.

- **Extras:** View and set the clock and alarm clock, view contacts, view your calendar, view notes, and play games.

- **Settings:** Set display settings, menu settings, the backlight timer, the clicker, and the date and time.

- **Shuffle Songs:** Play songs from your music library in random order.

- **Backlight:** Turn on or off the backlighting for the iPod display.

- **Now Playing:** This appears only when a song is playing — it takes you to the Now Playing display.

The iPod main menu for third-generation models offers the following selections:

- **Music:** Select music by playlist, artist, album, song, genre, or composer, or select an audio book.
- **Playlists:** Select a playlist to play.
- **Extras:** View and set the clock and alarm clock, view contacts, your calendar, or notes, and play games.
- **Settings:** Set display settings, menu settings, the backlight timer, the clicker, and the date and time.
- **Backlight:** Turn on or off the backlighting for the iPod display.
- **Now Playing:** This appears only when a song is playing — it takes you to the Now Playing display.

The main menu for first- and second-generation iPods and iPod mini offer the following selections:

- **Playlists:** Select a playlist to play.
- **Browse:** Select music by playlist, artist, album, song, genre, or composer, or select an audio book.
- **Extras:** View and set the clock and alarm clock, view contacts, view your calendar, view notes, and play games.
- **Settings:** Set display settings, menu settings, the backlight timer, the clicker, and the date and time.
- **Backlight:** Turn on or off the backlighting for the iPod display.
- **Now Playing:** This appears only when a song is playing — it takes you to the Now Playing display.

Pressing the iPod Buttons

The buttons on full-size iPod models do various tasks for song playback:

- **Previous/Rewind:** Press once to start a song over. Press twice to skip to the previous song. Press and hold to rewind through a song.
- **Menu:** Press once to go back to the previous menu. Each time you press, you go back to a previous menu until you reach the main menu.
- **Play/Pause:** Press to play the selected song, album, or playlist. Press Play/Pause when a song is playing to pause the playback.
- **Next/Fast-Forward:** Press once to skip to the next song. Press and hold Next/Fast-Forward to fast-forward through the song.

Figure 1-7:
The iPod color display main menu with backlight-ing on.

The buttons and scroll wheel on full-size iPods can do more complex functions when used in combination:

✔ **Turn on the iPod.** Press any button.

✔ **Turn off the iPod.** Press and hold the Play/Pause button.

✔ **Disable the iPod buttons.** To keep from accidentally pressing the buttons, push the Hold switch to the other side so that an orange bar appears (the Hold position). To reactivate the iPod buttons, push the Hold switch back to the other side so that the orange bar disappears (the normal position).

✔ **Reset the iPod.** Set the Hold switch to the Hold position, and then move it back to normal. Then, on first-, second-, or third-generation iPods or iPod mini, press the Menu and Play/Pause buttons simultaneously for about five seconds until the Apple logo appears in the iPod display; for fourth-generation and color-display iPods, press the Menu and Select buttons simultaneously for six seconds. You can reset the iPod if it gets hung up for some reason. (For example, it might get confused if you press the buttons too quickly.) This operation resets the iPod, essentially restarting the iPod's hard drive. It doesn't change the music or data on the iPod. See "Resetting Your iPod," later in this chapter.

✔ **Change the volume.** While playing a song (the display reads Now Playing), adjust the volume with the scroll wheel — clockwise turns the volume up, counterclockwise turns the volume down. A volume slider appears on the iPod display, indicating the volume level as you scroll.

✔ **Skip to any point in a song.** While playing a song (the display says Now Playing), press and hold the Select button until the progress bar appears to indicate where you are in the song, and then use the scroll wheel to scroll to any point in the song. Scroll clockwise to move forward, and counterclockwise to move backward.

Setting the Language

Wiedergabelisten? Übersicht? (Playlists? Browse?) If your iPod is speaking in a foreign tongue, don't panic — you're not in the wrong country. You might have purchased an iPod that's set to a foreign language. More likely, someone set it to a different language accidentally or on purpose (as a practical joke). Fortunately, you can change the setting without having to know the language that it's set to.

To set the language, no matter what language the menu is using, follow these steps:

1. **Press the Menu button repeatedly until pressing it doesn't change the words on the display, or until you see the word *iPod*.**

   If pressing the Menu button no longer changes the display, you're at the main menu. With fourth-generation models, the menu displays iPod no matter what language is selected — and you know you're at the main menu.

2. **Choose the third option from the top on fourth-generation iPods without color displays. Choose the fourth option from the top on iPod mini, iPod models with color displays, and older models. (In English, this is the Settings option.)**

   Scroll clockwise until the item is highlighted, and then press the Select button. The Settings menu appears.

3. **Choose the third option from the bottom of the Settings menu (which, in English, is the Language option).**

   The Language menu appears.

4. **Choose the language that you want to use. (English is at the top of the list.)**

If these steps don't do the trick, the menu may have been customized (something you can discover how to do in Chapter 22). Someone could have customized it previously, or perhaps you accidentally pressed buttons that customized the menu. To get around this problem, you can reset all the iPod settings back to the defaults. (Unfortunately, resetting your iPod settings back to the defaults wipes out any customizations that you've made; you have to redo any repeat/shuffle settings, alarms, backlight timer settings, and so on.)

Follow these steps to reset all your settings, no matter what language displays:

1. **Press the Menu button repeatedly until pressing it doesn't change the words on the display, or until you see the word *iPod*.**

   If pressing the Menu button no longer changes the display, you're at the main menu. With fourth-generation models, the menu displays iPod no matter what language is selected — and you know you're at the main menu.

2. **Choose the third option from the top on fourth-generation iPods without color displays. Choose the fourth option from the top on iPod mini, iPod models with color displays, and older models. (In English, this is the Settings option.)**

   The Settings menu appears.

3. **Choose the option at the bottom of the menu (in English, the Reset All Settings option).**

   The Reset All Settings menu appears.

4. **Choose the second menu option (in English, the Reset option; the first menu option is Cancel).**

   The Language menu appears.

5. **Choose the language you want to use. (English is at the top of the list.)**

The language you choose now applies to all the iPod menus. But don't pull that practical joke on someone else!

Resetting Your iPod

If your iPod doesn't turn on, don't panic — at least not yet. First check the Hold switch's position on top of the iPod. If it's in the locked position (with orange showing), slide it to the normal position. If it still doesn't work, check whether the iPod has enough juice. Is the battery charged up? Connect the iPod to a power source and see whether it works.

There are times when your iPod freezes up or seems confused, and it just won't start up. Pressing more than one iPod button at the same time might have caused this problem, or perhaps you disconnected the iPod from your computer before it had a chance to display the iPod's main menu (or in older models, the message saying it's okay to disconnect). In situations like this, you can *reset* the iPod.

Resetting the iPod isn't the same as resetting the *settings* of your iPod. If all you need to do is reset the settings on the Settings menu, you can choose Settings⇨Reset All Settings⇨Reset from the main menu. (We cover the settings on the Settings menu in Chapter 22.) All your menu and display settings return to their original values.

This section is about a different kind of reset — similar to pressing a reset button on a computer. This operation resets the operating system of the iPod and restarts the system. Sometimes when your iPod gets confused or refuses to turn on, you can fix it by resetting it. Follow these steps:

1. **Toggle the Hold switch to the locked position and then back to the unlocked position.**

   This step is like the beginning of a secret handshake.

2. **On fourth-generation models, including color-display models, press the Menu and Select buttons simultaneously.**

   On older models, press the Menu and Play/Pause buttons simultaneously.

3. **Hold these buttons for at least six seconds until the Apple logo appears; then release the buttons when you see the Apple logo.**

   The appearance of the Apple logo signals that your iPod is resetting itself, so you no longer have to hold down the buttons.

   Releasing the Menu and Select buttons (or Play/Pause on older models) as soon as you see the Apple logo is important. If you continue to hold down the buttons after the logo appears, the iPod displays the low battery icon (which looks like a slashed battery), and you must connect it to a power source before using your iPod again.

Set your iPod on a flat surface to press multiple buttons more easily. Make sure that when you press the Select button, you don't touch any part of the click wheel. Also make sure that you're pressing the Menu button toward the outside of the click wheel, and not near the center.

After resetting, everything should be back to normal, including your music and data files.

Chapter 2

Setting Up iTunes and Your iPod

. . . .

. . . .

*A*n iPod without iTunes is like a CD player without CDs. Sure, you can use utility programs from sources other than Apple to put music on an iPod. (See Chapter 26 if you don't believe us.) But iTunes gives you access to the vast online iTunes Music Store, and it's excellent for managing music on your computer and synchronizing your music library with your iPod.

On the Mac, iTunes is practically the only jukebox in town — it's not profitable to compete with something that's free. And yet, Apple hasn't abused its position by putting out a less-than-functional program. On Windows, iTunes has plenty of competition but is still one of the top five audio players.

This chapter explains how to set up your iPod with iTunes on the Mac or for Windows. It also explains how to set up the iPod Software, which provides the intelligence inside your iPod. With a history of 19 different model configurations and 10 different software configurations, getting the right iPod Software for your iPod would be downright confusing if Apple didn't provide one downloadable installer that takes care of everything. Fortunately, Apple provides exactly that: an updater/installer each for Mac and Windows that recognizes the type of iPod you have and installs the correct software.

Setting Up iTunes

As a Mac user, you probably already have iTunes installed because all Macs sold since 2003 (and many before that time) are preinstalled with iTunes and Mac OS X, and you also get iTunes if you install Mac OS X on an older machine. The most up-to-date version of iTunes as of this writing is version 4.8. If you've never used iTunes before, when you first launch it, you automatically get the iTunes Setup Assistant.

The version of iTunes that's provided with your iPod on a CD-ROM might be the newest version; then again, it might not be. Software updates occur very rapidly. If you really want the latest version, go directly to the Apple Web site to get it. You can download iTunes for free. Install iTunes first, and then install the iPod software.

You can set your Mac to automatically download the latest version of iTunes when it becomes available. Simply use Software Update from the Mac OS X System Preferences window. Click the Check Now button to check for a new version. If one exists, it appears in a window for you to select. Click the check mark to select it, and then click Install to download and install it.

If you use a PC with Windows, you most likely don't have iTunes yet. Go directly to the Apple Web site and download the latest version.

iPods that were sold before iTunes became available for Windows (in the fall of 2003) don't include iTunes on the CD-ROM. The older iPod CD-ROMs install MusicMatch Jukebox. If you plan on using iTunes for Windows, which requires Windows XP or Windows 2000, download the newer iTunes and iPod installers from the Apple Web site. If you're using MusicMatch, visit the companion Web site at www.dummies.com/go/ipod.

When you get your iPod, you might be tempted to go ahead and install from the CD-ROM. Our experience, especially with Windows PCs, is that you're better off going to the Apple Web site first and downloading the latest versions of the iTunes and iPod installers for Windows. Install iTunes first, and then install the iPod software.

To download iTunes for Mac or Windows, go to the Apple iTunes page on the Web (www.apple.com/itunes), select the appropriate version (Mac or Windows), and then click the Download iTunes button, as shown in Figure 2-1. Follow the instructions to download the installer to your hard drive. Pick a location on your hard drive to save the installer.

Figure 2-1:
Download
the newest
version of
iTunes from
the Internet.

Setting up iTunes on a Mac

If you downloaded the iTunes installer, launch the installer to unpack and install iTunes. To install iTunes from the CD-ROM, open the iTunes folder on the CD-ROM, and then double-click the iTunes package file (it has an `.mpkg` extension) to unpack and install it. Then follow these steps:

1. **Click Continue after the installer's Welcome page.**

   The installer needs to run a program to check your computer and make sure it's capable of running iTunes.

2. **Read the Important Information page and click Continue.**

   The installer displays important "read me" information about the latest iTunes features. Click Continue after reading it, or if you like, click the Save button to save the Important Information page as a document, the Print button to print it, or the Go Back button to quit the installer.

3. **Click Continue and then click the Agree button for Apple's License Agreement.**

   Apple's License Agreement appears in the installer.

Optional: Before you click the Agree button, you have a few other options. You can click the Save button to save the license agreement as a document, the Print button to print it, the Decline button to quit iTunes immediately, or simply go with the Agree button. No lawyers are present when you do this; it's all up to you.

4. **Select the destination volume for iTunes.**

   The installer asks for the destination volume (hard drive), as shown in Figure 2-2, which must be a Mac OS X startup drive — any other drive is marked by a red exclamation point indicating that you can't install iTunes there. iTunes is installed in the Applications folder on the Mac OS X startup drive.

5. **Click Install to proceed with the installation.**

   As an alternative, you can customize your installation by clicking Customize, selecting each package you want to install, and then clicking Install.

6. **Click Done when the installer finishes.**

Figure 2-2:
Choose a destination volume (hard drive) for the iTunes application.

Mac users can proceed by directly launching iTunes and setting it up with the iTunes Setup Assistant. Follow these steps:

1. **Launch iTunes by double-clicking the iTunes application or clicking the iTunes icon in the Dock.**

2. **Click Next in the iTunes Setup Assistant opening page.**

   The iTunes Setup Assistant takes you through the process of setting up iTunes for the Internet. After clicking Next, the iTunes Setup Assistant displays a window with questions, shown in Figure 2-3.

Figure 2-3:
Set up
iTunes to
connect to
the Internet
and handle
all audio
content
from the
Internet.

3. **Select Yes or No to answer the following questions:**

   • Would you like to use iTunes to handle audio content from the Internet?

   We suggest selecting Yes, allowing iTunes to organize and play all audio content, because iTunes offers more features than you typically find with browser plug-ins from other companies. On the other hand, if you're happy with your plug-ins and helper applications, select No and leave your Internet settings untouched.

   • Do you want iTunes to automatically connect to the Internet when it's necessary?

   If you use an always-on broadband Internet service, you probably want iTunes to connect automatically, and you can select Yes. If you use a dial-up modem, if your Internet service is intermittently off, or if your Internet service charges when you use it, you probably don't want this connection to be automatic. Selecting No forces iTunes to ask first.

   After you click Next, the iTunes Setup Assistant also asks another question:

   • Do you want iTunes to search your Home folder for music files?

   You might want to click the "No, I'll add them later myself" selection for now, because iTunes might find files that you don't want to add to your library (such as music for games).

4. **When the assistant asks whether you want to go straight to the iTunes Music Store, select either Yes or No. Then click Done.**

   We suggest selecting No. However, if you can't wait to go shopping, Chapter 4 gives you the scoop on the iTunes Music Store.

   After clicking Done, the iTunes window appears. (We unravel the wonders of this window in Chapter 3.) You can drag the bottom-right corner of your iTunes window to make it larger or smaller on your screen.

Whether or not you set iTunes to automatically connect to the Internet, be sure to connect to the Internet with iTunes at some point. Doing so allows you to buy music online and listen to Web radio. You can even retrieve track information when you insert a CD so that you don't have to type the information yourself.

Setting up iTunes for Windows

Before installing iTunes for Windows, make sure that you're logged on as a Windows Administrator user if you're using Windows 2000 or Windows XP. Quit all other applications before installing and disable any virus protection software.

To install iTunes for Windows, download the iTunesSetup.exe file from the Apple Web site, as we describe earlier in this chapter (refer to Figure 2-1).

The iTunes installer also installs the newest version of QuickTime, replacing any older version you may have. QuickTime is Apple's multimedia development, storage, and playback technology. While Windows users aren't required to use QuickTime beyond its use by iTunes itself, QuickTime is a bonus for Windows users because it offers digital video playback.

If for some reason you can't download this software from the Internet, and you know for certain that the CD-ROM includes iTunes for Windows, you can use the CD-ROM to install iTunes. The CD-ROM installation process installs both iTunes for Windows and the iPod Updater for Windows. See the section "Setting Up Your iPod with a Windows PC" for information about installing iTunes for Windows from the CD-ROM.

To install iTunes for Windows, follow these steps:

1. **Double-click the iTunesSetup.exe file, which you can download from the Apple Web site.**

   The installer comes to life, displaying its opening window.

2. **Click Next and then click the Yes button for Apple's License Agreement.**

   Apple's License Agreement page appears in the installer window, and you can use the PageDown key to scroll down the agreement. Click Yes after reading to agree to it, or click No to discontinue installation. You can also click Back to return to the first page. After clicking Yes, the installer displays the Important Information page.

3. Read the Important Information page and click Next.

The installer displays important "read me" information about the latest iTunes features. Click Next after reading it, or click Back to go back to the previous page. To quit the installer and stop the installation, click Cancel. After clicking Next, the installer displays the next page with questions about the type of setup, as shown in Figure 2-4.

Figure 2-4:
Setup options for the iTunes installation in Windows.

4. Select the appropriate options for your iTunes setup and then click Next.

The options follow:

- **Install Desktop Shortcuts:** You can install shortcuts for your Windows desktop for iTunes.

- **Use iTunes as the Default Player for Audio Files:** We suggest turning this on — allowing iTunes to be the default audio content player — because iTunes offers more features than you typically find with players and browser plug-ins from other companies. If you're happy with your audio player, you can deselect this option, leaving your default player setting unaffected.

- **Use QuickTime as the Default Player for Media Files:** We suggest turning this on — allowing QuickTime to be the default audio multimedia (including video and audio) player — because QuickTime for Windows can play just about any media format and is comparable to players and browser plug-ins from other companies. If you're happy with your media player, you can deselect this option, leaving your default media player setting unaffected.

After clicking Next, the installer displays the Choose Destination Location page, as shown in Figure 2-5.

Figure 2-5:
Choose a
Windows
destination
folder for
the iTunes
application.

5. **In the Choose Destination Location page, select a destination folder for iTunes, and then click Next.**

   By default, the installer assumes that you want to store the program in the Program Files folder of your C: drive (which is an excellent place to store it, unless you have other ideas). If you want to use a different folder, click Browse to use Windows Explorer to locate the desired folder.

   After you click Next, the installer displays information about the iTunes Music Store.

6. **Click Next.**

   After you click Next, the installer proceeds with the installation.

7. **When the installer finishes, click Finish.**

   iTunes for Windows and QuickTime are now installed on your PC.

To set iTunes up for your Internet connection and start using it, double-click the iTunes program or use your Start menu to locate iTunes and launch it. After that, follow these steps:

1. **If this is the first time you've used iTunes, click the Agree button for Apple's License Agreement.**

   Apple's License Agreement appears only when you start iTunes for the first time.

   Optional: Before you click the Agree button, you have a few other options. You can click the Save button to save the license agreement as a document, the Print button to print it, the Decline button to quit iTunes immediately, or simply go with the Agree button. If you don't agree, you can consult a lawyer, but you still won't be able to continue with the setup.

2. **Click Next in the iTunes Setup Assistant opening screen.**

   The iTunes Setup Assistant takes you through the process of setting up the Windows version of iTunes for the Internet. After clicking Next, the Setup Assistant displays a page that helps you find music files on your PC, as shown in Figure 2-6.

Figure 2-6:
Finding music files using iTunes Setup Assistant.

3. **Select or deselect the following options for finding music (by default they are selected):**

   • **Add MP3 and AAC Files:** Select this option if you already have music files in the AAC format that's used by iTunes and the iPod — this option copies those files automatically into iTunes. You might want to turn this off, however, because iTunes might find MP3 files that you don't want to add to your library (such as music for games).

   • **Add WMA Files:** Select this option if you want to add unprotected Windows Media audio files to your iTunes library. This option automatically converts the WMA files to the AAC format. (For more information about formats, see Chapter 17.) The original WMA files are left untouched.

   After clicking Next, the assistant displays choices for keeping your music files and folders organized, as shown in Figure 2-7.

Figure 2-7:
Set iTunes
to rename
files and
folders as
you edit
song infor-
mation to
keep music
organized
auto-
matically.

4. **The assistant asks whether you want to keep your iTunes music folder organized. Select Yes or No, and then click Next.**

   The default is Yes, which tells iTunes to keep your music files organized automatically — iTunes renames and moves files into appropriate folders when you edit the artist name, song title, album name, or track number. If you don't want automatic renaming or you want to rename files and folders manually, click No.

5. **The assistant asks whether you want to go straight to the iTunes Music Store. Select Yes or No, and then click Finish.**

   We suggest selecting No until you are ready to go to the store. (Chapter 4 covers the iTunes Music Store in depth.)

   After clicking Finish, the iTunes window appears. (Chapter 3 gives you the full scoop on this window.) You can drag the bottom-right corner or the edges of your iTunes window to make it larger or smaller on your screen.

Setting Up Your iPod with a Mac

As with the iTunes software, the version of the iPod software that's provided with your iPod on CD-ROM might not be the newest version — especially if the iPod sat on a store shelf for a few months. Even minor changes to the software might mean new iPod features or better performance with your battery. Updates to the iPod software occur frequently. If you want the latest version, go directly to the Apple Web site to get it. You can download the iPod software for free.

You can set your Mac to automatically download the latest version of the iPod software when it becomes available — just use Software Update from the Mac OS X System Preferences window. Click the Check Now button to check for a new version. If one exists, it appears in a window for you to select. Select it and click Install to download and install it.

To download the iPod software, go to Apple's iPod download page on the Web (www.apple.com/ipod/download) and select the appropriate version (Mac or Windows). Follow the instructions to download the installer to your hard drive. Pick a location on your hard drive to save the installer. Then launch the installer to unpack and install the iPod software.

Apple pre-installs the iPod software on Apple-branded models so that you can use it right away with iTunes on a Mac. The extra step of downloading and installing iPod software ensures that you have the newest version and that you can restore the iPod if necessary (as we describe in Chapter 27).

To set up your iPod with a Mac, connect it to the Mac as described in Chapter 1. When you first connect your iPod to a Mac, the iTunes Setup Assistant appears like a butler, ready to help you set it up, as shown in Figure 2-8 for a color-display iPod. In this dialog you can give your iPod a name, which is a good idea if you plan on sharing several iPods among several computers.

Figure 2-8:
Set up your
iPod with
the iTunes
Setup
Assistant.

In the iTunes Setup Assistant, you can decide whether to update your iPod automatically or manually. If you want to copy your entire iTunes music library, leave the "Automatically update songs on my iPod" option selected. This option creates a mirror image of your library on the iPod, including all playlists and audio files, every time you connect your iPod. (Don't worry. You can always change this setting later; see Chapter 10.) If you want to copy only a portion of your library to the iPod, deselect (clear) this option.

The color-display iPod models also let you "Automatically copy photos to my iPod;" refer to Figure 2-8. Turn this option on if you want to copy all the photos in your iPhoto library to your iPod, or leave it off if you want to transfer photos later. This option copies (or updates) your entire iPhoto library to the iPod every time you connect your iPod.

If you turn on the option to copy photos automatically, and you also turn on the option to copy songs automatically, iTunes copies the songs first, then copies photos from the iPhoto library up to the limit of the iPod's capacity. iTunes tries to fit the entire photo library if your iPod has room. But if all the photos can't fit, iTunes fills the iPod with photos in the order specified by album list in the iPod pane of the iTunes Preferences window. See Chapter 24 to read all about transferring photos to your color-display iPod.

If you have an iPod shuffle, the iTunes Setup Assistant displays an option to copy songs randomly, as shown in Figure 2-9. If you leave the "Automatically choose songs for my iPod" option on, iTunes copies a random selection of songs to the iPod shuffle. You can always choose to fill the iPod shuffle with a different selection by clicking the Autofill button, as we describe in Chapter 10.

Figure 2-9:
Set up your
iPod shuffle
with the
iTunes
Setup
Assistant.

The iTunes Setup Assistant allows you to register your iPod with Apple to take advantage of Apple support. When you reach the last dialog, click Done. iTunes automatically launches, and your iPod's name appears in the iTunes Source pane under the Music Store. If you selected the automatic update feature in the iTunes Setup Assistant, the iPod name appears grayed out in the Source pane, and you can't open it. However, your iPod quickly fills up with the music from your iTunes music library — that is, if you *have* music in your library.

If you deselected the automatic update feature, the iPod name appears just like any other source in the Source pane, and you can open it and play songs on the iPod through iTunes and your Mac speakers, as we describe in Chapter 16. Of course, if you're just starting out, you probably have no tunes in your library. Your next step is to import music from CDs, buy music online, or import music from other sources.

After finishing setup, the iPod icon also appears on the Finder Desktop. If you leave your iPod connected to the Mac, the iPod appears on the Desktop and in iTunes whenever you start iTunes.

To see how much free space is left on the iPod, click the iPod icon on the desktop and choose File⇨Get Info. The Finder displays the Get Info window with information about capacity, amount used, and available space. You can also use the About command on the iPod, which is available in the Settings menu: Choose Settings⇨About. The iPod information screen appears with capacity and available space.

Setting Up Your iPod with a Windows PC

Before installing the iPod Software for Windows, make sure you're logged on as a Windows Administrator user if you're using Windows 2000 or Windows XP. Quit all other applications before installing, and disable any virus protection software.

The version of iPod Software for Windows provided on the CD-ROM with your iPod might not be the newest version. Therefore, we recommend going directly to the Apple Web site and downloading the latest version.

If you bought your iPod before the fall of 2003, the CD-ROM that came with it installs MusicMatch Jukebox. Don't use the CD-ROM from older iPods if you plan on using iTunes for Windows — download the newer iTunes and iPod installers from the Apple Web site.

If you use Windows 2000 or Windows XP, you can use iTunes for Windows. If you use any other Windows version, you need to install MusicMatch Jukebox from the iPod CD-ROM.

Setting up your iPod with Windows is a two-step process: installing the iPod Software and using the iTunes Setup Assistant. As of this writing, the CD-ROMs supplied with iPods offer iTunes for Windows and iPod Software in one installation. However, the CD-ROM might not contain the newest versions — especially if the iPod sat on a store shelf for a few months. The Apple Web site offers free downloads of the most up-to-date versions.

If you have no other choice, you can install from the CD-ROM and then update your software later from the Apple Web site.

Installing the iPod Software

To install iPod Software for Windows from the CD-ROM, *do not* connect the iPod to your computer — leave it disconnected, but be ready to connect it when the instructions say so. Follow these steps first:

1. **Double-click the CD-ROM icon in Windows Explorer.**

   The CD-ROM's AutoPlay feature starts the installation process; if the installer doesn't open automatically, right-click the CD-ROM icon in the My Computer window and choose AutoPlay from the shortcut menu that appears.

2. **In the first dialog that appears, choose the language that you want to use and then click OK.**

   The language shortcut menu lets you choose from quite a number of languages. After clicking OK, the InstallShield Wizard, so familiar to Windows users, takes over and launches the installer.

3. **Click Agree for the license agreement and type in your iPod serial number. Then click Next (or Cancel to quit).**

   Follow the instructions to type in your iPod serial number, and click Next for each window. The CD-ROM installation performs the same process as installing iTunes and the iPod software separately.

4. **In the Choose Destination Location pane, select a destination folder for the iPod Updater, and then click Next.**

   The iPod folder contains the iPod Updater program. By default, the installer assumes that you want to store the iPod folder in the Program Files folder of your C: drive (which is just peachy, unless you like to defy the system designers at Microsoft by putting programs in other places). Click Browse to use Windows Explorer if you dare locate a different folder.

   After selecting a folder (or keeping the default), click Next. The installer displays the next page, which asks you to connect your iPod to check its hard drive format.

5. **Connect your iPod and reformat its hard drive if necessary, then press Next.**

6. **When the iTunes Setup Assistant appears, click Next again.**

   Connect your iPod as described in Chapter 1. The installer checks to see if it needs to be reformatted, and if it does, it reformats the iPod for Windows. When finished, press Next, and iTunes starts up with the iTunes Setup Assistant dialog inside the iTunes window. You can skip to the next section on using the iTunes Setup Assistant.

If you purchased an older model without a CD-ROM, or a model with an outdated CD-ROM, you can install iPod Software for Windows, which is available on the Internet. To download iPod Software for Windows and install the downloaded version, go to Apple's iPod download page on the Web (`www.apple.com/ipod/download`) and click the iPod software link. Follow the instructions to download the installer to your hard drive. Pick a location on your hard drive to save the installer.

To install the downloaded version of iPod Software for Windows, *do not* connect the iPod to your computer — leave it disconnected, but be ready to connect it when the instructions say so. Follow these steps first:

1. **Double-click the `iPodSetup.exe` file, which you can download from the Apple Web site.**

2. **In the first dialog that appears, choose the language that you want to use, and then click OK.**

   The language menu lets you choose from quite a number of languages. After clicking OK, the InstallShield Wizard, so familiar to Windows users, takes over and launches the installer.

3. **Click Agree for the license agreement, and then click Next (or Cancel to quit).**

4. **In the Choose Destination Location pane, select a destination folder for the iPod Updater, and then click Finish.**

   The iPod folder contains the iPod Updater program. By default, the installer assumes that you want to store the iPod folder in the Program Files folder of your C: drive (which is just peachy, unless you like to defy the system designers at Microsoft by putting programs in other places). Click Browse to use Windows Explorer to locate a different folder if you dare.

   After selecting a folder (or keeping the default), click Finish.

After the installer finishes installing the iPod Updater, follow these steps:

1. **Start iPod Updater by choosing it from the iPod menu in your Start menu.**

   Launch the iPod Updater program by double-clicking the program icon or choosing it from the Start menu (Start⇨iPod⇨iPod Updater). The iPod Updater displays "Plug in an iPod to update it" in the iPod Updater window. You can now plug your iPod into the computer.

2. **Connect your iPod and wait for iPod Updater to recognize it.**

   Connect your iPod as described in Chapter 1. The installer checks to see if it needs to be reformatted; if it does, it activates the Restore button shown in Figure 2-10. This leaves you no other option except to restore the iPod to its factory condition, which includes reformatting the iPod for Windows. If your iPod is formatted for Mac use, it displays N/A for Name and Capacity. Refer to Figure 2-10.

Figure 2-10:
Use iPod
Updater to
restore an
iPod and
reformat
it for
Windows
use.

Figure 2-10:
Use iPod Updater to restore an iPod and reformat it for Windows use.

3. **Click the Restore button to restore the iPod, and click Restore again to continue.**

After you click Restore, the iPod Updater displays a warning dialog. Click Restore to continue with the restoration. iPod Updater erases and reformats the hard drive and restores the iPod to its factory settings. When it finishes restoring, it displays "Restore is complete. Please disconnect iPod from PC and connect it to the external power supply to allow firmware reflash."

4. **Disconnect the iPod from the computer and connect it to AC power.**

The iPod needs AC power to do a firmware refresh. (*Firmware* is software encoded in hardware.) Disconnect your iPod carefully, and then connect it to your power adapter. The iPod performs a firmware refresh operation that takes a few minutes. After the operation is complete, the iPod Updater displays its opening dialog.

5. **Connect the iPod to the computer again.**

iPod Updater should now recognize your iPod.

6. **Close iPod Updater, but leave your iPod connected.**

Close the iPod Updater by clicking the X-marked close box in the upper-right corner. Since your iPod is still connected, iTunes should start automatically and display the iTunes Setup Assistant dialog inside the iTunes window. If iTunes doesn't start automatically, start iTunes and wait for it to recognize your iPod. If your computer or iTunes has trouble recognizing your iPod, see Chapter 27.

Using iTunes Setup Assistant

If you started your installation from CD-ROM, as most people do, the iTunes Setup Assistant automatically appears after installing the iPod Software — just follow the steps given here. If you instead started your installation from the downloaded iPod Updater, as many of you savvy folks do because you want to use the latest version, leave your iPod connected and iTunes should start automatically; otherwise, you can start iTunes and connect your iPod when you're ready to continue setup — and as soon as iTunes recognizes your iPod, it displays the Setup Assistant. Then follow these steps:

1. **Click Next when the Setup Assistant opening dialog displays.**

   After clicking Next, the Setup Assistant displays the next page, which lets you give your iPod a name, as shown in Figure 2-11.

2. **Give your iPod a name, set automatic options, then click Next.**

   In this dialog you can give your iPod a name, which is a good idea if you plan on sharing several iPods among several computers.

Figure 2-11:
Give your Windows-based iPod a name and set the automatic update option with the iTunes Setup Assistant.

You can also decide whether to update your iPod automatically or manually. If you want to copy your entire iTunes music library, leave the "Automatically update songs on my iPod" option selected. This option creates a mirror image of your library on the iPod, including all playlists and audio files, every time you connect your iPod. (Don't worry. You can always change this setting later; see Chapter 10.) If you want to copy only a portion of your library to the iPod, deselect (clear) this option.

If you have an iPod shuffle, the iTunes Setup Assistant displays an option to copy songs randomly. If you leave the "Automatically choose songs for my iPod" option on, iTunes copies a random selection of songs to the iPod shuffle. You can always choose to fill the iPod shuffle with a different selection by clicking the Autofill button, as we describe in Chapter 10.

The color-display iPod models also let you "Automatically copy photos to my iPod." Turn this option on if you want to copy all the photos in your Adobe Photoshop Album (version 1.0 or newer) or Photoshop Elements (version 3.0 or newer) library to your iPod. Leave it off if you want to transfer photos later. This option copies (or updates) your entire photo library to the iPod every time you connect your iPod.

Click Next when you're finished with setting options and the iPod's name. iTunes Setup Assistant moves on to the page for registering your iPod.

3. **Click the Register button to register your iPod, and then click Finish.**

   The iTunes Setup Assistant allows you to register your iPod with Apple to take advantage of Apple support. When you reach the last dialog, click Finish. iTunes automatically launches, and your iPod's name appears in the iTunes Source pane under the Music Store.

If you turn on the option to copy photos automatically, and you also turn on the option to copy songs automatically. iTunes copies the songs first, then copies photos up to the limit of the iPod's capacity. iTunes tries to fit the entire photo library if your iPod has room. But if all the photos can't fit, iTunes fills the iPod with photos in the order specified by album list in the iPod pane of the iTunes Preferences window. See Chapter 24 to read all about transferring photos to your color-display iPod.

If you selected the automatic update feature in the iTunes Setup Assistant, the iPod name appears grayed out in the Source pane, and you can't open it. However, your iPod quickly fills up with the music from your iTunes music library.

If you deselected the automatic update feature, the iPod name appears just like any other source in the Source pane. You can open it and play songs on the iPod through iTunes and your PC speakers, as we describe in Chapter 16. Of course, if you're just starting out, you probably have no tunes in your library. Your next step is to import music from CDs, buy music online, or import music from other sources.

Chapter 3

Getting Started with iTunes

More than half a century ago, jukeboxes were the primary and most convenient way for people to select the music they wanted to hear and share with others, especially newly released music. Juke joints were hopping with the newest hits every night. You could pick any song to play at any time, but you had to insert a coin and pay for each play. Radio eventually supplanted the jukebox as the primary means of releasing new music to the public, and the music was free to hear — but you couldn't choose to play any song you wanted at any time.

Today, using iTunes, you can have a digital jukebox *and* a radio in your computer. Click a button to play any song anytime you want, or click a radio station and play a broadcast. Connect your computer to a stereo amplifier in your home or connect speakers to your computer, and suddenly your computer is the best jukebox in the neighborhood.

This chapter explains what you can do with iTunes and how you can use iTunes to play music tracks on a CD, just like a jukebox, only better — you don't have to pay for each song you play, and you can play some or all of the songs on an album in any order.

What You Can Do with iTunes

You can download songs from the Internet and copy them to iTunes, or copy songs from CDs directly into your iTunes library. You can also buy music and music videos online at the iTunes Music Store, or subscribe to *podcasts,* which are feeds that transfer new audio files automatically, such as weekly radio broadcasts. iTunes downloads content from the store and puts it in your library, making it immediately available for playing. You can then burn the audio content onto a CD or transfer it to an iPod. You can even use iTunes to listen to Web radio stations and add your favorite stations to your music library.

Transferring songs from a CD to your computer is called *ripping* a CD (to the chagrin of the music industry old-timers who think that users intend to destroy the discs or steal the songs). Ripping an entire CD's worth of songs is quick and easy, and track information, such as artist name and title, arrives automatically over the Internet.

iTunes gives you the power to organize songs into playlists and burn any set of songs in your library to CD, in any order. You can even set up dynamic smart playlists that reflect your preferences and listening habits. iTunes offers an equalizer with preset settings for all kinds of music and listening environments, and it gives you the ability to customize and save your own personalized settings with each song.

The Mac and Windows versions of iTunes are virtually identical, with the exception that dialogs look a bit different between the two operating systems. There are also a few other differences, mostly related to the different operating environments — the Windows version lets you import Windows Media (WMA) songs, while the Mac version, like most Mac applications, can be controlled by Applescripts. Nevertheless, as Apple continues to improve iTunes, the company releases upgrades to both versions at the same time, and the versions are free to download.

Opening the iTunes Window

You can run iTunes anytime to add music, audio books, podcasts, Web radio stations, and music videos, and to manage your iTunes library. You don't have to connect your iPod until you're ready to transfer music, audio books, and podcasts to it (as we describe in Chapter 11), or play the content on the iPod rather than the content in the library (as we describe in Chapter 18).

When you launch iTunes, your library and other sources of content appear. Figure 3-1 shows the iTunes window on the Mac, and Figure 3-2 shows it in Windows.

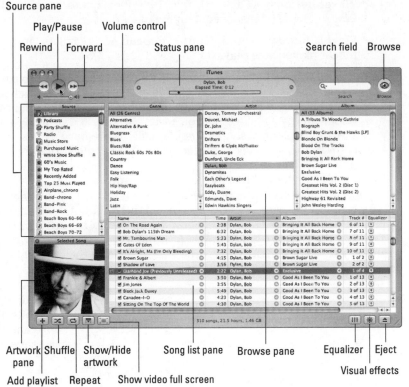

Source pane

Play/Pause   Volume control

Rewind   Forward   Status pane   Search field   Browse

Figure 3-1:
The iTunes
window on
a Mac.

Artwork Shuffle Show/Hide   Song list pane   Browse pane   Equalizer Eject
pane   artwork

Add playlist Repeat   Show video full screen   Visual effects

The iTunes window offers a view of your library and your sources for content, as well as controls for organizing, importing, and playing content, as follows:

- **Source pane:** Displays the source — Library (your iTunes library), Party Shuffle (a dynamic playlist), Radio (access to Web radio), Music Store (the iTunes Music Store), your iPod (if it's connected), and your playlists.

- **Song List pane and Browse pane:** Depending on the source that's selected in the Source pane, these panes display a list of the content in your library, your playlist, your iPod, the iTunes Music Store, the podcast directory, or Web radio stations. The Browse button in the upper-right corner toggles between Browse view (with the Song List pane below and the Browse pane above with genre, artist, and album) and the Song List pane by itself. Browse view isn't available when viewing a playlist or the Radio selection.

- **Status pane:** When a song, audio book, radio station, podcast, or video is playing, this displays the artist name, piece title (if known), and the elapsed time.

- **Search field:** Type characters in this field to search your library. You can also use the search field to peruse a playlist or to look within the iTunes Music Store.

✔ **Player buttons — Forward/Next, Play/Pause, and Previous/Rewind:** Control the playback of content in iTunes.

✔ **Playlist buttons — Add, Shuffle, Repeat:** Add playlists, and shuffle or repeat playback of playlists.

✔ **Miscellaneous buttons — Show/Hide Artwork, Equalizer, Turn on visual effects, Eject:** Display or hide artwork (either your own or the artwork supplied with purchased songs and videos), the equalizer, and visual effects. The Eject button ejects a CD or iPod — while a CD will actually pop out of some computers, iPods are hard drives, and ejecting them simply removes (a.k.a. *un-mounts*) the drives from the system.

If you don't like the width of the Source pane, you can adjust it by dragging the shallow dot on the vertical bar between the Source pane and the Song List pane and Browse pane. You can also adjust the height of the Song List and Browse panes by dragging the shallow dot on the horizontal bar between them. To resize the iTunes window in Windows, drag the edges of the window horizontally or vertically. On a Mac, drag diagonally from the bottom-right corner.

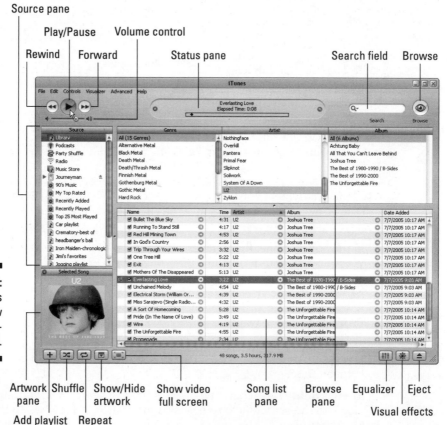

Source pane

Play/Pause   Volume control

Rewind   Forward   Status pane   Search field   Browse

Figure 3-2: The iTunes window on a Windows PC.

Artwork Shuffle Show/Hide Show video   Song list   Browse   Equalizer   Eject
pane   artwork   full screen   pane   pane
                                                                   Visual effects
Add playlist Repeat

Playing CD Tracks in iTunes

iTunes needs content. You can get started right away with ripping music from CDs into your library, but for more instant gratification, you can *play* music right off the CD without importing it. Maybe you don't want to put the music into your library yet. Maybe you just want to hear it first, as part of your Play First, Rip Later plan.

Insert any music CD or even a CD-R that someone burned for you. The music tracks appear in the iTunes song list. The Browse button changes to an Import button when a CD is inserted, in anticipation of importing (a.k.a. *ripping*) the CD.

The songs first appear in your song list as generic, unnamed tracks. If your computer is connected to the Internet, you may be able to grab the song information automatically, without your having to type anything — that is, if you turned on the "Connect to Internet when needed" option in the General tab of the Preferences dialog (as described in Chapter 8).

After you insert the CD, iTunes displays a message about accessing the Gracenote CDDB database on the Internet, and then presents the track information for each song automatically, as shown in Figure 3-3. (Gracenote CDDB is a song database on the Internet that knows the track names of most commercial CDs, but not homemade mix CDs. You can read about it and editing song information, in Chapter 8.)

Figure 3-3: CD track info appears after iTunes consults the Internet.

When you play a CD in iTunes, it's just like using a CD player. To play a CD from the first track, click the Play button. (If you clicked somewhere else after inserting the disc, you may have to click the first track to select it before clicking the Play button.) The Play button then turns into a Pause button, and the song plays.

When the song finishes, iTunes continues playing the songs in the list in sequence until you click the Pause button (which then toggles back into the Play button), or until the song list ends. You can skip to the next or previous song by using the arrow keys on your keyboard, or by clicking the Forward button or the Back button next to the Play button. You can also double-click another song in the list to start playing it.

You can press the space bar to perform the same function as clicking the Play button; pressing it again is just like clicking the Pause button.

The Status pane above the list of songs tells you the name of the artist or the song title (if known), as well as the elapsed time of the track. When you click the artist name, the artist name disappears, and the song title appears; if you click the song title, the artist name comes back up. If you click the Elapsed Time status, the status changes to the remaining time and then, with another click, to the total time. (One more click brings you back to the elapsed time.)

Eject a CD by clicking the Eject button or by choosing Controls⇨Eject Disc. Another way to eject the CD is to click the eject icon next to the CD's name in the Source pane. You can also right-click the CD's name and choose Eject from the contextual menu.

Rearranging and repeating tracks

You can rearrange the order of the tracks to automatically play them in any sequence you want — similar to programming a CD player. Click the upward-pointing arrow at the top of the first column in the song list, and it changes to a downward-pointing arrow, and the tracks appear in reverse order.

To change the order of tracks that you're playing in sequence, just click and hold on the track number in the leftmost column for the song, and then drag it up or down in the list. You can set up the tracks to play in a completely different sequence.

Skipping tracks

To skip tracks so that they don't play in sequence, deselect the check box next to the song names. iTunes skips deselected songs when you play the entire sequence.

To remove all check marks from a list, simultaneously hold down the ⌘ key on a Mac (or the Ctrl key in Windows) while clicking a check mark. Select an empty check box while pressing ⌘/Ctrl to add check marks to the entire list.

Repeating a song list

You can repeat an entire song list by clicking the Repeat button below the Source pane on the left side of the iTunes window (or by choosing Controls➪ Repeat All). When it's selected, the Repeat button icon changes to show blue highlighting. Click the Repeat button again to repeat the current song (or choose Controls➪Repeat One). The icon changes to include a blue-highlighted numeral 1. Click it once more to return to normal playback (or choose Controls➪Repeat Off).

The Shuffle button, located to the left of the Repeat button, plays the songs in the list in random order, which can be fun. You can then press the arrow keys on your keyboard or click the Back and Forward buttons to jump around in random order.

Displaying visuals

The visual effects in iTunes can turn your display into a light show that's synchronized to the music in your library. You can watch a cool visual display of eye candy while the music plays — or leave it on like a lava lamp.

Click the Visual Effects button on the bottom-right side of the iTunes window to display visual effects. The visual animation appears in the iTunes window and synchronizes with the music.

In addition to the animation replacing the iTunes song list, an Options button replaces the Import button in the upper-right corner of the iTunes window. You can click the Options button to open the Visualizer Options dialog, as shown in Figure 3-4.

The Visualizer Options dialog offers the following options that affect the animation (but not the performance of iTunes when it's playing music):

- ✔ **Display Frame Rate:** Displays the frame rate of the animation along with the animation.

- ✔ **Cap Frame Rate at 30 fps:** Keeps the frame rate at 30 fps (frames per second) or lower, which is roughly the speed of video.

- ✔ **Always Display Song Info:** Displays the song name, artist, and album for the song currently playing, along with the animation.

✔ **Use OpenGL (Mac only):** You can choose to use OpenGL, the most widely used standard for three-dimensional graphics programming, to display very cool animation with faster performance.

✔ **Faster but Rougher Display:** The animation plays faster, with rougher graphics. Select this option if your animation plays too slowly.

Figure 3-4: Set options for visual effects.

The Visualizer menu in iTunes gives you even more control over visual effects. You can choose Visualizer➪Small or Visualizer➪Medium to display the visual effects in a rectangle inside the iTunes window, or choose Visualizer➪Large to fill the iTunes window. Choosing Visualizer➪Full Screen sets the visual effects to fill up the entire screen. When displaying the full-screen visual effects, you can click the mouse or press Escape (Esc) to stop the display and return to iTunes. Choosing Visualizer➪Turn Visualizer On is the same as clicking the Visual Effects button: It displays the visual effects.

While the animated visual effects play, press Shift-/ (like when you type a question mark) to see a list of keyboard functions. Depending on the visual effect, you might see more choices of keyboard functions by pressing Shift-/ again.

To turn off the visual effects display, click the Visual Effects button again. You can leave the effects on (except when in full-screen mode) even while opening the equalizer because you still have access to the playback controls.

Chapter 4

Shopping at the iTunes Music Store

● ●

In This Chapter

▶ Setting up an account with the iTunes Music Store

▶ Previewing and buying songs

▶ Sending and receiving gift certificates

▶ Setting up allowance accounts

▶ Authorizing computers to play purchased music

● ●

*W*hen Apple announced its new music service, Apple chairman Steve Jobs remarked that other services put forward by the music industry tend to treat consumers like criminals. Steve had a point. Many of these services cost more and add a level of copy protection that prevents consumers from burning more than one CD or using the music they bought on other computers or portable MP3 players.

Record labels had been dragging their feet for years, experimenting with online sales and taking legal action against online sites, such as Napster, that allowed free downloads and music copying. Although the free music attracted millions of listeners, the free services were under legal attack in several countries, and the digital music that was distributed wasn't of the highest quality (not to mention the widespread and sometimes intentional misspellings in the song information and artist names). Consumers grew even warier when the Record Industry Association of America (RIAA), a lobbying organization looking out for the interests of record companies, began legal proceedings against people for illegal copyright infringement — people who possibly thought they were downloading free music.

No one should go to jail for being a music junkie. Consumers and the industry both needed a solution, so Apple did the research on how to make a service that worked better and was easier to use, and the company forged ahead with the iTunes Music Store. By all accounts, Apple has succeeded in offering the easiest, fastest, and most cost-effective service for buying music online for your computer and your iPod. The iTunes Music Store even offers gift certificates that you can e-mail to others and allowance accounts that you can set up for others (such as children) with credit limits but without the need to use a credit card. Apple adds new features to the store almost every week.

In this chapter, we show you how to sign in and take advantage of what the iTunes Music Store has to offer.

Visiting the iTunes Music Store

You can visit the iTunes Music Store by connecting to the Internet and using either iTunes or America Online (AOL).

As of this writing, the iTunes Music Store offers at least 1.5 million songs, with most songs available for download at the price of 99 cents each and entire albums available for download at less than the CD price. You can play the songs on up to five different computers, burn your own CDs, and use them on the iPod. The store also offers audio books from Audible.com, and *podcasts,* which are similar to syndicated radio shows but can be downloaded into iTunes and listened to at your convenience on your computer and iPod.

The iTunes Music Store is part of iTunes version 4 and newer. If you're running an older version of iTunes, download the newest version, as we describe in Chapter 2.

You can preview any song for up to 30 seconds (and audio books up to about 90 seconds), and if you have an account set up, you can buy and download the song immediately. We don't know of a faster way to purchase a song.

To open the iTunes Music Store, you have three options:

  ✔ **Click the Music Store option in the Source pane.** This opens the Music Store's home page, as shown in Figure 4-1.

  ✔ **Follow a music link in iTunes.** Click the *music link* (the gray-circled arrow next to a song title, artist name, or album title) to go to a Music Store page related to the song, artist, or album. iTunes performs a search in the Music Store by using the song information. If nothing closely related turns up, at least you end up in the Music Store, and you might even find music you like that you didn't know about.

  ✔ **Go to iTunes on AOL and click the iTunes link.** If you use AOL, you can browse or search the AOL music area for songs and click the <u>iTunes</u> link to automatically launch iTunes and go to the Music Store.

If you need to fire up your modem and log on to your Internet service to go online, do so before clicking the Music Store option or following a music link.

The Music Store replaces the iTunes Song List and Browse panes. You can check out artists and songs to your heart's content although you can't buy songs unless you have a Music Store account set up. You can use the Choose Genre pop-up menu to specify music genres, or click links for new releases, exclusive tracks, and so on.

We use the term *pop-up menu* for menus on the Mac that literally pop up from dialogs and windows; the same type of menu in Windows actually drops down and is also called a *drop-down menu*. We use pop-up menu for both.

The iTunes Music Store also provides buttons on a gray bar just above the Song List pane and Browse pane. The left and right triangle buttons work just like the Back and Forward buttons of a Web browser, moving back a page or forward a page. The button with the Home icon takes you to the iTunes Music Store home page. The Browse button in the upper-right corner switches the view between Browse view (with the Song List and Browse panes both open) and Song List view (with only the Song List pane open).

Figure 4-1:
The iTunes
Music Store
home page.

Setting up an account

To create an iTunes Music Store account, follow these steps:

1. **In iTunes, click the Music Store option in the Source pane or follow a music link.**

   The Music Store's home page appears (refer to Figure 4-1), replacing the iTunes Song List pane and Browse pane.

2. **Click the Sign In button in the upper-right area of the window to create an account or sign in to an existing account.**

   If you don't have an account, the button next to Account on the gray bar reads "Sign In." If you already have an account, the account name appears in place of the Sign In button. You need an account to buy music. After clicking the Sign In button, iTunes displays the account sign-in dialog, as shown in Figure 4-2.

   If you already set up an account with the iTunes Music Store, with the .Mac service, with other Apple services (such as the Apple Developer Connection), or with AOL, you're halfway there. Type in your ID and password, and then click the Sign In button. Apple remembers the personal information that you put in previously, so you don't have to re-enter it every time you visit the Music Store. If you forgot your password, click the Forgot Password? button, and iTunes provides a dialog to answer your test question. If you answer correctly, iTunes then e-mails your password to you.

Figure 4-2:
Sign in to
the iTunes
Music
Store.

3. **If you aren't signed up yet, click the Create New Account button.**

   iTunes displays a new page, replacing the iTunes Music Store home page with the terms of use and an explanation of steps to create a new account.

4. Click the Agree button, and then fill in your personal account information.

iTunes displays the next page of the setup procedure, shown in Figure 4-3, which requires you to type your e-mail address, password, test question and answer (in case you forget your password), birth date, and privacy options.

5. Click the Continue button to go to the next page of the account setup procedure, and then enter your credit card information.

The entire procedure is secure, so you don't have to worry. The Music Store keeps your personal information (including your credit card information) on file, and you don't have to type it again.

6. Click Done to finish the procedure.

You can now use the iTunes Music Store to purchase and download music to play in iTunes and use on an iPod.

If you use AOL and the AOL Wallet feature, you can assign payment for your Music Store account to your AOL Wallet. AOL Wallet contains your billing and credit card information for purchases. Use AOL Wallet to fill out your personal information. AOL Wallet automatically fills information into the text boxes of the account setup pages so that you don't have to.

Figure 4-3:
Create
a new
account for
the iTunes
Music
Store.

Click the Choose Store button in the top-left corner of the iTunes Music Store page to choose online music stores in other countries. iTunes displays a page of buttons with flags of other countries — click one to go to the home page for the iTunes Music Store for that country. For example, the music store in France displays menus in French and features hit songs for the French market.

Browsing for artists, songs, and albums

The iTunes Music Store home page is loaded with specials and advertisements to peruse. You can also use the Genre pop-up menu to see only those specials and ads for a particular genre. You can click just about anything on the home page to get more information: today's top ten songs, exclusive offerings, albums, artists' names, and more.

What if you're looking for music in a particular genre? You can browse the store by genre and artist name in a method similar to browsing your iTunes library. To browse the store, click the Browse button in the top-right corner of the iTunes window. iTunes displays the store's offerings categorized by genre, and within each genre, by artist and album. Click a genre in the left column, then a subgenre in the middle-left column, then an artist in the middle-right column, and finally an album in the right column, which takes you to the list of songs from that album that are available to preview or purchase, as shown in Figure 4-4.

Figure 4-4: Browsing the Music Store for artists and albums.

To see more information about a song or the album that it came from, click the music link (one of the gray-circled arrow buttons in the song list):

- ✔ Clicking the arrow in the Artist column takes you to the artist's page of albums.
- ✔ Clicking the arrow in the Album column takes you to the album page.
- ✔ Clicking the arrow in the Genre column takes you back to the genre's specials page (or the home page).

Our only complaint about browsing by artist is that artists are listed alphabetically by first name — you have to look up Bob Dylan under *Bob*.

If you know specifically what you're looking for, you can search rather than browse. The Search field in the top-right corner of the iTunes window lets you search the iTunes Music Store for just about anything. Type part of a song title or artist name to quickly search the store, or use the Power Search feature to narrow your search. (See the "Power-searching" section later in this chapter.)

Browsing the charts

What do Louis Armstrong, Roy Orbison, the Beach Boys, Dean Martin, and Mary Wells have in common? Each one had a top-ten hit in the charts for 1964. So says *Billboard,* the weekly magazine for the entertainment industry that has kept tabs on song popularity for more than half a century. The iTunes Music Store offers pop charts for each year going back to 1946, so you can probably find some of the songs that you grew up with.

You can't find *every* song that made the charts — only the songs that the iTunes Music Store offers.

To find the charts, click the Billboard Charts link in the list of Music Store links on the home page, or browse the store and select Charts at the very top of the Genre column. From the Charts column, you can select Billboard Hot 100, Billboard Top Country, or Billboard Top R&B (rhythm & blues).

Don't like the songs that *Billboard* chose? Try selecting Radio Charts from the Genre column, and then pick a city in the United States in the middle column. Now you can find out what songs are hits in your hometown, no matter where you are at the moment.

Power-searching

You're serious about music, and you want the power to search for exactly what you want. Click the <u>Power Search</u> link on the iTunes Music Store home page to go to the Power Search page, as shown in Figure 4-5.

You can fill in the song title, the artist name, and the album title, or just fill in one of those text boxes (for example, if all you know is the song title). You can narrow your search by picking a genre from the Genre pop-up menu and by adding a composer name. After you fill in as much as you know, click the Search button.

Playing music videos and movie trailers

Music videos and movie trailers are just a click away, and they're free to watch. The <u>Music Video</u> link on the iTunes Music Store home page takes you to a Music Store page. Click a thumbnail or title to select a video. Then either click Small to select a small video window size for quicker downloading, or Large for a larger video window size for better viewing.

It might take some time to download the video before it starts to play. After the QuickTime player controls appear in the iTunes window, as shown in Figure 4-6, you can click the movie's Play button (the right triangle next to the Sound button) to play the video.

Figure 4-5: Use Power Search to find a song in the Music Store.

Figure 4-6:
Play the music video in a small window.

You can play music in your iTunes library while waiting for a Music Store page or video to download over the Internet. Double-click the Music Store option in the Source pane to open the Music Store in a separate window. With two windows, you can use the first window to play music in your library while using the second to browse the Music Store and download a video. The first windows stops playing music when you use the second window to play a video or select a song to preview or buy.

Browsing celebrity and published playlists

Do you want to be influenced? Do you want to know what influenced some of today's music celebrities and buy what they have in their record collections? Scroll down the iTunes Music Store home page and click a celebrity name in the Celebrity Playlists panel, or click the Celebrity Playlists link to go to the page of celebrity playlists.

A typical celebrity playlist offers about an album's worth of songs from different artists. You can preview or buy any song in the list or follow the music links to the artist or album page.

The Music Store home page lists some of the celebrity playlists, but a lot more aren't listed there (204 the last time we checked). To see all the celebrity playlists, click the See All button at the bottom of the panel of Celebrity Playlist links on the home page.

You can also be influenced by other Music Store buyers and do a little influencing yourself. Click the <u>iMix</u> link on the Music Store home page to check out playlists that have been contributed by other consumers and published in the Music Store. iMixes offer 30-second previews of any songs in the playlist. To learn how to publish your own iMix playlist, see Chapter 9.

Do you want to turn someone else on to some music quickly by sending an e-mail? Include a reference to a song in the Store in a document or a Web page? You can also include a Web link (URL) to an iTunes Music Store page in an e-mail message or other document so the reader can click the link to go directly to the store page. Drag any link, track, or graphic from a Music Store page to an e-mail message or document you are composing, and iTunes copies the link. You can also Ctrl-click the item and choose Copy iTunes Music Store URL.

Previewing a song

The cool thing about record stores, besides being able to hang out and meet people, is the ability to preview CDs before you buy them. You can't meet flesh-and-blood people in the online iTunes Music Store, but you can preview songs before you buy them. To preview a song, click the song title in the song list, and then click the Play button or press the space bar.

By default, the previews play on your computer off the Internet in a stream, so you might hear a few hiccups in the playback. Each preview lasts about 30 seconds. Just when you start really getting into the song, it ends — but if the song is irresistible, you can buy it on the spot.

If you have a slow Internet connection — especially slower than 128 kbps — the preview may stutter. Choose iTunes⇨Preferences on a Mac or Edit⇨ Preferences on a Windows PC and click Store. In the Store pane click the "Load complete preview before playing" option to turn it on.

Buying and Downloading Songs

After setting up an account, you can purchase songs and download each one to your computer immediately, or gather them in a virtual shopping cart first, to see your choices and decide whether or not to purchase them before downloading them all at once.

Depending on how you set up your account, you can download the song immediately with the 1-Click option or place the song in your Music Store Shopping Cart temporarily, to purchase and download later. You can change your Music Store shopping method at any time.

After the song downloads, it appears in your iTunes song list. Purchased songs also appear in a special Purchased Music playlist under the Music Store option in the Source pane. You can see the list of all the songs that you purchased by clicking the triangle to expand the Music Store option in the Source pane, and then clicking the Purchased Music option. The Song List pane and Browse pane change to show the list of songs that you purchased.

Using 1-Click

Apple offers 1-Click technology in the iTunes Music Store so that with one click, the song immediately starts downloading to your computer — and the purchase is done.

With 1-Click, you select a song and click the Buy Song button at the far right of the song. (You might have to scroll down your iTunes Music Store window.) The store displays a warning dialog to make sure that you want to buy the song, and you can then go through with it or cancel. If you click the Buy button to purchase the song, the song downloads automatically and shows up in your iTunes library. The Music Store keeps track of your purchases over a 24-hour period and charges a total sum rather than for each single purchase.

1-Click seems more like two clicks. If you really want to use only one click to buy a song, select the Don't Warn Me About Buying Songs option in the warning dialog so that you never see it again.

Your decision to download each song immediately or add to a Shopping Cart and download later is likely based on how your computer connects to the Internet. If you have a slow connection such as a phone line, you probably want to use the Shopping Cart, to avoid tying up the phone with each download.

Using the Shopping Cart

You don't have to use the 1-Click technology. Instead, you can add songs to the Shopping Cart to delay purchasing and downloading until you're ready. With the Shopping Cart, the store remembers your selections, allowing you to browse the store at different times and add to your Shopping Cart without making any purchases final. You can also remove items from the cart at any time. When you're ready to buy, you can purchase and download the songs in your cart at once.

If you switch to the Shopping Cart method (see the following section, "Changing your Store preferences"), the Buy Song button toggles to an Add Song button. After adding songs, you can view your Shopping Cart by clicking the triangle next to the Music Store option in the Source pane to show the Music Store selections (see Figure 4-7), and click the Shopping Cart option. The Shopping Cart appears with your purchases listed in the Song List pane, and recommendations from the store appear along the top of the window.

When you're ready to purchase everything in your Shopping Cart, click the Buy Now button in the lower-right corner of the Shopping Cart window to close the sale and download all the songs at once. You can alternatively click the Buy (for an album) or Buy Song buttons for each item that you want to purchase.

To delete items from your Shopping Cart, select them and press Delete/ Backspace. A warning appears asking whether you're sure that you want to remove the selected items. Click Yes to go ahead and remove the selections from your Shopping Cart.

Changing your Store preferences

You can change your shopping method by choosing iTunes⇨Preferences on the Mac or by choosing Edit⇨Preferences on a Windows PC. In the Preferences window, click the Store button. The Store Preferences window appears. You can set the following features:

- ✔ Change from 1-Click to Shopping Cart or vice versa. 1-Click is the default.

- ✔ If you select the Play Songs After Downloading option, the songs that you buy start playing as soon as they complete download to your iTunes library.

- ✔ For better playing performance (fewer hiccups) with previews over slow Internet connections, select the Load a Complete Preview before Playing option. (It's deselected by default.)

If you use more than one computer with your Music Store account, you can set the preferences for each computer differently and still use the same account. For example, your home computer might have a faster connection than your laptop on the road, and you can set your iTunes preferences accordingly — the home computer could be set to 1-Click, and the laptop could be set to Shopping Cart.

Figure 4-7:
View your
Shopping
Cart before
checking
out of the
Music
Store.

Resuming interrupted downloads

All sales are final — you can't return the digital merchandise. However, you have to receive all of it before the Music Store charges you for the purchase. If for any reason the download is interrupted or fails to complete, your order remains active until you connect to the store again.

iTunes remembers to continue the download when you return to iTunes and connect to the Internet. If for some reason the download doesn't continue, choose Advanced⇨Check for Purchased Music to continue the interrupted download. You can also use this command to check for any purchased music that hasn't downloaded yet.

If your computer's hard drive crashes and you lose your information, you also lose your songs — you have to purchase and download them again. However, you can mitigate this kind of disaster by backing up your music library, which we describe in detail in Chapter 11. You can also burn your purchased songs onto an audio CD, as we describe in Chapter 12.

Redeeming gift certificates and prepaid cards

If you're the fortunate recipient of an iTunes Music Store gift certificate, all you need to do is go to the Music Store in iTunes and set up a new account if you don't already have one. Recipients of gift certificates can set up new accounts without having to provide a credit card number. As a recipient of a gift, you can simply click None for the credit card option and use the gift certificate as the sole payment method.

You can receive gift certificates on paper, delivered by the postal service, or by e-mail; you can also receive a prepaid card with a fixed balance. To redeem a certificate, click the <u>Gift Certificate</u> link on the iTunes Music Store home page, and then click the Redeem Now button. Then type the number printed on the lower-right edge of the certificate or supplied in the e-mail, click the Redeem button to credit your account, and then sign in to your account or set up an account. To redeem the amount of a prepaid card, click the <u>Prepaid Cards</u> link on the iTunes Music Store home page, click the Redeem button now, and then sign in or set up your account.

If you use Apple's Mail program, you can redeem a gift certificate that was sent by e-mail by clicking the Redeem Now button at the bottom of the e-mail message. This button launches iTunes with the Music Store option selected in the Source pane, and the certificate's number shows up automatically. Click the Redeem button to credit your account, and then sign in to your account (if you already have an account), or set up an account (see "Setting up an account," earlier in this chapter).

The balance of your gift certificate (how much you have left to spend) appears right next to your account name in the iTunes Music Store window and is updated as you make purchases.

Managing Your Account

Online stores record necessary information about you, such as your credit card number, your billing address, and so forth. You can change this information at any time, and you can also take advantage of Music Store account features, such as sending gift certificates and setting up allowance accounts.

Viewing and changing account information

Life is unpredictable. As John Lennon sang in "Beautiful Boy (Darling Boy)," "Life is what happens to you while you're busy making other plans." So if your billing address changes, or you need to switch to another credit card, or you need to change your password for any reason, you can edit your account information at any time.

To see your account information in the Music Store, click the Account button that shows your account name. iTunes displays a dialog for you to enter your account password. You then click the View Account button to see your account in the store.

Your account page displays your Apple ID, the last four digits of the credit card that you use for the account, your billing address, your most recent purchase, and your computer authorizations. (See "Authorizing computers to play purchased music," later in this chapter.) You can click buttons to edit your account information and credit card and to buy or redeem gift certificates and set up allowances.

Viewing your purchase history

In the rock 'n' roll lifestyle, you might recall songs from the 60s but not remember what you bought last week. To view your purchase history, go to your account page by clicking the Account button and typing your password in the dialog that appears. Click the View Account button, and on your account page, click the Purchase History button.

The Music Store displays the songs that you purchased, starting with the most recent. If you bought a lot of songs, not all of them appear on the first page. To see the details of previous purchases, click the arrow to the left of the order date. After viewing your history, click Done at the bottom of the history page to return to your account page.

Setting up allowances

Do you trust your kids with your credit card? You don't have to answer that — you can sidestep the entire issue by providing an *allowance account* for that special someone who wants to buy music on your credit card. With an allowance account, you can set the amount of credit to allow for the account each month — from $10–$200 in increments of $10. You can change the amount of an allowance or stop it at any time.

To use an allowance account, the recipient must be using iTunes version 4 or newer and live in a country where the iTunes Music Store is available on the Internet (such as the United States).

You can set up the allowance account yourself or define an allowance on an existing account. The recipient signs in to the account and types his or her password — no credit card required. When the recipient reaches the limit of the allowance, that account can't buy anything else until the following month. iTunes Music Store saves any unused balance until the next Music Store purchase.

To set up an allowance account, click the <u>Allowance</u> link on the Music Store home page. iTunes takes you to the Allowance page in the Music Store, where you can enter your name, your recipient's name, the monthly allowance amount (using the Monthly Allowance pop-up menu), and your recipient's Apple ID and password.

Click Continue to proceed with the account setup process, and then follow the instructions to finish setting up the account.

To stop an allowance or change the amount of an allowance account, go to your account page by clicking the Account button that shows your account name, and then type your password in the dialog that appears. Click the View Account button and scroll the account page until you see the Setup Allowance button; click this button to go to the Allowance page.

Sending gift certificates

A song is a gift that keeps on giving every time the recipient plays the song. You can't go wrong giving a Music Store gift certificate to that special person who has everything. New songs are introduced every day, and another half-million songs are available spanning every type of musical genre.

Before sending a gift certificate, first make sure that the recipient can run iTunes 4. (You might want to subtly suggest to the future recipient, in an e-mail, that it's time to download iTunes, just to find out whether he or she has the requisite system configuration — see Chapter 1.)

To buy a gift certificate to send to someone, click the Gift Certificate link on the Music Store home page. iTunes takes you to the Gift Certificate page in the Music Store.

Click the Buy Now button to purchase a gift certificate. You can send a printed certificate by snail mail or as an e-mail message. Supply the address, set the amount of the gift certificate, and even add a personal message if you want; then click Continue and follow the instructions to finish the process.

To set up or change the amount of a gift certificate, go to your account page by clicking the Account button that shows your account name and typing your password in the dialog that appears. Click the View Account button and scroll the account page until you see the Gift Certificate button; click it to go to the Gift Certificate page.

Authorizing computers to play purchased music

The computer that you use to set up your account is automatically authorized by Apple to play the songs that you buy. Fortunately, the songs aren't locked to that computer — you can copy them to other computers and play them with iTunes. When you first play the songs on the other computers, iTunes asks for your Music Store account ID and password to authorize that computer. You can have up to five computers authorized at any one time.

If you want to delete one computer and add another computer, you can remove the authorization from a computer by choosing Advanced⇨Deauthorize Account on that computer. If you need to deauthorize a computer that no longer works, you can contact Apple through its Music Store support page (www.apple.com/support/itunes/authorization.html).

Remember to deauthorize your computer before you upgrade, sell, or give it away. Also, make sure you deauthorize your computer before upgrading your RAM, hard drive, or other system components. Otherwise, the upgraded system might count as another authorized computer. If you've reached five authorizations due to system upgrades or failed computers, you can reset your authorization count by clicking Deauthorize All in the Account Information screen. (See "Viewing and changing account information" earlier in this chapter.) You can do this only once a year — the Deauthorize All button appears only if you have at least five authorized computers and you haven't used the option in the last 12 months.

After you set up an account, you can sign in to the Music Store at any time to buy music, view or change account information, and see your purchase history. Each time you buy music, you get an e-mail from the iTunes Music Store with the purchase information. It's nice to know right away what you bought.

Chapter 5

Importing Music into iTunes

To immortalize your music, you need to import it into iTunes from your audio CDs and other sources. After the music is in your iTunes library, you can preserve it forever. A song in digital format can be kept in that format in a file on any number of digital media storage devices — so even if your CDs, DVDs, and hard drive fail, your backup copy (assuming that you made a backup copy on a safety CD or disk) is still as perfect as the original digital file. You can make any number of digital copies, and there are no technical limitations on *playing* the copies except those imposed by the iTunes Music Store for songs that you purchased.

Importing tracks from a CD is called *ripping* a CD. We're not sure why it's called that, but Apple certainly took the term to a new level with an ad campaign for Macs a while back that featured the slogan *Rip, Mix, Burn*. Burning a mix CD was the hip thing to do a few years ago. With iTunes, you can still rip and mix, but if you have an iPod, you no longer need to burn CDs to play your music wherever you go.

Ripping, in technical terms, is the process of extracting the song's digital information from an audio CD, but in common terms it also includes the process of compressing the song's digital information and encoding it in a particular sound file format. The ripping process is straightforward, but the import settings that you choose affect sound quality, hard drive space (and iPod space), and compatibility with other types of players and computers. In this chapter, we show you how to rip CDs, import music from the Internet, and provide suggestions for settings.

Setting the Importing Preferences

Although importing music from an audio CD takes a lot less time than playing the CD, it still takes time, so you want your import settings to be correct before starting. Pay a visit to the Importing Preferences window (iTunes⇨ Preferences on a Mac, or Edit⇨Preferences in Windows), and then click the Importing button. The Importing preferences appear, as shown in Figure 5-1.

Figure 5-1:
Set your importing preferences for ripping CDs.

The Import Using pop-up menu gives you the opportunity to set the type of encoding — this is perhaps the most important choice — and the Setting pop-up menu offers different settings depending on your choice of encoder. For example, in Figure 5-1, we've chosen the AAC Encoder with a high-quality setting; in Figure 5-2, we've switched to the MP3 Encoder in the Import Using menu, and we're in the process of choosing Higher Quality in the Setting menu.

Encoding is a complicated subject and requires a whole chapter of its own. (In fact, Chapter 17 provides a more in-depth look if you want to know more.) For a quick and pain-free ripping session, select from among the following encoders in the Import Using pop-up menu based on how you plan to use your iTunes library:

✔ **AAC Encoder:** We recommend the AAC for all uses. (However, AIFF is better if you plan to burn another CD with the songs and not use them in your iPod.) Select the High Quality option from the Setting pop-up menu.

You can convert a song that's been ripped in AIFF, Apple Lossless, or WAV to AAC or MP3, as we describe in Chapter 18. However, ripping a CD with one encoder might be more convenient — and after that, you can rip it *again* with a different encoder. For example, you might import *Sgt. Pepper* with the AAC encoder for use in your Mac and iPod, and then import it again with the AIFF encoder, calling the album "Sgt. Pepper-2" or something, in order to burn some songs on a CD. After burning the CD, you can delete "Sgt. Pepper-2" to reclaim the hard drive space.

Figure 5-2:
Set the quality setting for the encoder you've chosen for importing.

- **AIFF Encoder:** Use AIFF if you plan on burning the song to an audio CD using a Mac (see WAV for Windows). AIFF offers the highest possible quality, but AIFF also takes up lots of space. If you use AIFF, select the Automatic option from the Setting pop-up menu. Don't use AIFF format for songs to be transferred to your iPod — convert them first to AAC or MP3, as we describe in Chapter 18.

- **Apple Lossless Encoder:** Use the Apple Lossless encoder for songs that you intend to burn onto audio CDs *and* for playing on iPods — the files are just small enough (about 60-70 percent of the size of the AIFF versions) that they don't hiccup on playback.

- **MP3 Encoder:** Use the MP3 format for songs that you intend to burn on MP3 CDs or use with MP3 players or your iPod — it's universally supported. If you use MP3, we recommend selecting the Higher Quality option from the Setting pop-up menu.

✔ **WAV Encoder:** WAV is the high-quality sound format that's used on PCs (like AIFF), and it also takes up a lot of space. Use WAV if you plan on burning the song to an audio CD or using it with PCs. If you use WAV, select the Automatic option from the Setting pop-up menu. Don't use WAV for songs to be transferred to your iPod — convert them first to AAC or MP3, as we describe in Chapter 18.

The Importing Preferences window offers the following options, which you set *before* ripping a CD:

✔ **Import Using:** Set this pop-up menu to the encoder. For more information about encoders, see Chapter 17.

✔ **Setting:** Set this pop-up menu to High Quality or better for most music. You can change this setting to get better quality or use hard drive space more efficiently, as we describe in Chapter 18.

✔ **Play Songs While Importing:** Select this check box to play the songs at the same time that you start ripping them. This option slows down the speed of importing, but hey — you get to listen to the music right away.

✔ **Create File Names with Track Number:** Select this check box to include the track number in the file names created by iTunes for the songs that you rip. Including the track number makes it easier to find tracks on an iPod using a car's audio controls — if you've connected your iPod to a car stereo system as described in Chapter 15.

✔ **Use Error Correction When Reading Audio CDs:** While it reduces the speed of importing, select this check box to use error correction if you have problems with audio quality or if the CD skips. (Not every skipping CD can be imported even with error correction, but it may help.)

Ripping Music from CDs

After checking your Importing Preferences to be sure that your settings are correct, you are ready to rip. To rip a CD, follow these steps:

1. **Insert an audio CD.**

   The songs appear in your song list as generic, unnamed tracks at first. If your computer is connected to the Internet and the CD is in the Gracenote database, iTunes retrieves the track information automatically. If you need to connect to the Internet, go ahead and establish your connection, and then choose Advanced⇨Get CD Track Names to get the track information. If you don't want to connect to the Internet, or if your CD isn't recognized by the Gracenote database, you can type the track information yourself. That's described in Chapter 8.

2. *Optional:* **Deselect the check boxes next to any songs on the CD that you don't want to import.**

   iTunes imports the songs that have check marks next to them; when you remove the check mark next to a song, iTunes skips that song.

3. *Optional:* **To remove the gap of silence between songs that segue together, select those songs and choose Advanced⇨Join CD Tracks.**

   This happens often with music CDs — the tracks are separate, but the end of one song merges into the beginning of the next song. You don't want an annoying half-second gap between the songs. For example, in Figure 5-3, we already joined the first two songs of the *Sgt. Pepper's Lonely Hearts Club Band* album because they run together, and we're in the process of using Join CD Tracks to join the last three songs.

Figure 5-3:
Join songs to avoid the audible gap between them.

To select multiple songs, click the first one, hold down ⌘/Ctrl, and click each subsequent one. To select several consecutive songs in a row, click the first one, hold down Shift, and then click the last one.

Be sure to check the importing preferences before actually ripping the CD.

4. **Click the Import button.**

   The Import button is at the top-right corner of the iTunes window. The status display shows the progress of the operation. To cancel, click the small *x* next to the progress bar in the status display.

iTunes plays the songs as it imports them. You can click the Pause button to stop playback (but the importing continues). If you don't want to listen to the songs as they import, choose Preferences from the iTunes menu on a Mac or from the Edit menu in Windows. In the Preference window, click the Importing button. In the Importing Preferences window, deselect the "Play songs while importing" check box.

iTunes displays an orange, animated waveform icon next to the song that it's importing. As iTunes finishes importing each song, it displays a check mark next to the song, as shown in Figure 5-4. (On a color monitor, you see that the check mark is green.) iTunes chimes when it finishes the import list. When all the songs are imported, eject the CD by clicking the Eject button at the lower-right corner of the iTunes window. You can also choose Controls➪Eject Disc to eject the disc, or click the Eject icon next to the disc's name in the Source pane.

Figure 5-4:
iTunes
shows a
check mark
to indicate it
is done
ripping the
song.

Importing Music Files

The quality of the music that you hear depends initially on the quality of the source. Web sites and services offering music files vary widely. Some sites provide high-quality, legally derived songs that you can download, and some provide only streaming audio, which you can play but not save on your hard drive or on a CD (such as a Web radio station). The allegedly illegal file-sharing services offering MP3 files can vary in quality. Unauthorized copies of songs might be saved in a lower quality format to save space and download time, so beware of less-than-high-quality knockoffs.

You can download the music file or copy it from another computer to your hard drive. After you save or copy an MP3 file — or for that matter an AIFF or WAV file — on your hard drive, you can simply drag it into the iTunes window to import it to your library. If you drag a folder or disk icon, all the audio files that it contains are added to your iTunes library. You can also choose File⇨ Add to Library as an alternative to dragging.

When you add a song to your iTunes library, a copy of the song file is placed inside the iTunes Music folder — as long as you have your preferences set for iTunes to "Copy files to iTunes music folder when adding to library" (the default setting).

If you want iTunes to store only links to song files on the hard drive and not copy the files when you add songs, you can turn off the default copy files option by choosing iTunes ⇨Preferences on a Mac, or Edit ⇨Preferences on a Windows PC, clicking Advanced in the Preferences dialog, and turning off the "Copy files to iTunes music folder when adding to library" setting.

You can check out the contents of your music folder using the Finder on a Mac or Windows Explorer on a Windows PC. On the Mac, the iTunes Music folder lives in the iTunes folder inside the Music folder in your Home folder. The path to this folder is *your home folder*/Music/iTunes/iTunes Music. On a Windows PC, the iTunes Music folder resides in the iTunes folder inside the My Music folder of the My Documents folder in your user folder. The path to this folder is *Your User folder*\My Documents\My Music\iTunes\iTunes Music. These are the default locations — unless you turn off the default organization in iTunes by choosing iTunes ⇨Preferences on a Mac, or Edit ⇨Preferences on a Windows PC, clicking Advanced in the Preferences dialog and choosing a new location for the music folder.

When you import a song file into iTunes, the song is copied into a new file in the iTunes library without changing or deleting the original file. You can then convert the imported song to another format — for example, you can convert an AIFF file to an MP3 file — while leaving the original intact. Find out about converting your songs to a different format in Chapter 18.

MP3 CDs are easy to import — since they are essentially data CDs, simply insert them into your CD-ROM drive, open the CD in the Finder, and drag-and-drop the MP3 song files into the iTunes window. Downloaded song files are even easier — just drag-and-drop the files into iTunes. If you drag a folder or CD icon, all the audio files it contains are added to your iTunes library.

You can import any sound into iTunes, even music from scratchy old vinyl records or sound effects recorded through a microphone. You might want to import unusual sounds or digitize and preserve rare music that can't be found anywhere else.

How do you get stuff like that into iTunes? On a Mac, you can use GarageBand, which is part of the iLife suite (available from the Apple Store and preinstalled on all new Macs), or use a sound-editing program such as CD Spin Doctor (part of the Toast package) or Sound Studio. These programs typically record from any analog source device, such as a tape player or even a turntable. Sound Studio lets you record and digitize directly to your hard drive on a Mac running OS X. Some Mac models include a free copy of Sound Studio (you can find it in the Applications folder). You can also download a copy from Felt Tip Software (www.felttip.com/products/soundstudio) and use it for two weeks before having to pay $49.99 for it. Toast 6 Titanium from Roxio (www.roxio.com) for Mac OS X includes the CD Spin Doctor application for recording sounds.

There are many commercial applications to choose from that work on Windows PCs, including Roxio's Easy CD Creator 5 Platinum package, which includes CD Spin Doctor. You can also use MusicMatch Jukebox to record sound through a PC's line-in connection. If you're using MusicMatch, visit the companion Web site at www.dummies.com/go/ipod.

AIFF- or WAV-encoded sound files occupy too much space in your music library and iPod. Voice recordings and sound effects tend to be low-fidelity and typically don't sound any better in AIFF or WAV format than they do in formats that save hard drive space. Also, sound effects and voice recordings are typically mono rather than stereo. You can save hard drive and iPod space and still have quality recordings by converting these files to MP3 or AAC formats, changing them from stereo to mono in the process and leaving the original versions intact. We describe converting songs in Chapter 18.

Importing Audio Books

Do you like to listen to audio books and spoken magazine and newspaper articles? Not only can you bring these sounds into iTunes, but you can also transfer them to an iPod and take them on the road, which is much more convenient than taking cassettes or CDs.

Audible is a leading provider of downloadable spoken audio files. Audible lets you authorize computers to play the audio files, just like the iTunes Music Store; see Chapter 4. Audible does require that you purchase the files, and its content is also licensed by Apple to be included in the iTunes Music Store in the Audio Books category. Audible content includes magazines and radio programs as well as books.

To import Audible files, follow these steps:

1. **Go to www.audible.com and set up an account if you don't already have one.**

2. **Select and download an Audible audio file.**

   Files that end with .aa are Audible files.

3. **Drag the Audible file to the iTunes window.**

   If this is the first time that you've added an Audible file, iTunes asks for your account information. You need to enter this information once for each computer that you use with your Audible account.

To disable an Audible account, open iTunes on the computer that you no longer want to use with the account, and choose Advanced⇨Deauthorize Computer. In the Deauthorize Computer dialog that appears, select the Deauthorize Computer for Audible Account option and click OK.

You need to be online to authorize a computer or to remove the authorization from that computer.

Chapter 6

Sharing Music sans a Lawyer

. . . .

. . . .

*H*ey, it's your music after you buy it — that is, to the extent that you can make copies for yourself. You want to play your music anywhere and even share the music with your friends. It's only natural.

You can easily share the music that you rip from your CDs: After the music becomes digital, you can copy it endlessly with no loss in quality. You can also share the songs that you download from a service. Of course, if the songs are in a protected format (such as music bought from the iTunes Music Store), the computers that access the shared library must be authorized to play the music. However, iTunes lets you share a library over a local area network (LAN) with other computers running iTunes. Whether the computers are connected to the LAN by cable (such as thin Ethernet cabling) or by wireless technology such as Apple's AirPort, you can share your library with other computers — up to *five* other computers in a single 24-hour period.

In this chapter, we show you how to bend the rules and share music with others. (After all, your parents taught you to share, didn't they?)

Sharing the iTunes Music Store Wealth

To a limited extent, you can share the music that you buy online from the iTunes Music Store. Apple uses a protected form of the AAC encoder for the songs — the music filenames use the extension m4p for protected music, rather than m4a for music in the regular AAC format. (Read all about format encoders in Chapters 17 and 18.) Thus, more than with most other services, the rights of artists are protected while also giving you more leeway in using the music (although by the time you read this, other services might have adopted this format with similar privileges).

I fought the law and the law won: Sharing and piracy

Apple CEO Steve Jobs gave personal demonstrations of the iTunes Music Store and the iPod to Paul McCartney and Mick Jagger before introducing the online music store. According to Steven Levy at *Newsweek* (May 12, 2003), Jobs said, "They both totally get it." The former Beatle and the Stones' frontman are no slouches — both conduct music-business affairs personally and both have extensive back catalogs of music. They know all about the free music-swapping services on the Internet, but they agree with Jobs that most people are willing to pay for high-quality music rather than download free copies of questionable quality.

We think the solution to piracy is not technology because determined pirates always circumvent it with newer technology, and only consumers are inconvenienced.

Giving music away is, of course, the subject of much controversy, with services such as the original Napster closed by court order while others flourish in countries that don't have copyright laws as strict as the United States has. (Napster is back, but it no longer provides the same type of music sharing.)

The songs that you hear from free sharing services such as KaZaa are (for the most part) low quality, on a par with FM radio broadcasts. They're nice for listening to new songs to see whether you like them, but they're not useful for acquiring as part of your real music collection. The iTunes Music Store is clearly superior in quality and convenience, and we prefer the original authorized version of the song — not some knock-off that might have been copied from a radio broadcast.

As for making copies for personal use, the law is murky at best. It depends on what you mean by *personal use.* The iLife package allows you to use these music files in creative projects. You can, for example, put together a music video to show your friends by using iMovie to combine some video footage that you shot with your camcorder along with the latest hit by Eminem. However, don't expect to see it on MTV or VH1. Your local public access cable TV station can't even play it unless you first obtain the broadcast rights (which typically includes contacting the music publisher, the record label, and the artist — good luck).

Can you legally use a pop song as a soundtrack for a high school yearbook slideshow? It sounds legal to us, given the ability to use music for educational purposes, but you should ask a lawyer. If you're interested in obtaining the rights to music to use in semi-public or public presentations, or even movies and documentaries for public distribution, you can contact the music publisher or a licensing agent. Music-publishing organizations, such as the Music Publishers' Association (www.mpa.org), offer information and lists of music publishers, as well as explanations of various rights and licenses.

The protected form of AAC used with iTunes Music Store songs lets you do the following:

✔ **Create backups.** You can download the music files and make as many copies as you want.

- ✔ **Copy music to iTunes libraries on other computers.** Play songs on up to five separate computers. See Chapter 4 to find out how to authorize your computers.

- ✔ **Copy music to iPods.** Copy the music files to as many iPods as you want. See Chapter 10 for automatic and manual iPod updating.

- ✔ **Burn up to seven CDs.** Burn seven copies of the same playlist containing protected songs to an audio CD, but no more. See Chapter 12 for tips on CD burning.

- ✔ **Share music over a network.** Up to five computers running iTunes on a LAN can play the music in your shared library in the same 24-hour period.

You can also play music in your library over a wireless connection to a stereo amplifier or receiver by using AirTunes and AirPort Express, as we describe in Chapter 16.

Regardless of whether you manage files on your hard drive on a regular basis, you might want to know where these songs are stored so that you can copy the music to other computers and back up the entire library. You might also want to move the library to another computer — after all, these computers just keep getting better year after year.

You can play your purchased music on any authorized computer, you can authorize up to five at once, and you can remove authorization from any computer that you don't use. Also, up to five computers can share your music library on a LAN in a given 24-hour period.

Sharing Music in a Network

If you live like the Jetsons — with a computer in every room, connected by a wireless or wired network — iTunes is made for you. You can share the music in your library with other computers in the same network. These computers can be PCs running Windows or Macs, as long as they are all running iTunes. If they can communicate with each other over the network, iTunes can share a music library with up to five PCs in a single 24-hour period. The restriction to five in a 24-hour period is yet another one imposed by the record labels.

When you share songs on a network, the song is *streamed* from the computer that contains the songs in its library (the *library computer*) to your computer over the network. A *stream* arrives in your computer bit by bit; the computer starts playing the stream as soon as the first set of bits arrive, and more sections are transferred while you listen, so you hear it as a continual stream. Broadcasters use this technology to continually transmit new content (like a radio station). The song is not copied to your music library. From your computer, you can't burn the shared-library songs onto a CD or copy the songs to your iPod.

You can share radio links, MP3, AIFF, and WAV files — and even AAC files and music purchased from the iTunes Music store — but not Audible spoken word files or QuickTime sound files.

To share your music library — turning your computer into the library computer — follow these steps:

1. **Choose Preferences (from the iTunes menu on a Mac or from the Edit menu on a Windows PC) and click the Sharing tab.**

   The Sharing pane appears, as shown in Figure 6-1, offering options for sharing music.

Figure 6-1: Share your music library with other computers on the same network.

2. **Select the Share My Music option.**

3. **In the same dialog, select either the Share Entire Library option or the Share Selected Playlists option (and then choose the playlists to share).**

4. **Type a name for the shared library and add a password if you want.**

   The name that you choose appears in the Source list for other computers that share it. The password restricts access to those who know it. Use a password that you don't mind letting others know — not the password for the online music store or any other secret password.

   Pick a password that you don't mind sharing with others; for example, your name is a good password, but your ATM PIN is not.

iTunes displays a `Reminder: Sharing music is for personal use only` message.

5. Click OK.

You can access the music from the other computers on the network by following these steps:

1. Choose Preferences (from the iTunes menu on a Mac or from the Edit menu on a Windows PC) and click the Sharing tab.

The Sharing window appears, offering options for sharing music. Refer to Figure 6-1.

2. Select the Look for Shared Music option.

The shared libraries or playlists appear in the Source pane. Figure 6-2 shows a shared library in the Source pane.

Figure 6-2: Select the music library that's shared by iTunes running on another network computer.

3. Click the shared library to select it.

Click the shared library in the Source pane; refer to Figure 6-2. iTunes fills the view on the right with the artists and songs from the shared library. Click the triangle next to a shared library entry in the Source pane, as shown in Figure 6-3, to see the shared playlists.

Figure 6-3:
Open the list of playlists in the shared music library.

When you are finished sharing a music library, click the tiny Eject button that appears to the right of the shared library name in the Source pane.

Before turning off sharing for your library, you must first notify anyone sharing the library to eject the shared library before turning off the sharing feature. Otherwise, iTunes displays a warning dialog allowing you to either continue (and break off the connection to the shared library) or to leave sharing turned on for the moment.

Sharing a music library can be incredibly useful for playing music on laptops, such as PowerBooks, that support the wireless AirPort network.

Copying Songs to Other Computers

You can copy songs freely from your iTunes window to other hard drives and computers, or copy the song folders from the iTunes Music folder to other hard drives and computers. On the Mac, you can use the Finder to copy song files as well as dragging songs out of the iTunes window into folders or hard drives. Windows PCs offer several methods, including using Windows Explorer to copy files.

By default, the files are organized in folders by artist name and by album within the iTunes Music folder — unless you change options in the Advanced section of iTunes Preferences, as described in Chapter 11. Copying an entire album, or every song by a specific artist, is easy — just drag the folder to a folder on another hard drive.

You can find out the location of any song by selecting the song in iTunes and choosing File➪Get Info. Click the Summary tab in the Get Info dialog to see the Summary pane.

Although you can change the location of your music library as described in Chapter 11, most people leave the music library in its default location — inside the iTunes Music folder in the iTunes folder.

On the Mac, the iTunes Music folder can be found by default at *your home folder*/Music/iTunes/iTunes Music. On a Windows PC, the iTunes Music folder can be found at *your user folder*/My Documents/My Music/iTunes/iTunes Music.

Your playlists, including the library itself (which is in some ways a giant playlist), are stored as eXtensible Markup Language (XML) files in the iTunes folder along with your iTunes Music folder.

The easiest way to copy an album from a folder on a hard drive into your iTunes library is to drag the album's folder over the iTunes window and drop it there. If you drop it into the Source pane, iTunes creates a playlist of the album's songs using the album name. To copy individual songs, you can drag the song files over the iTunes window and drop them. When you add a song to your iTunes library, a copy is placed inside the iTunes Music folder.

Copying Songs between PCs and Macs

Song files are not small, and album folders filled with songs are quite large. Copying a music library from a Mac to a PC, or vice versa, is not a simple task because of the enormity of the file sizes.

Attaching a file to an e-mail message is the most popular method of transferring a file to someone, but there is a limit as to what you can attach. Most e-mail servers in the world won't accept an attachment larger than 5MB; some won't accept larger than 3MB. Don't even think about e-mail. *If the file is over four, it won't go through the door.* (Four megabytes, that is; and the door is the limitation of your Internet service provider's e-mail server.) If you use a .Mac e-mail account, the limitation is 10MB.

Well, heck, just about every jazz tune and Grateful Dead jam we listen to in iTunes is larger than 3MB. A song compressed in the AAC or MP3 format is typically between 2 and 10MB, so you might get by with one pop song attached to an e-mail, but that's it.

How do you transfer larger amounts of music? One way would be with an external FireWire or a USB hard drive formatted for a PC — an iPod installed for Windows would do nicely, and you can learn all about using an iPod as a hard drive in Chapter 23. The Mac should recognize it when you plug it in, even though the drive is formatted for Windows, and you can copy files directly to the hard drive, and then take the hard drive over to your PC. You need FireWire or USB to connect an external drive. (USB is much slower.)

On a LAN you can share forever — if your computers communicate over a local-area network, they can share files . . . even large ones. To copy large song files or entire album folders between two Macs in a LAN, all you need to do is allow personal file sharing on your Mac. This sounds like a liberal thing to do, inviting all sorts of mischief and voyeurism, but you can control what others can do. (The converse is true: If someone wants to make a file or folder available to *you* over a LAN, all he has to do is enable personal file sharing.)

Mac OS X makes it very easy to share files and folders with Windows computers. You can enable Windows file sharing on the Mac, or access the Windows computer from a Mac. To access a Windows PC from a Mac, you need a valid user ID and password for an account on the Windows computer. You can go right to that account's Home directory on the Windows computer and use your Mac to copy folders and files to and from the Windows computer. For more information about file sharing on a Mac (specifically between Mac and Windows computers on a network), see *Mac OS X Panther All-in-One Desk Reference For Dummies,* by Mark L. Chambers (Wiley).

Copying very large song files over the Internet is a bit more complex, involving use of a communication application such as iChat AV, or one that offers the File Transfer Protocol (FTP). Although it's easy to download an MP3 song file from a Web page or an FTP site with any browser (all you need is the Web or FTP address — and a user ID and password if the site is protected), you can't *send* the file to a protected site with most browsers unless the site is set up for this function. One easy way to share your files from a Mac is to use the .Mac service to create a Web page that accommodates anyone with the right password, even Windows-using folks, to visit and download files you put there. For information about setting up a .Mac account, see *iLife All-in-One Desk Reference For Dummies,* by yours truly (Wiley).

To make it easy for others to copy files to and from a Mac at their convenience, enable FTP access for the Mac. To do this, open System Preferences, click the Sharing icon, and click the Services button. Select the FTP Access option. A message at the bottom of the Sharing window provides the address of your FTP server on your Mac — something like `ftp://192.168.1.246/`. Give this address to those with an account on your computer, and they can access files and folders by using a Web browser, an FTP client such as Fetch, or Mac OS X. If you've turned on the firewall in Mac OS X, click the Firewall button and select the FTP Access option; this allows FTP access through the firewall.

How about transferring song files to other FTP sites, such as a password-protected site that requires use of an FTP client? You have several options:

- ✔ **Use an FTP client,** such as Fetch or Rbrowser 4 for Mac OS X, or FTP Explorer for Windows. You can find Fetch at `http://fetchsoftworks.com` for $25 as of this writing. You can use it for several weeks before paying for it. Rbrowser 4 (`www.rbrowser.com`) is free to download and use, and looks a bit like the Mac Finder. FTP Explorer (`www.ftpx.com`) is shareware you can use for a month before paying $35. (Students and faculty members can use it for free.)

- ✔ **Use the FTP function inside another application,** such as Macromedia Dreamweaver.

- ✔ **Use a free Terminal application,** such as the one supplied with Mac OS X, found in the Utilities folder inside your Applications folder, which offers FTP. For instructions, see *Mac OS X Panther All-in-One Desk Reference For Dummies,* by Mark L. Chambers (Wiley).

Most FTP utilities and functions within applications provide an easy way to copy files; for example, Fetch provides a drag-and-drop interface for transferring any type of file with FTP servers. After you establish a connection with the FTP server by typing the appropriate information (the FTP server name, your ID, your password, and the directory that you have access to), you can drag files to and from the FTP server window via the Finder, or you can browse folders to select files and then use the Get and Put Files buttons.

You can send an entire folder of files, such as an album of songs or an artist folder with multiple albums, by stuffing the folder (or even a set of folders) into a compressed Zip file. (Zip is a standard compression format.) Select the files or folders and right-click the selection. In Mac OS X, choose Create Archive; in Windows, choose WinZip (or similar Zip utility that installs itself into Windows menus).

You can then transfer the Zip file to the FTP server in one step. While the Zip file formats compress other types of files, the files won't get any smaller if your music files are already compressed as MP3 or AAC. However, the format offers a compact way of sending an entire folder of files.

Part II
Managing Your Music

"I could tell you more about myself, but I think the playlist on my iPod says more about me than mere words can."

In this part . . .

*V*isit this part to find out how to organize your music.

- ✔ Chapter 7 describes how to browse your iTunes music library, change viewing options, and search for songs or artists.

- ✔ Chapter 8 describes how to add song information, artwork, and ratings, and then edit the info in iTunes.

- ✔ Chapter 9 shows you how to build playlists of songs and entire albums in iTunes, including smart playlists.

- ✔ Chapter 10 describes updating your iPod or iPod shuffle automatically or manually with iTunes and how to edit playlists and song information directly on your iPod.

- ✔ Chapter 11 shows you how to make backup copies of your iTunes.

- ✔ Chapter 12 is a guide to burning audio and MP3 CDs and printing CD jewel-case inserts and song listings.

Chapter 7

Searching, Browsing, and Sorting in iTunes

*Y*ou rip a few CDs, buy some songs from the iTunes Music Store, and then watch your music library fill up with songs. That song list keeps getting longer and longer — and as a result, your library is harder to navigate.

The iTunes Library is awesome even by everyday jukebox standards. Though previous versions were limited to a paltry (!) 32,000 songs per library and you had to create multiple libraries to get around that limit, version 4 and up can hold a virtually unlimited number of songs (depending on how much space you have on your hard drive).

Consider that a 60GB iPod can hold about 15,000 songs in the AAC format — enough music to last at least a month if played 24 hours a day! Even if you keep your iTunes library down to the size of what you can fit on your iPod, you still have a formidable collection at your fingertips. If you're a music lover and your music collection is getting large, you'll want to organize your collection to make finding songs easier. After all, finding U2's "I Still Haven't Found What I'm Looking For" is a challenge even in a library of only 32,000 songs.

This chapter shows you how to search, browse, and sort your music library in iTunes. You can find any song in seconds and display songs sorted by artist, album, genre of music, or other attributes. You can change the viewing options to make your library's display more useful.

Browsing by Artist and Album

Overwhelmed by the long list of songs? Try browsing: Switch from Song List view to Browse view to find songs more easily. When you select an album in Browse view, iTunes displays only the songs for that album.

If you don't get track information from the Internet for each song (as we show in Chapter 5) or type it in yourself (as described in Chapter 8), iTunes displays a blank space for Artist and Album name and "Track 01" and so on for each track. That would make it difficult to browse for a song or artist by name.

To view albums in Browse view, click the Browse button in the upper-right corner. iTunes organizes your music library by genre, artist, and album, which makes finding just the right tunes easier, as shown in Figure 7-1. Click the Browse button again to return to the Song List view — the Browse button toggles between Browse view and the Song List view.

Figure 7-1: Click the Browse button to browse the iTunes library.

The Browse view sorts the songs by genre, artist, and album. Click a genre in the Genre column to see artists in that genre, or click All at the top of the Genre column to see all artists for all genres.

When you click an artist in the Artist column in the middle column (as shown in Figure 7-2), the album titles appear in the Album column on the right. At the top of the Album column, the All selection is highlighted, and the songs from every album by that artist appear in the song list below the Genre, Artist and Album columns.

Figure 7-2:
Select an
artist to see
the list of
albums for
that artist.

To see more than one album from an artist at a time, hold down the Ctrl on a
Windows PC (⌘ key on a Mac), and click each album name.

As you click different albums in the Album column, the song list displays the
songs from that album. The songs are listed in proper track order, just as the
artist, producer, or record label intended them — assuming the track information has been downloaded from the Internet or typed in manually.

This is great for selecting songs from albums, but what if you want to look
at *all* the songs by *all* the artists in the library at once? You can see all the
songs in the library in Browse view by selecting All at the top of each of the
columns — Genre, Artist, and Album.

Note that iTunes considers Clash and The Clash to be different groups,
although it sorts them properly under C. We show you how to edit the artist
name and other information in Chapter 8.

Understanding the Song Indicators

As you make choices in iTunes, it displays an action indicator next to each
song to show you what it's doing. Here's a list of the song indicators and what
they mean:

   ✔ **Orange waveform:** iTunes is importing the song.

   ✔ **Green check mark:** iTunes has finished importing the song.

- **Exclamation point:** iTunes can't find the song. You might have moved or deleted the song accidentally. You can move the song back to iTunes by dragging it from your hard drive into the iTunes window.

- **Broadcast icon:** The song is on the Internet and plays as a music stream.

- **Black check mark:** The songs are marked for the next operation, such as importing from an audio CD or playing in sequence. Click to remove the check mark.

- **Speaker:** The song is playing.

- **Chasing arrows:** iTunes is copying the song from another location or downloading the song from the Internet.

Changing Viewing Options

iTunes lets you customize the song list view. The list starts out with the Song Name, Time, Artist, Album, Genre, My Rating, Play Count, and Last Played categories. You might have to drag the horizontal scroll bar along the bottom of the song list to see all these columns. You can display more or less information, or different information, in your song list. You can also display columns in a different order from left to right.

To make a column wider or narrower, drag the dividing line between the column and the next column to its right. As you move your cursor over the divider, it changes to a vertical bar with opposing arrows extending left and right; you can click and drag the divider to change the column's width.

You can also change the order of columns from left to right by clicking a column heading and dragging the entire column to the left or right — except that you can't change the position of the Song Name column and the narrow column to its left (which displays indicators). In addition, you can Control-click (Ctrl-click) or right-click any of the column headings to display a shortcut menu offering the same options as the View Options window, the Auto Size Column option, and the Auto Size All Columns option.

Maybe you don't like certain columns, like when they take up too much valuable screen space; or perhaps you want to display some other information about the song. You can add or remove columns such as Size (for file size), Date and Year (for the date the album was released, or any other date you choose for each song), Bit Rate, Sample Rate, Track Number, and Comment. To add or delete columns, choose Edit⇨View Options.

The View Options dialog appears, as shown in Figure 7-3, and you can select the columns that you want to appear in the song list. To pick a column, mark the check box next to the column's heading, indicating that column will be shown. Any unchecked column headings are columns that do *not* appear in the song list in iTunes. ***Note:*** The Song Name column always appears in the iTunes song list and can't be removed, which is why it doesn't appear in the View Options dialog. You can also change the view options by ⌘-clicking on a Mac (Ctrl-clicking on a PC) any of the column headings in the song list in either Browse or Song List view.

Figure 7-3:
The viewing
options for
the song list.

Change the viewing options to suit your needs. You might want to display the Time column to know at a glance the duration of any song. Or maybe you want the Date or Year columns to differentiate songs from different eras, or the Genre column to differentiate songs from different musical genres.

Browse view includes a Genre column on the left side. If you don't need a Genre column, you can remove it from the Browse view (or add it back) by choosing Preferences (from the iTunes menu on a Mac, or the Edit menu in Windows). Click the General button at the top of the Preferences window. In the General dialog, disable the "Show genre when browsing" option, which is on by default.

Sorting Songs by Viewing Options

Knowing how to set viewing options is a good idea because you can use the viewing options to sort the listing of songs. Whether you're in Browse view or viewing the song list in its entirety, the column headings double as sorting options.

For example, clicking the Time heading reorders the songs by their duration in ascending order from shortest to longest. If you click the Time header again, the sort is reversed, starting with the longest song. You can sort by any column heading, such as Artist, Album, Track, and Ratings. You might want to add the Date Added column to the Song List or Browse view, so that you can sort your library by the date you added the song.

You can tell which way the sort is sorting — ascending or descending order — by the little arrow indicator in the heading. When the arrow points up, the sort is in ascending order; when pointing down, it's in descending order.

Alternatively, you can sort the song list in alphabetical order. Click the Artist heading to sort all the songs in the list by the artist name, in alphabetical order (arrow pointing up). Click it again to sort the list in reverse alphabetical order (arrow pointing down).

Searching for Songs

As your music library grows, you might find locating a particular song by the usual browsing and scrolling methods that we describe earlier in this chapter too time-consuming. Let iTunes find your songs for you!

If you want to search the entire library in Browse view, first click the All selections at the top of the Genre and Artist columns to browse the *entire* library before typing a term in the Search field. Or, if you prefer, click the Browse button again to return to the Song List view, which lists the entire library.

Locate the Search field — the oval field in the top-right corner, to the left of the Browse button — and follow these steps:

1. **Click in the Search field, and then type several characters of your search term, using these tips for best searching:**

   • You can search for a song title, an artist, or an album title.

   • Typing very few characters results in a long list of possible songs, but the search narrows down as you type more characters.

   • The Search features ignore case — for example, when we search for *miles,* iTunes finds "Eight Miles High," "She Smiles Like a River," and everything by Miles Davis.

2. **The results display as you type.**

   The search operation works immediately, as shown in Figure 7-4, displaying in the song list any matches in the Song Name, Artist, and Album columns.

   If you're in Browse view with an artist and a particular album selected, you can't search for another artist or song. Use browsing *with* searching to further narrow your search.

Figure 7-4:
Search for
any song
titles, album
titles, or
artists.

3. **Scroll through the search results and click a song to select it.**

   The search operation works immediately, searching for matches in the
   Song Name, Artist, and Album columns of the listing.

To back out of a search so that the full list appears again, you can either click
the circled X in the Search field (which appears only after you start typing
characters) or delete the characters in the Search field. You then see the
entire list of songs in the library's song list, just as before you began your
search. All the songs are still there and remain there unless you explicitly
remove them. Searching only manipulates your view of the songs.

Showing the Current Song and Song File

Getting lost in a large library is easy. As you browse your song library, you
may want to return quickly to view the current song playing. While the song
is playing, choose File➪Show Current Song (or use ⌘-L or Ctrl-L as a shortcut). iTunes switches the view back to show you the currently playing song.

You can also show the location of the song file for any song. This trick can
come in handy if you want to copy the song file to another hard drive or over
a network, or open it in another application. Choose File➪Show Song File (or
use ⌘-R or Ctrl-R as a shortcut), and iTunes switches control back to the
operating system (Mac or Windows), which displays the folder containing the
song file. You can show the song file if it is on your hard drive, but not if it is
in a shared library on another computer.

Showing Duplicate Songs

As your library grows larger, you may want to check for duplications — some songs that appear on artist CDs also appear on compilation or soundtrack CDs. If you rip them all, you could have duplicate songs that take up space on your hard drive.

On the other hand, maybe you want to find different versions of the same song by the same artist. iTunes can find all the songs with the same title by the same artist quickly, even when the songs appear on different albums.

To show duplicate songs in the song list, choose Edit➪Show Duplicate Songs. iTunes displays all the duplicate songs in alphabetical order in the song list. If you are in Browse view, iTunes displays all the duplicate songs in artist order — click the artist to see the duplicate songs for that artist, as shown in Figure 7-5.

Figure 7-5: Show duplicate songs for each artist.

To stop showing duplicate songs and return to your previous view (either song list or Browse view), click the Show All Songs button below the list of duplicate songs.

Chapter 8

Adding and Editing Song Information in iTunes

In This Chapter

▶ Retrieving information online

▶ Putting in song information

▶ Adding more information, album artwork, comments, and ratings

*O*rganization depends on information. You expect your computer to do a lot more than just store a song with *Track 01* as the only identifier.

Adding all the song information for your tracks seems like a lot of trouble, but you can get most of the information automatically from the Internet — without all that pesky typing. Adding song information is important because you don't want your ripped CD music to have vague song titles like Track 03. You certainly don't want to mistakenly play "My Guitar Wants to Kill Your Mama" by Frank Zappa when trying to impress your classical music teacher with Tchaikovsky's 3rd Movement, Pathétique Symphony, do you?

This chapter shows you how to add song information to your music library in iTunes, and edit it for better viewing, so that you can organize your music by artist, album name, genre, composer, and ratings, and then sort the Song List or Browse view using this information by clicking the column headings.

Retrieving Information from the Internet

Why bother entering song information if someone else has already done it for you? You can easily get information about most music CDs from the Internet — if you can connect to the Internet.

Retrieving information automatically

During the iTunes setup process that we describe in Chapter 2, you specify whether iTunes connects automatically to the Internet. If you have an always-on Internet connection, you probably set up iTunes to connect automatically; if you use a modem to manually connect, you probably set up iTunes to not connect automatically.

Even with a manual modem connection to the Internet, though, you can temporarily change the setup of your Internet connection to connect automatically at any time. Just follow these steps:

1. **Choose Preferences (from the iTunes menu on a Mac, or the Edit menu on a Windows PC).**

   The Preferences dialog appears.

2. **Click the General button.**

   The General dialog appears.

3. **Select the Connect to Internet When Needed option.**

   With this option enabled for a modem connection, iTunes triggers your modem automatically (like a Web browser), calls your Internet service provider (ISP), and completes the connection process before retrieving the track information. With this option disabled (cleared), iTunes asks first before connecting to the Internet.

You can always stop an automatic modem connection at any time — a good idea if your ISP or phone service charges extra fees based on timed usage. When iTunes finishes grabbing the song information from the Internet, switch to your remote connection program without quitting iTunes, terminate the Internet connection, and then switch back to iTunes. That way, you can leave your Preferences setting to connect when needed and still terminate any connection right after using it.

Retrieving information manually

You can connect to the Internet at any time manually (such as with a modem connection) and retrieve the song information when you are ready to use it. After you connect to the Internet, choose Advanced➪Get CD Track Names.

Even if you automatically connect to the Internet, the song information database on the Internet (Gracenote CDDB) might be momentarily unavailable, or you might have a delayed response. If at first you don't succeed, choose Advanced➪Get CD Track Names again.

Long distance information: Using the Gracenote database

The first time we popped an audio CD into the computer, song information appeared like magic. iTunes displayed the song names, album title, and artist names automatically. How did it know? This information isn't stored on a standard music CD in digital form — iTunes has to recognize the disc somehow.

The magic is that the software knows how to reach out and find the information on the Internet — in the Gracenote CDDB service. (CDDB stands for — you guessed it — *CD Database*.) The site (www.gracenote.com) hosts CDDB on the Web and offers the ability to search for music CDs by artist, song title, and other methods. The iTunes software already knows how to use this database, so you don't have to!

Gracenote recognizes an audio CD by taking into account the number, sequence, and duration of tracks (which is why the database can recognize CD-Rs that are burned with the identical songs in the same order). The database keeps track of information for most of the music CDs that you find on the market.

Although the database doesn't contain any information about personal or custom CDs, people can submit information to the database about CDs that the database doesn't know. You can even do this from within iTunes — type the information for each track while the audio CD is in your computer, and then choose Advanced⇨ Submit CD Track Names. The information that you enter is sent to the Gracenote CDDB site, where the good people who work tirelessly on the database check out your information before including it. In fact, if you spot a typo or something erroneous in the information that you receive from the Gracenote CDDB, you can correct it, and then use the Submit CD Track Names command to send the corrected version back to the Gracenote site. The good folks at Gracenote appreciate the effort.

After connecting and retrieving track information using a modem, your Internet service might still be connected until the service hangs up on you. You might want to switch to a browser, without quitting iTunes, and surf the Web to make use of the connection — and use iTunes to play music while you surf.

Entering Song Information

You have to manually enter the song information for CDs that are not known by the Gracenote CDDB or for custom CD-Rs. No big deal, though — just enter a song's information in either Browse view or song list view. Click directly in the information field, such as Artist, and then click again so that the mouse pointer turns into an editing cursor. You can then type text into the field.

After grabbing the song information from the Internet or typing it yourself, iTunes keeps track of the information for the CD even if you just play the CD without importing it. The next time you insert the CD, the song information is automatically filled in.

After you enter the information for a rare CD, consider submitting the song information to the Gracenote CDDB for others to use. Enter the information for each track while the audio CD is in your computer, and then choose Advanced⇨Submit CD Track Names. The information that you type is sent to the Gracenote CDDB site, where it is checked first for accuracy and then posted for others to use.

Editing the Information

Retrieving ready-made song information off the Internet is a great help, but you might not always like the format it comes in. At some time or another, you might want to edit artist and band names. For example, we like to list solo artists by last name rather than by first name (as listings from the Gracenote CDDB often are) — we routinely change *Miles Davis* to *Davis, Miles.*

Other annoyances sometimes occur in the CDDB, such as bands with *The* at the beginning of their names, such as The Who, The Band, The Beatles, and The Beach Boys. Even though these names sort correctly (in alphabetical order under their proper name), we dislike having *The* before the band name, so we routinely remove it.

In either Browse view or the Song List view, you can edit a song's information by clicking directly in the specific track's field (such as the Artist field), and clicking again so that the mouse pointer turns into an editing cursor. You can then select the text and type over it, or use the Copy, Cut, and Paste commands in the Edit menu, to move tiny bits of text around within the field. As you can see in Figure 8-1, we changed the Artist field to be *Beck, Jeff.*

You can edit the Song Name, Artist, Album, Genre, and My Ratings fields right in the song list. However, editing this information with File⇨Get Info is easier. Keep reading to find out.

Editing multiple songs at once

Editing in the song list is fine if you're editing the information for one song, but typically you need to change all the tracks of an audio CD. For example, if a CD of songs by Bob Dylan is listed with the artist as *Bob Dylan,* you might want to change all the songs at once to *Dylan, Bob.* Changing all the song information in one fell swoop is fast and clean, but like most powerful short-cuts, you need to be careful because it can be dangerous.

Figure 8-1:
Click inside
a field to
edit the
information.

You can change a group of songs in either Browse view or the song list view.
Follow these steps to change a group of songs at once:

1. **Select a group of songs by clicking the first song and then holding
   down the Shift key as you click the last song.**

   All the songs between the first and last are highlighted. You can extend a
   selection by Shift-clicking other songs or add to a selection by ⌘-clicking
   on a Mac, or Ctrl-clicking on a Windows PC. You can also remove songs
   already selected by ⌘-clicking on a Mac or Ctrl-clicking on a PC.

2. **Choose File⇨Get Info or press ⌘-I (Mac) or Ctrl-I (PC).**

   A warning message displays: Are you sure you want to edit
   information for multiple items?

   Speed-editing the information in multiple songs at once can be dangerous for your library organization. If, for example, you change the song
   title, the entire selection then has that song title. So be careful about
   what you edit when doing this. We recommend leaving the Do Not Ask
   Me Again check box cleared so that the warning appears whenever you
   try this.

3. **Click Yes to edit information for multiple items.**

   The Multiple Song Information dialog appears, as shown in Figure 8-2.

Multiple Song Information

Artist
☑ Beck, Jeff

Year
☐

Album
☐

Track Number
☐ of ☐

Grouping
☐

Disc Number
☐ of ☐

Composer
☐

BPM
☐

Comments
☐

Artwork
☐

Genre
☐ Rock

Part of a Compilation
☐ No

My Rating
☐ · · · · ·

Volume Adjustment
-100%   None   +100%

Equalizer Preset
☐ None

Cancel   OK

Figure 8-2:
Change the
field info for
multiple
songs at
once.

4. **Edit the field you want to change (typically the Artist field) for the multiple songs.**

   When you edit a field, a check mark appears automatically in the check box next to the field. iTunes assumes that you want that field changed in all the selected songs. Make sure that no other check box is selected except the field that you want, which is typically the Artist field (and perhaps the Genre field).

5. **Click OK to make the change.**

   iTunes changes the field for the entire selection of songs.

You can edit the song information *before* importing the audio tracks from a CD. The edited track information for the CD imports with the music. What's interesting is that when you access the library without the audio CD, the edited version of the track information is still there — iTunes remembers CD information from the CDs you previously inserted. Even if you don't import the CD tracks, iTunes remembers the edited song information until the next time you insert that audio CD.

Editing fields for a song

Although the track information grabbed from the Internet is enough for identifying songs in your iTunes library, some facts — such as composer credits — are not included. Composer information is important for iPod users because the iPod allows you to scroll music by composer as well as by artist, album, and song. Adding composer credits is usually worth your while because you can then search and sort by composer and create playlists.

After your songs import into the music library, locate a single song and choose File⇨Get Info (or press ⌘-I). You see the song's information dialog, as shown in Figure 8-3.

While My Guitar Gently Weeps

Summary | Info | Options | Artwork

No Artwork Available

While My Guitar Gently Weeps (4:45)
Beatles
The Beatles [White Album] (Disc 1)

Kind: AAC audio file	**Profile:** Low Complexity
Size: 11 MB	**Channels:** Stereo
Bit Rate: 320 kbps	**Encoded with:** iTunes v4.0, QuickTime 6.2
Sample Rate: 44.100 kHz	
Date Modified: 5/25/03 3:53 PM	
Play Count: 3	
Last Played: 4/21/05 3:11 PM	

Where: Macintosh HD:Users:TBone:Music:iTunes:iTunes Music:Beatles:The Beatles [White Album] (Disc 1):07 While My Guitar Gently Weeps.m4a

Previous | Next | Cancel | OK

Figure 8-3:
The song's information dialog.

When you select one song, the Song Information dialog appears; when you select multiple songs, the Multiple Song Information dialog appears. Be careful when selecting multiple songs and using the Get Info command.

The Song Information dialog offers the following tabs:

- **Summary:** The Summary tab (as shown in Figure 8-3) offers useful information about the music file's format and location on your hard drive; the music file size; and information about the digital compression method (bit rate, sample rate, and so on).

- **Info:** The Info tab allows you to change the song name, artist, composer, album, genre, year, and other information, and you can also add comments, as shown in Figure 8-4.

- **Options:** The Options tab offers volume adjustment, choice of equalizer preset, ratings, and start and stop times for each song. You can assign up to five stars to a song (your own rating system, equivalent to the Top 40 charts).

- **Artwork:** The Artwork tab allows you to add or delete artwork for the song. The iTunes Music Store supplies artwork with most songs. Read how to add artwork in the upcoming section, "Adding Album Cover Art or Images."

While My Guitar Gently Weeps

Summary | Info | Options | Artwork

Name
While My Guitar Gently Weeps

Artist   **Year**
Beatles   1968

Album   **Track Number**
The Beatles [White Album] (Disc 1)   7 of 17

Grouping   **Disc Number**
                                                          of

Composer   **BPM**
George Harrison

Comments
Eric Clapton on lead guitar.

Genre
Rock   ☐ Part of a compilation

Previous   Next   Cancel   OK

Figure 8-4:
View and edit song information from the Info tab.

You can edit the song information one song at a time and still move quickly one song at a time through an album (without having to close the song information dialog and reopen it) by clicking the Previous or Next buttons in the bottom-left corner of the dialog to jump from song to song in an album.

Adding a rating

iTunes also allows you to rate songs, and the cool thing about ratings is that they're *yours*. You can use them to mean anything you want. For example, you can rate songs based on how much you like them, whether your mother would listen to them, or how they blend into a work environment. Then you can use the My Top Rated playlist to automatically play the top-rated songs in the library. You find out more about playlists in Chapter 9.

To add a rating to a song, click the Options tab, as shown in Figure 8-5. Drag inside the My Rating field to add stars — the upper limit is five stars (for best).

You might have noticed the My Top Rated playlist in the Source pane. This playlist is an example of a *smart playlist* — a playlist that updates itself when ratings are changed. The My Top Rated playlist plays all the top-rated songs in the library.

You can also add a rating to a song: Select the song in the song list, choose File⇨My Rating, and select a set of stars for the rating (or None). If you include a Rating column in your song list, you can drag within the Rating column to add a rating to a song.

While My Guitar Gently Weeps

Summary Info **Options** Artwork

Volume Adjustment: |————————●————————|
                    -100%   None   +100%

Equalizer Preset: [None   ⬍]

My Rating: [★★★★★]

☐ Start Time: [0:00]
☐ Stop Time: [4:45.257]

Figure 8-5:
Add a rating
to a song
from the
Options tab.

(Previous) (Next)   (Cancel) (OK)

Adding Album Cover Art or Images

Songs that you buy from the iTunes Music Store typically include an image of the album cover art or a photo of the artist. You can see the artwork in the lower-left corner of the iTunes window by clicking the Show/Hide Artwork button, as shown in Figure 8-6. The artwork changes for each song or album that you select.

Figure 8-6:
Show the
artwork for
a song.

Unfortunately, you don't get free artwork like this when you rip an audio CD — the discs aren't manufactured with digital cover art stashed somewhere on an empty track. With a scanner, however, you can scan the cover art and save it in a graphics format that iTunes (and its underlying graphics technology, QuickTime) understands — JPEG, GIF, PNG, TIFF, or Photoshop. Or with a Web browser, you can visit Web pages to scout for suitable art; just Ctrl-click (Mac) or right-click an image (PC) to download and save the image on your hard drive. (Most graphics on the Web are in JPEG or GIF format, so you don't have to convert anything.)

To add artwork to one or more songs, select the song or songs in your iTunes library and drag the artwork's image file from a folder into the artwork viewing area. That area is in the bottom-left corner of the iTunes window.

To add the same image as artwork for an entire album of songs (rather than just individual songs), select the album in Browse view first (or select all the songs in the album in song list view), and then drag the image file into the artwork viewing area.

To add artwork to a single song, you can choose File⇨Get Info to open the song information window, click the Artwork tab, click the Add button, browse your hard drive or network for the image file, and select the file. Click OK to close the song information window.

You can also add the artwork to an album while editing multiple songs at once. Follow these steps:

1. **In Browse view, select the album in your iTunes library.**

   Click the Browse button to switch to Browse view so that an Album column appears on the right side of the iTunes window. Click an album to select it.

2. **Choose File⇨Get Info or press ⌘-I (Mac) or Ctrl-I (PC).**

   A warning message displays: `Are you sure you want to edit information for multiple items?`

3. **Click Yes to edit information for multiple items.**

   The Multiple Song Information dialog appears.

4. **Enable the Artwork field by selecting its check box.**

   When you add a check mark to a field, iTunes assumes you want that field changed in all the selected songs. Make sure that no other check box is selected except Artwork.

5. **Drag the graphics file to the Artwork panel.**

   Drag the graphics file directly over the blank Artwork well in the Multiple Song Information dialog.

6. **Click OK to make the change.**

   A warning message displays: `Are you sure you want to change the artwork for multiple items?`

7. **Click Yes to change the artwork.**

   iTunes adds the artwork for the entire album.

To remove the artwork from a song, view the artwork in a larger window, or resize the artwork, choose File➪Get Info and click the Artwork tab. You can add a different image, add several images, delete the images with the Add or Delete buttons, or resize images with the size slider.

You can remove the artwork for an entire album by opening the Multiple Song Information dialog (choose File➪Get Info after selecting the album), enabling the Artwork field, and then clicking OK. Because you haven't added anything to the Artwork field, iTunes replaces the artwork with nothing, effectively deleting the artwork.

Chapter 9

Organizing Music with Playlists

In This Chapter

▶ Creating a playlist of multiple songs

▶ Creating a playlist of albums

▶ Creating and editing smart playlists

▶ Deleting songs, albums, artists, and playlists

▶ Creating an iMix playlist for the iTunes Music Store

*T*o organize your music for different operations, such as copying to your iPod or burning a CD, you make a *playlist* — a list of the songs that you want.

You can use playlists to organize your music playback experience. For example, you can make a playlist of love songs from different albums to play the next time you need a romantic mood or compile a playlist of surf songs for a trip to the beach. We create playlists specifically for use with an iPod on road trips, and we generate other playlists that combine songs from different albums based on themes or similarities. For example, we have a jazz playlist for cruising around at night in the city, a classic rock playlist for jogging in the morning, and a playlist of rain songs to celebrate rainy days.

You can create as many playlists of songs, in any order, as you like. The song files themselves don't change, nor are they copied — the music files stay right where they are, with their names stored in the playlists.

You can even create a *smart playlist* that automatically includes songs in the playlist based on the criteria you set up and removes from the playlist songs that don't match the criteria. The song information you edited in Chapter 8 is very useful for setting up the criteria — for example, you can define the criteria for a smart playlist to automatically include songs from a particular artist, or songs that have the highest rating or fit within a particular musical genre.

Creating Playlists

You need to create a playlist in order to burn a CD, but playlists can also make it easier to play songs you like without having to browse the entire library looking for them. You can create playlists of individual songs or entire albums. You can also include video files, podcasts, and Web radio stations in playlists, just like songs.

Playlists of songs

You can drag individual songs into a playlist and rearrange the songs to play in any sequence you want.

To create a playlist, follow these steps:

1. **Click the + button or choose File⇨New Playlist.**

   The + button, in the bottom-left corner of the iTunes window under the Source pane, creates a new playlist in the Source pane named *untitled playlist*.

2. **Type a descriptive name for the playlist.**

   The playlist appears in the Source pane. After you type a new name, iTunes automatically sorts it into alphabetical order in the Source pane, underneath the preset smart playlists and other sources.

3. **Select the library in the Source pane, and then drag songs from the library to the playlist.**

   Drag one song at a time (as shown in Figure 9-1) or drag a selection of songs, dropping them onto the playlist name in the Source pane. The initial order of songs in the playlist is based on the order in which you drag them to the list. Of course, you can rearrange the songs in any order after dragging them, as we show in the next step.

4. **Select the playlist in the Source pane, and then drag songs to rearrange the list.**

   To move a song up the list and scroll at the same time, drag it over the up arrow in the first column (the song number); to move a song down the list and scroll, drag it to the bottom of the list. You can move a group of songs at once by selecting them first (holding down Shift to select a range of songs, or press ⌘ on a Mac or Ctrl on a PC to select specific songs), and then dragging them into a new position.

Figure 9-1:
Drag a song
to the
playlist
named "Car
playlist."

You can drag songs from one playlist to another playlist. Only links are copied, not the actual files. Besides dragging songs, you can also rearrange a playlist by sorting the list — click the Song Name, Time, Artist column headings, and so on. And when you double-click a playlist, it opens in its own window, displaying the song list.

To open a playlist in a new window, double-click the playlist icon in the Source pane. You can then easily browse your iTunes library and drag songs to the playlist window.

To create a playlist quickly, select the group of songs that you want to make into a playlist, and then choose File⇨New Playlist from Selection — or drag the selection to the white area underneath items in the Source pane. A new playlist appears in the Source pane, and you can then type a name for the playlist.

Playlists of albums

It's simple to make a playlist of an album. Select the library in the Source pane and drag an album from the Album list in the Browse view to the white area below the items in your Source pane. iTunes automatically creates a new playlist named after the album.

You might want to play several albums of songs without having to select each album as you play them. For example, you might want to use an iPod on that long drive from London to Liverpool to play Beatles albums in the order they were released (or perhaps the reverse order, reversing the Beatles' career from London back to Liverpool).

To create a playlist of entire albums in a particular order, follow these steps:

1. **Create a new playlist.**

   Create a playlist by clicking the + sign under the Source pane or by choosing File⇨New Playlist. Type a descriptive name for the new playlist.

2. **Select the library in the Source pane, and click the Browse button to find the artist.**

   The Album list appears in the right panel.

3. **Drag the album name over the playlist name.**

4. **Select and drag each subsequent album over the playlist name.**

   Each time you drag an album, iTunes automatically lists the songs in the proper track sequence.

You can rename a playlist at any time by clicking inside its name and typing a new one. Also, in case you forget which songs are in which playlists, you can see all the playlists that include a particular song. In Browse or song List view, on a Mac press the Control key and click the song; in Windows use the right mouse button to right-click the song, and then drag down to Playlists in the pop-up menu. The playlists that include the song are listed in the submenu.

Using Smart Playlists

At the top of the Source pane, indicated by a gear icon, you can find what Apple (and everyone else) calls a *smart playlist*. iTunes comes with a few sample smart playlists, such as the My Top Rated and Recently Added playlists, and you can create your own. Smart playlists add songs to themselves based on prearranged criteria. For example, as you rate your songs, My Top Rated changes to reflect your new ratings. You don't have to set anything up — My Top Rated and Recently Added are already defined for you.

Of course, smart playlists are ignorant of your taste in music — you have to program them with criteria using the song information you edited in Chapter 8. For example, you can create a smart playlist that uses the Year field to grab all the songs from 1966, only to find that the list includes the Beatles ("Eleanor Rigby"), Frank Sinatra ("Strangers in the Night"), the Yardbirds ("Over Under Sideways Down"), and Ike and Tina Turner ("River Deep, Mountain High") in no particular order. Use other fields of the song information you entered, such as ratings, artist name, or comment to fine-tune your criteria. You can also use built-in functions such as the Play Count (the number of times the song was played) or the Date Added (the date the song was added to the library).

Creating a smart playlist

To create a new smart playlist, choose File⇨New Smart Playlist. The Smart Playlist dialog appears (as shown in Figure 9-2), offering the following choices for setting criteria:

Figure 9-2:
Set the first match condition for a smart playlist.

✔ **Match the Following Conditions:** From the first pop-up menu (refer to Figure 9-2), you can select any of the categories used for song information. From the second pop-up menu, you can choose an operator, such as the greater than or less than operators. The selections that you make in these two pop-up menus combine to express a condition such as `Year is greater than 1966`. You can also add multiple conditions by clicking the + button, and then decide whether to match all or any of these conditions.

✔ **Limit To:** You can limit the smart playlist to a specific duration, measured by the number of songs, time, or size in megabytes or gigabytes, as shown in Figure 9-3. The songs can be selected by various methods such as random, most recently played, and so on.

✔ **Match Only Checked Songs:** This option selects only those songs that have a check mark beside them, along with the rest of the criteria. Checking and unchecking songs is an easy way to fine-tune your selection for a smart playlist.

✔ **Live Updating:** This allows iTunes to automatically update the playlist continually as you play songs, add or remove them from the library, change their ratings, and so on.

A smart playlist for recent additions

Setting up multiple criteria gives you the opportunity to create playlists that are way smarter than the ones supplied with iTunes. For example, we created a smart playlist with criteria shown in Figure 9-3 that does the following:

✔ Adds any song added to the library in the past week that *also* has a rating greater than three stars.

✔ Limits the playlist to 72 minutes of music (to fit on one audio CD), and refines the selection to the most recently added if the entire selection becomes greater than 72 minutes.

✔ Matches only checked songs.

✔ Performs live updating.

Figure 9-3:
Use multiple conditions and a time limit for a smart playlist.

After setting up the criteria, click OK. iTunes creates the playlist with a gear icon and the name *untitled playlist* or whatever phrase you used for the first condition (such as the album or artist name). You can click in the playlist field and type a new name for it.

Editing a smart playlist

To edit a smart playlist, select the playlist and choose File➪Edit Smart Playlist (or right-click the playlist with a two-button mouse and select Edit Smart Playlist from the pop-up menu). The Smart Playlist window appears, with the criteria for the smart playlist.

To modify the smart playlist so that songs with a higher rating are picked, simply add another star or two to the My Rating criteria.

You can also choose to limit the playlist to a certain number of songs, selected by various methods such as random, most recently played, and so on.

Deleting Songs, Albums, Artists, and Playlists

Deleting songs can seem counterproductive when you're trying to build up your iTunes library, but there are times when you have to do it, such as the following:

- **Deleting versions of songs:** You might have ripped a CD twice — once in AIFF format to burn the songs onto another CD, and another in AAC format for your library and iPod. You can delete the AIFF versions in your library after burning your CD (as we describe in Chapter 12).

- **Deleting songs from playlists:** You can delete songs from playlists while keeping the songs in your Library. When you delete a song from a playlist, the song is simply deleted from the list — not from the library. You can delete playlists as well, without harming the songs in the library. You have to switch to the Library in the Source pane to delete songs from the library.

- **Deleting a song, album, or artist from the library:** With the Library selected in the Source pane, you can select any song, group of songs, album, group of albums, artist, or group of artists, and then press Delete/Backspace or choose Edit➪Clear. After clicking Yes to the warning message, the songs are gone from iTunes. (Why did you rip them in the first place? See Chapter 3 about how to play tracks first, before importing them.)

To delete a song from a playlist, select the playlist in the Source pane, and then select the song. Press Delete/Backspace (that's Delete on a Mac or Backspace on a Windows PC), or choose Edit➪Clear. In the warning dialog that appears, click Yes to remove the selected item from the list.

To delete a playlist, select the playlist in the Source pane and press Delete/Backspace, or choose Edit➪Clear.

To delete a song from the library, select Library in the Source pane, and then select the song. Press Delete/Backspace, or choose Edit➪Clear. In the warning dialog that appears, click Yes to remove the selected item from the list.

Deleting a song from the iTunes Library removes the song from your Library song list, but it doesn't remove it from your hard drive until you agree. iTunes displays another warning — Some of the selected files are located in your iTunes Music folder. Would you like to move these files to the Trash? — and you can click Yes to trash them, No to keep them in your music folder, or Cancel to cancel the operation.

You can delete multiple songs by first selecting them. Just hold down Shift as you click to select a range of songs, or hold down ⌘ (Mac) or Ctrl (PC) as you click each song to add it to the selection. Then press Delete/Backspace, or choose Edit➪Clear.

To delete an entire album, first select the album in Browse view, press Delete/ Backspace, or choose Edit➪Clear. To delete everything by an artist, first select the artist in Browse view, and then press Delete/Backspace or choose Edit➪Clear. If you choose to move the album or artist folder to the Trash, the album or artist folder is deleted from your hard drive; otherwise, it remains in your iTunes Music folder.

If you leave music files and folders in your iTunes Music folder, you can add them back to your iTunes library by dragging and dropping them into the iTunes window.

Creating an iMix

Amateur disk jockeys, rejoice! The iTunes Music Store offers the iMix section for sharing your iTunes playlists with other iTunes users. While you can submit a playlist of any songs to be published in the iMix section of the store, only songs available from the store are actually published — unavailable songs are skipped. You can include in the playlist any song from any ripped CD, and if the song is also available in the store, the song will be included in the published iMix playlist.

Browsers in the iTunes Music Store can view the playlist by entering the iMix section and clicking any playlist. See Chapter 4 for information about navigating the iTunes Music Store, playing short preview clips, and buying songs.

To create an iMix, follow these steps:

1. **Select the playlist in your iTunes library and choose File➪Create an iMix.**

   iTunes displays a warning message before accessing the iTunes Music Store to publish your playlist.

2. **Click the Create button in the warning message.**

   Click Create to start the process. iTunes displays the music store sign-in dialog shown in Figure 9-4.

3. **Sign in to the iTunes Music Store with your ID and password.**

   Provide your Apple or AOL ID and password to log into the store. iTunes selects the Music Store in the Source pane and displays the iMix Music

Store page shown in Figure 9-5. You see the iMix playlist that will be pub-lished, which includes only songs that are available from the store.

4. **Edit the title and description for the iMix playlist and click the Publish button.**

iTunes publishes the playlist in the iMix section of the store. Others can browse the playlist and buy any songs, as we describe in Chapter 4.

Chapter 10

Updating Your iPod with iTunes

*i*Tunes is the software that puts music on your iPod (more than just music, of course — you can include audio books, podcasts, or anything stored as a song in iTunes). iTunes can fill your iPod with sounds very quickly and keep it updated every time you connect it. (iTunes can also keep your iPod synchronized with new or edited contacts and calendars, as we describe in Chapter 26, and keep a color-display iPod synchronized with your photo library, as we describe in Chapter 24.)

If you're too busy to copy specific songs to your iPod and your entire iTunes music library fits on your iPod anyway, why not just copy everything? Copying your library is just as fast as copying individual songs, if not faster, and you don't have to do anything except connect the iPod to your computer. This chapter shows you how to set up iTunes to automatically update your iPod.

This chapter also shows how you can update your iPod manually, choosing which songs to copy. iTunes is flexible in that you can use either option or *both* options to update your iPod. For example, you can update automatically with all the songs in playlists, and then copy other music not in playlists directly to your iPod, and delete songs from your iPod if you need to make room.

This chapter explains how to set your preferences for updating and change them when you need to. It also explains how to fill an iPod shuffle automatically or manually and how to manage space on an iPod shuffle.

Changing Your Update Preferences

If you've changed your iPod preferences to update manually, you can change them back to update automatically any time and vice versa. Change your iPod preferences by following these steps:

1. **Connect the iPod to your computer.**

   Your iPod must be connected for you to change the update preferences.

   iTunes starts automatically. If this is the first time connecting your iPod, it synchronizes automatically with the iTunes library. If you want to prevent this from happening, hold down the Ctrl and Alt keys on a PC (⌘ and Option keys on a Mac) as you connect the iPod, keeping them pressed until the iPod name appears in the iTunes Source pane.

2. **Select the iPod in the iTunes Source pane.**

   Your iPod appears in the Source pane using the name you gave it when you installed the iPod software. See Chapter 2.

3. **Click the iPod Options button on the bottom-right side of the iTunes window, or click the iPod button in the iTunes Preferences window.**

   The iPod Options button appears only when an iPod is connected and selected in the Source pane. You can also choose iTunes➪Preferences on a Mac or Edit➪Preferences on a Windows PC, and click the iPod button — whether or not the iPod is selected in the Source pane (although it has to be connected). The iPod preferences dialog appears, as shown in Figure 10-1.

4. **Click the Music button in the iPod preferences dialog to select music update preferences.**

   The Music button may already be selected; if not, click it to show the music preferences.

5. **Select the update preferences you want.**

   Set the update preferences, and click OK to the warning message that appears. For example, if you select the Automatically Update All Songs and Playlists option, iTunes displays a warning message asking you to confirm the update preference you chose (see Figure 10-2). Be sure that you want to use this option before selecting it; see "Updating Your iPod Automatically" later in this chapter.

6. **Click OK to go ahead (confirming that you want to change to automatic update).**

Figure 10-1:
Switch iPod
updating
methods in
the iPod
preferences
dialog.

Figure 10-2:
Confirm that
you want to
update your
music
library
automat-
ically.

7. **Change other iPod music preferences as you wish.**

   Other preferences that you might want to change include the "Open
   iTunes when this iPod is attached" option, which launches iTunes automatically when turned on. If this is off, you have to start iTunes by
   launching it yourself. Other options appear depending on the iPod
   model — for example, the option "Display album artwork on your iPod"
   appears only for iPod models with color displays.

8. **Click OK to close the Preferences dialog.**

9. **Click the iPod Eject button, which appears in the bottom-right side of the iTunes window.**

   Another way to eject the iPod on a Mac is to drag the iPod icon on the Desktop to the Trash — or in Mac OS X 10.3, click the eject icon next to the iPod icon in the Finder Sidebar. In either Mac OS X or Windows, you can right-click the iPod icon and choose Eject.

   After you eject the iPod, the iPod displays an OK to disconnect message in first- and second-generation models, or the iPod main menu in third-generation models. You can then disconnect the iPod from its dock, or disconnect the dock from the computer.

While the updating is in progress, don't disconnect your iPod from the computer until it tells you it is safe to do so. The iPod is a hard drive, after all, and hard drives need to be closed down properly in order for you not to lose any critical data. When it's safe, the iPod displays an OK to disconnect message in first- and second-generation models, or the iPod main menu in third-generation and fourth-generation models.

Updating Your iPod Automatically

The default setting for a new iPod is to update itself automatically, *synchronizing* to your iTunes library: The iPod matches your library exactly, song for song, playlist for playlist. If you made changes in iTunes after the last time you synchronized, those changes are automatically made in the iPod when you synchronize again. If you added or deleted songs in your library, those songs are added or deleted in the iPod library. (A color-display iPod also synchronizes automatically with your photo library. To read all about updating with photos, see Chapter 24.)

If your iTunes music library is too large to fit on your iPod, you can still update automatically and keep your iPod synchronized to a subset of your library, adding new material under your control. For example, you can let iTunes select the music automatically according to your ratings, as described in the upcoming section, "Updating from a library larger than your iPod." You can even create a *smart playlist* that does it for you, as described in the later section, "Updating by playlist."

Before you actually connect your iPod to a computer to automatically update the iPod, keep these things in mind:

   ✔ iTunes remembers your updating preferences for each iPod you connect from the last time you updated the iPod. If you already set your preferences to update automatically, iTunes remembers and starts to automatically update the iPod. If you already set your preferences to update manually, iTunes remembers and makes the iPod active in the iTunes Source pane.

✔ To prevent an iPod from automatically updating, hold down the ⌘ and Option keys on a Mac (Ctrl and Alt keys on a PC) as you connect the iPod, and keep pressing until the iPod name appears in the iTunes Source pane. This works even if you choose to automatically update the iPod in the Setup Assistant.

✔ If you connect your iPod to another computer running iTunes, you might be in for a surprise. When you connect an iPod previously linked to another computer, iTunes displays the message: `This iPod is linked to another iTunes music library. Do you want to change the link to this iTunes music library and replace all existing songs and playlists on this iPod with those from this library?` If you don't want to change your iPod to have this other music library, click No. Otherwise, iTunes erases your iPod and updates your iPod with the other computer's iTunes library. By clicking No, you change that computer's iTunes preferences to manually update, thereby avoiding automatic updating.

✔ Songs stored remotely (such as songs shared from other iTunes libraries on a network) are not synchronized because they are not physically on your computer. See Chapter 6 for more info on how to share music over a network with iTunes.

When your iPod is set to update automatically (the entire library, or by either playlist or selected song), the iPod song list and the iPod entry in the Source pane are grayed out in the iTunes window. Because you manage the contents automatically, you don't have direct access to the songs in the iPod using iTunes. For direct access, see "Updating Your iPod Manually," later in this chapter.

Synchronizing with your library

Your iPod is set up by default to automatically update itself from your iTunes library so that it can synchronize with it. Just follow these simple steps:

1. **Connect the iPod to your computer.**

   When you first connect the iPod to the computer, your iPod automatically synchronizes with your iTunes music library — unless you turned off the "Automatically update songs on my iPod" option in the Setup Assistant, or unless you hold down the ⌘ and Option keys on a Mac (Ctrl and Alt keys on a PC) while connecting the iPod.

2. **Wait for the updating to finish and then eject the iPod.**

   Wait until the iTunes status pane (up at the top) reads `iPod update is complete`. You can then click the iPod Eject button, which appears in the bottom-right side of the iTunes window.

You can also eject the iPod by dragging the iPod icon on the Desktop to the Trash on the Mac; in OS X 10.3, you can click the eject icon next to the iPod icon in the Finder Sidebar. In Windows, you can use various methods, including right-clicking the iPod icon and choosing Eject from the contextual menu.

While the updating is in progress and right after ejecting the iPod, don't disconnect your iPod from your computer until it tells you that it's safe to do so. As a reminder, the iPod displays the message `Do not disconnect`.

Updating from a library larger than your iPod

If your iTunes music library is too large to fit on your iPod, you can still update automatically and keep your iPod synchronized to a subset of your library. When you first use your iPod (which is set by default to automatic update), iTunes displays a message if your library is too large to fit, telling you that it has created a special playlist for your iPod. This playlist is specially designed for updating your iPod automatically. For example, if your iPod is named GigaMojo, you find a new playlist named GigaMojo Selection filled with all the songs that iTunes could fit in your iPod.

If, on the other hand, you have already been using your iPod and it's set to automatically update, iTunes displays a message that gives you a choice of automatically creating a new playlist, or letting iTunes choose for you:

- ✔ If you click Yes, iTunes creates a new playlist (titled GigaMojo Selection, if your iPod is named GigaMojo like one of ours) and displays a message telling you so. Click OK, and iTunes updates your iPod using the new playlist.

- ✔ If you click No, iTunes updates automatically until it fills up your iPod. iTunes decides which songs and albums to include in this playlist using the ratings that you can set for each song in the iTunes song information, as we describe in Chapter 8. iTunes groups album tracks together and computes an average rating and play count for the album. It then fills the iPod, giving higher priority to albums with play counts and ratings greater than zero. You can therefore influence the decisions that iTunes makes by adding ratings to songs or entire albums.

Updating by playlist

Updating by playlist is useful when you want to copy selected sets of songs to your iPod every time you connect it to your computer. For example, you can define a set of playlists in your iTunes library to use just for updating an iPod that doesn't have enough capacity to hold your entire library. To do this, set up the iPod to update only selected playlists automatically.

 Updating automatically by playlist is also an easy way to automatically update an iPod from an iTunes library that is larger than the iPod's capacity.

Before using this update option, create the playlists in iTunes (see Chapter 9) that you want to copy to the iPod. Then follow these steps:

1. **Connect the iPod to your computer.**

   If your iPod is set to automatically update, hold down the ⌘ and Option keys on a Mac (Ctrl and Alt keys on a PC) while connecting the iPod.

2. **Select the iPod name in the iTunes Source pane.**

3. **Click the iPod Options button or click the iPod button in the iTunes Preferences window.**

   The iPod Options button appears only when an iPod is connected and selected in the Source pane. You can also choose iTunes➪Preferences on a Mac or Edit➪Preferences on a Windows PC, and click the iPod button. The iPod preferences dialog appears.

4. **Click the Music button in the iPod preferences dialog to select music update preferences.**

5. **Select the Automatically Update Selected Playlists Only option.**

6. **In the list box, select each playlist that you want to copy in the update.**

   Select the check box next to each playlist to select it for the update, as shown in Figure 10-3.

7. **Click OK to close Preferences.**

   iTunes automatically updates the iPod by erasing its contents and copying only the playlists that you selected in Step 6.

8. **Wait for the updating to finish, and then eject the iPod.**

   Wait until the iTunes status pane reads `iPod update is complete`. Then you can click the iPod Eject button (the one with the eject triangle), which appears in the bottom-right side of the iTunes window.

Updating selected songs

You might want to update the iPod automatically but only with selected songs — especially if your iTunes library is larger than the capacity of your iPod. To use this method, you must first deselect the songs you don't want to transfer, since all the songs in your iTunes library are selected by default.

To deselect a song, click the check box next to the song so that the check mark disappears. To select a song, mark the check box so that the mark appears.

You can quickly select or deselect an entire album by selecting an album in Browse view and holding down the ⌘ key (Mac) or the Ctrl key (PC).

After you deselect the songs that you don't want to transfer and make sure that the songs you *do* want to transfer are selected, follow these steps:

1. **Connect the iPod to your computer.**

   If your iPod is set to automatically update, hold down the Ctrl and Alt keys on a PC (⌘ and Option keys on a Mac) while connecting the iPod.

2. **Select the iPod name in the iTunes Source pane.**

   You can select the iPod name even when it's grayed out.

3. **Click the iPod Options button or click the iPod button in the iTunes Preferences window.**

   The iPod Options button appears only when an iPod is connected and selected in the Source pane. You can also choose iTunes⇨Preferences on a Mac or Edit⇨Preferences on a Windows PC, and click the iPod button. The iPod preferences dialog appears; refer to Figure 10-1.

4. **Click the Music button in the iPod preferences dialog to select music update preferences.**

5. **Select the Automatically Update All Songs and Playlists option and click OK for the `Are you sure you want to enable automatic updating` message that appears.**

6. **Select the Only Update Checked Songs check box and then click OK to close Preferences.**

   iTunes automatically updates the iPod by copying only the songs in the iTunes library that are selected.

7. **Wait for the updating to finish, and then eject the iPod.**

   Wait until the iTunes status pane reads `iPod update is complete`, and you can then click the iPod Eject button, which appears in the bottom-right side of the iTunes window.

Updating Your iPod Manually

With manual updating, you can add music to your iPod directly via iTunes, and you can delete music from your iPod as well. The iPod name appears in the iTunes Source pane, and when selected, its contents appear in the iTunes song list replacing the library contents.

You might have one or more reasons for updating manually, but some obvious ones are the following:

- ✔ Your entire music library is too big for your iPod, and you want to copy individual albums, songs, or playlists to the iPod directly.

- ✔ You want to share a single music library with several iPods, and you have different playlists that you want to copy to each iPod directly.

- ✔ You share an iPod with others, and you want to copy your music to the iPod without wiping out their music.

- ✔ You want to copy some music from another computer's music library without deleting any music from your iPod.

- ✔ You want to edit the playlists and song information directly on your iPod without changing anything in your computer's library.

✔ You want to play the songs on your iPod using iTunes on the computer, where you can play your iPod through the computer's speakers and take advantage of iTunes playback features (such as cross-fading between two tracks — see Chapter 16).

When you set your iPod to update manually, the entire contents of the iPod is active and available in iTunes. You can copy music directly to your iPod, delete songs on the iPod, and edit the iPod playlists directly.

To set your iPod to update manually, follow these steps:

1. **Connect the iPod to your computer, holding down the Ctrl and Alt keys on a PC (⌘ and Option keys on a Mac) to prevent automatic updating.**

   Continue holding the keys down until the iPod name appears in the iTunes Source pane.

2. **Select the iPod name in the iTunes Source pane.**

3. **Click the iPod Options button or click the iPod button in the iTunes Preferences window.**

   The iPod Options button appears only when an iPod is connected and selected in the Source pane. You can also choose iTunes⇨Preferences on a Mac or Edit⇨Preferences on a Windows PC, and click the iPod button. The iPod preferences dialog appears (refer to Figure 10-1).

4. **Click the Music button in the iPod preferences dialog to select music update preferences.**

5. **Select the Manually Manage Songs and Playlists option.**

   iTunes displays the `Disabling automatic update requires manually unmounting the iPod before each disconnect` message.

6. **Click OK to accept the new iPod preferences.**

   The iPod contents now appear active in iTunes and not grayed out.

Don't disconnect your iPod while it is active in iTunes with the manual updating method. You have to eject the iPod and wait until the iPod displays the message `OK to disconnect` (in first- and second-generation models) or the iPod main menu.

Copying music directly

As soon as you set your iPod to manual updating, you can copy music directly. To copy music to your iPod directly, follow these steps (with your iPod connected to your computer):

1. **Select the iTunes music library or a library playlist in the Source pane.**

   The library's or playlist's songs appear in a List view or in Browse view.

2. **Drag items directly from your iTunes library or playlist over the iPod name in the Source pane, as shown in Figure 10-4.**

   When you drag a playlist name, all the songs associated with the playlist copy along with the playlist itself. When you drag an album title, all the songs in the album are copied.

Figure 10-4: Copy an album of songs directly from the iTunes library to the iPod.

3. **Wait for the copy operation to finish and then eject the iPod.**

   Wait until the iTunes status pane reads `iPod update is complete`; you can then click the iPod Eject button, which appears in the bottom-right side of the iTunes window.

   "Jeanne" has to be highlited in order to use eject (lower rt. corner)

Deleting music on your iPod

With manual updating, you can delete songs from the iPod directly. Manual deletion is a nice feature if you just want to go in and delete a song or an album to make room for more music.

Automatic synchronization with your iTunes library means that anything you delete in your iTunes library is also deleted when you update your iPod. However, if you update manually, you can delete songs from your iPod without changing your iTunes library.

To delete any song in the song list with your iPod set to manual updating, follow these steps:

1. **Select the iPod in the iTunes Source pane.**

   The iPod's songs appear in the List or Browse view, replacing the view of your library songs.

2. **Select a song or album on the iPod and press Delete/Backspace or choose Edit⇨Clear.**

   iTunes displays a warning to make sure you want to do this; click OK to go ahead or Cancel to stop. If you want to delete a playlist, select the playlist and press Delete or choose Edit⇨Clear.

Like in the iTunes library, if you delete a playlist, the songs are not deleted — they are still on your iPod unless you delete them from the iPod song list or update the iPod automatically with other songs or playlists.

Managing Playlists on Your iPod

The song information and playlists for your iPod are automatically copied to your iPod when you update the iPod. However, you might want to edit your iPod's music library separately, perhaps creating new playlists or changing the song information manually, just on your iPod.

First you must connect your iPod to your computer, open iTunes, and set your iPod to update manually, as we describe earlier in "Updating Your iPod Manually."

Creating playlists directly on the iPod

You can create a playlist just on the iPod itself, using songs that are on the iPod. The songs must already be on the iPod.

To create a new playlist, follow these steps:

1. **Select the iPod in the iTunes Source pane.**

2. **Click the triangle next to the iPod name to open the iPod list of playlists, as shown in Figure 10-5.**

Figure 10-5:
Create a
playlist
here.

3. **Create a new playlist by clicking the + button in the bottom-left corner of iTunes under the Source list or choose File⇨New Playlist.**

   Untitled playlist appears in the Source pane under the iPod entry.

4. **Type a name for the untitled playlist.**

   After you type a new name, iTunes automatically sorts it into alphabetical order in the list under the iPod.

5. **Click the name of the iPod in the Source pane and drag songs from the iPod song list to the playlist.**

   You can also click the Browse button to find songs on the iPod more easily.

The order of songs in the playlist is based on the order in which you drag them to the list. You can rearrange the list by dragging songs within the playlist.

You can create smart playlists on the iPod in exactly the same way as in the iTunes music library. A *smart playlist* updates itself when you create it using iTunes, and then updates itself every time you connect and select your iPod with iTunes. Read all about smart playlists in Chapter 9.

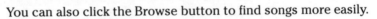

Editing playlists

To edit an existing playlist on your iPod, do the following:

1. **Select the iPod in the iTunes Source pane.**

   The iPod songs appear in the List or Browse view, replacing the view of your library songs.

2. **Click the triangle next to the iPod name to open the iPod list of playlists.**

3. **Scroll the Source pane to locate the playlist.**

4. **Select the playlist to rearrange songs.**

   You can rearrange songs by dragging them within the List view for the playlist — just as if the playlist were in the iTunes library.

5. **Click the name of the iPod in the Source pane and drag more songs from the iPod song list to the iPod playlist.**

   You can also click the Browse button to find songs more easily.

The songs and albums that you drag to an iPod playlist must already be on the iPod. If you want to copy songs from your iTunes library, see "Updating Your iPod Manually," earlier in this chapter.

Editing Song Information on Your iPod

With the iPod selected in iTunes and set for updating manually, you can edit song information just like you do in the iTunes library by scrolling down the song list and selecting songs.

After selecting the iPod in the Source pane, click the Browse button. In Browse view, you can browse the iPod library, and find the songs by artist and album.

You can edit information such as the Song Name, Artist, Album, Genre, and My Ratings information for the iPod songs directly in the columns in the song list. To edit song information, locate the song and click inside the text field of a column to type new text.

You might find it easier to edit this information by choosing File⇨Get Info and typing the text into the Song Information dialog, as shown in Figure 10-6.

Nowadays Clancy Can't Even Sing

| Summary | Info | Options | Artwork |

Name
Nowadays Clancy Can't Even Sing

Artist   **Year**
Buffalo Springfield   1966

Album   **Track Number**
Buffalo Springfield   4 of 23

Grouping   **Disc Number**
                                                          4 of 4

Composer   **BPM**
Neil Young

Comments

Genre
Rock   ☐ Part of a compilation

Previous   Next   Cancel   OK

Figure 10-6:
Type the
composer
credits here.

iTunes grabs song information from the Internet (as we describe in Chapter 7), but this information typically doesn't include composer credits. If you have the time and inclination to add composer credits, doing so is worth your while because you can then search, sort, and create playlists based on this information. This is particularly important for classical music lovers because iTunes and the iPod make it easy to find songs by the performer/artist but not by the composer — and sorting by composer is what many classical music fans prefer.

Updating an iPod Shuffle

The iPod shuffle is designed for quick and convenient music updating — just plug it into your computer and click Autofill. It also offers automatic compression to manage and fit more songs into your iPod shuffle space.

While Apple proudly advertises its capability to shuffle songs randomly, the key to its success is that you cannot only shuffle the songs already there, but can copy random songs to it every time you connect it to your computer. Eventually you can shuffle through everything in your library if you so wish, by randomly filling your iPod shuffle every time. On the other hand, you can fine-tune your random selection, and even reorder the iPod shuffle's playlist to play back in a specific order.

While you can add songs to your iPod shuffle manually by dragging a playlist or song, you can also automatically fill it without having to set options for automatic updating. Autofill automatically picks songs from your entire iTunes music library, or from a playlist you select in the Source pane. You can also manage the playlist for your iPod shuffle directly, after using Autofill, to fine-tune your selection.

Using Autofill

To use Autofill to copy songs to your iPod shuffle, follow these steps:

1. **Connect the iPod shuffle to your computer.**

   When you connect an iPod shuffle to your computer, it shows up in the Source pane.

2. **Select the iPod shuffle in the iTunes Source pane.**

   After selecting the iPod shuffle in the Source pane, the Autofill pane appears below the Song List pane, as shown in Figure 10-7. The iPod shuffle's songs appear in the List or Browse view, replacing the view of your library songs

3. **Choose your source of music in the "Autofill from" pop-up menu.**

   Choose either a playlist or library (for the entire library). If you choose a playlist, Autofill uses only the playlist as the source of music.

4. **To pick random songs, select the "Choose songs randomly" option.**

5. **To pick only the best songs (if you are choosing them randomly), select the "Choose higher rated songs more often" option.**

6. **To replace songs already on the iPod shuffle, select the "Replace all" option.**

   If you don't select this option, iTunes adds the songs without replacing existing songs.

7. **Click the Autofill button to start copying songs.**

   iTunes grabs a subset of your music, creates a playlist, and copies the contents of the playlist to the iPod shuffle.

8. **Wait for the copy operation to finish and then eject the iPod shuffle.**

   Wait until the iTunes Status pane reads `iPod update is complete`; you can then click the iPod eject button, which appears in the bottom-right side of the iTunes window.

Figure 10-7:
Autofill your
iPod shuffle
from an
iTunes
playlist.

You can click Autofill over and over to create different random playlists. When you get one you like, select all its contents and choose File➪New Playlist From Selection to create a new playlist that contains the songs generated by Autofill. When you next connect your iPod shuffle, select this new playlist from the Autofill From pop-up menu and click Autofill to load the music from the playlist to your shuffle.

The iPod shuffle can play type 2, 3, and 4 Audible.com audio books (including audio books sold by the iTunes Music Store). Unfortunately, iTunes won't automatically add them to the iPod shuffle — you have to add them manually.

Updating manually

The iPod shuffle is always set for manual updating. When you connect an iPod shuffle to your computer, you can copy music directly to it, delete songs from it, and edit its playlist.

To copy music to your iPod shuffle directly, connect your iPod shuffle to your computer and follow these steps:

1. Select the iTunes Music Library in the Source pane.

The library's songs appear in a List or Browse view.

2. **Drag items directly from your iTunes music library over the iPod shuffle name in the Source pane, as shown in Figure 10-8.**

   When you copy a playlist, all the songs in the playlist are copied. When you copy an album, all the songs in the album are copied.

Figure 10-8: Copy songs directly from the iTunes library to the iPod shuffle.

3. **Wait for the copy operation to finish and then eject the iPod.**

   Wait until the iTunes status pane reads `iPod update is complete`; you can then click the iPod Eject button, which appears in the bottom-right side of the iTunes window.

To delete any song in your iPod shuffle, follow these steps:

1. **Select the iPod shuffle in the iTunes Source pane.**

   The iPod shuffle songs appear in the List or Browse view, replacing the view of your library songs.

2. **Select a song or album on the iPod shuffle and press Delete/Backspace or choose Edit⇨Clear.**

   iTunes displays a warning to make sure you want to do this; click OK to go ahead or Cancel to stop.

Managing an iPod shuffle playlist

You may not want to make a random choice or even fine-tune a random choice — you may want to take a more deterministic approach to updating the song choices and sequence of your iPod shuffle. You can do this by managing your iPod shuffle playlist manually, and you can manage even without connecting the iPod shuffle.

Connect the iPod shuffle and select it in the iTunes Source pane so you can see its playlist in the List view. The song order in the playlist is based either on the order Autofill selected them or the order in which you dragged them. You can rearrange the playing order by dragging songs within the iPod shuffle playlist to new positions in the list. You can also copy songs to the iPod shuffle at any position in the list and delete songs from the iPod shuffle playlist, as described in the previous section, "Updating manually."

The cool thing about an iPod shuffle is that you can also do these things *without* connecting the iPod shuffle. Follow these steps:

1. **Connect the iPod shuffle and select it in the Source pane.**

2. **Click the iPod Options button or click the iPod button in the iTunes Preferences window.**

   The iPod Options button appears only when an iPod is connected and selected in the Source pane. You can also choose iTunes⇨Preferences on a Mac or Edit⇨Preferences on a Windows PC, and click the iPod button. The iPod preferences dialog appears, as shown in Figure 10-9.

3. **Click the Music button in the iPod preferences dialog to select music update preferences.**

4. **Select the "Keep this iPod in the source list" option.**

   Click this option's check box to turn it on. That way when you disconnect your iPod shuffle, it remains in the Source pane and you can continue changing its playlist. Your iPod shuffle is automatically updated the next time you connect it.

5. *Optional:* **Select the "Only update checked songs" option.**

   Click this option's check box if you want iTunes to copy only songs that are marked in the iTunes library as selected. To use this option effectively, you must first *deselect* songs you don't want to copy. To deselect a song, deselect the check box next to the song in the iTunes library. To select a song, mark the check box so the mark appears.

6. **Click OK to close the Preferences dialog.**

7. Eject the iPod shuffle before disconnecting it.

Click the iPod Eject button, which appears in the bottom-right side of the iTunes window, or click the eject icon next to the iPod shuffle name in the Source pane.

Your iPod shuffle remains in the Source pane even after you disconnect it, as shown in Figure 10-10. Select the iPod shuffle's name in the Source pane and rearrange the playlist as you wish, including copying and deleting songs. When you are finished, iTunes saves the iPod shuffle playlist so when you reconnect your iPod shuffle, it is automatically updated to match this playlist.

Managing space on your iPod shuffle

It's a nifty song player! No, it's an external flash drive for data backup! Either way, you can wear the iPod shuffle around your neck, which makes it quite convenient for either music or data. To maximize its data potential, see Chapter 21. To maximize its music potential, connect your iPod shuffle and open iPod preferences — either select the iPod shuffle in the Source pane and click the iPod Options button, or choose iTunes⇨Preferences (on a Mac) or Edit⇨Preferences (in Windows), and click the iPod button.

Figure 10-10:
Keep the iPod shuffle's playlist active after disconnecting the iPod shuffle.

The iPod preferences dialog (refer to Figure 10-9) includes a storage allocation slider with More Songs on the left side and More Data on the right side. Drag the slider to the left to open up more space for music. Don't worry — adding more space won't affect any data files already stored on the iPod shuffle.

If the storage allocation slider is as far left as it can go, or as far left as you want to take it (leaving space for data), you still have one more method of squeezing music onto the iPod shuffle: the "Convert higher bitrate songs to 128 kbps AAC for this iPod" option. This option does just what it says: converts songs with higher bit rates in either protected or unprotected AAC files or MP3 files into smaller AAC files using 128 kbps as the bit rate. It performs this conversion on the fly, while copying songs to the iPod shuffle, without changing the songs in your library. Protected AAC songs retain their protection.

You can save considerable space by doing this. An iPod shuffle holding an average of 180 songs encoded at 192 Kbps in MP3 can hold an average of 260 songs by setting this option. The conversion reduces an uncompressed AIFF file to about seven percent of its original size.

Chapter 11

Gimme Shelter for My Music

*Y*ou might think that your music is safe, stored as it is on both your iPod and your hard drive. However, demons in the night are working overtime to render your hard drive useless, while at the same time someone left your iPod out in the rain. (No, not really, but it could happen.)

Copyright law and common sense prohibit you from copying copyrighted music and selling it to someone else. However, you *are* allowed to make copies of music, audio books, and podcasts for your personal use, including copies for your iPod and copies for backup.

In this chapter, you find out how to make a backup of your entire library — a very important operation, especially if you purchase songs that don't exist anywhere else. That way, even if your hard drive fails, you still have your iTunes library.

You can't copy music from your iPod to your computer — that is, using iTunes. It's a one-way trip from iTunes to your iPod. The reason you can't copy music from your iPod using iTunes is that record companies didn't want to allow indiscriminate copying, and Apple complied with their request. You can, however, use third-party utility programs (not supported by Apple) to copy music both ways. (More on this topic in Chapter 26.) According to record labels, most music is copyrighted and shouldn't be copied in this manner anyway. Instead, keep a backup of your iTunes library on your computer and on another hard drive or backup medium — don't rely on your iPod as your sole music storage device.

Some music that you can use in iTunes and with your iPod is protected. The iTunes Music Store uses Apple's FairPlay technology that protects the rights of copyright holders while also giving you some leeway in how you can use the music. You can copy the music files freely, so backup is easy and straightforward on either a PC or a Mac. The question of whether you can *play* the music after copying it is answered by reading the section on authorizing computers to play purchased music in Chapter 4. (You can play iTunes Music Store songs on up to five computers at the same time.)

Studying Files in the iTunes Library

If you are like that guy who, in the movie *Diner,* couldn't stand to have his records misfiled, you'll love iTunes and its nice, neat file storage methods. Songs can be saved with descriptive filenames within album folders, which are, in turn, saved within artist folders. These folders are stored in the iTunes Music folder — unless you change your storage preferences.

Finding the iTunes library

The default method of storing content in the iTunes library is to store all audio files, including music, podcasts, and audio books, in the iTunes Music folder. Music videos purchased from the iTunes Music Store are also stored here. With this method, music and video files that you drag to the iTunes window are copied into the iTunes Music folder without deleting the original files. You need to know where this folder is to copy content folders or back up your library.

iTunes maintains a separate iTunes folder (with a separate iTunes Music folder) in each Home folder (Mac) or user folder (PC). If you share your computer with other users who have Home folders, each user can have a separate music library on the same computer (and, of course, a separate iPod that synchronizes with it).

On a Mac, iTunes stores your content library inside your Home folder. The path to this folder is *your home folder*/Music/iTunes/iTunes Music.

On a Windows PC, iTunes stores your content library inside your user folder. The path to this folder is *your user folder*/My Documents/My Music/iTunes/iTunes Music.

Changing the location of the library

You can store your iTunes library in a different location on your hard drive, as long as you tell iTunes where to find it. To change where iTunes stores your music library, choose Preferences (from the iTunes menu on a Mac or from the Edit menu on PCs), click Advanced, and then click the Change button shown in Figure 11-1. You can then browse to select another location — on a hard drive or any computer on a network.

Figure 11-1:
Change the
location of
the iTunes
music
library.

After selecting a new location, the songs you bring into iTunes (by ripping CDs, downloading music from the iTunes store, or dragging music files) are stored in the new location — but songs previously imported stay where they are. To move the previous songs to the new library location, drag the songs into the iTunes window to add them to the new library, so iTunes stores them automatically in the new location and updates its library file properly. You can then delete the song files you copied from the old library location.

To change the storage location back to the iTunes folder inside the Music folder, choose Preferences, click Advanced, and then click the Reset button.

Changing how files are stored in the library

The default method of organizing files in the iTunes library is to store content files in album and artist folders, naming the files according to the disc number, track number, and title.

For example, the song "Here, There and Everywhere" has the track name and song title in the filename (05 Here, There And Everywhere.mp3). The filename extension even tells you the type of encoding format — in this case, MP3. *Note:* Songs encoded in AAC have the extension .m4a or .m4p (for protected songs purchased from the iTunes Music Store). This song is saved in the Revolver folder (for the album), which is in the Beatles folder (for the artist).

What about songs performed by multiple artists, such as duets, or soundtrack albums with multiple artists? Albums and songs designated as part of a compilation are stored in album folders within the Compilations folder rather than within individual artist folders. You can designate a song as part of a compilation by selecting the song and opening the Song Information dialog (File⇨Get Info), clicking the Info tab, and then selecting the Part of a Compilation option. You can designate an entire album as a compilation album (so that the album folder is stored in the Compilations folder) by selecting the album, opening the Multiple Song Information dialog (File⇨Get Info), clicking Yes to edit multiple songs at once, and then selecting the Part of a Compilation option by choosing Yes (in the pop-up menu on a Mac or the drop-down menu in Windows). Even if the choice is already made, choose Yes again to set the check mark for updating.

When you change the song information for a song (or music video, audio book, or podcast), the filename and location within artist and album folders changes if you revise those information fields. For example, if you change the song title, the filename also changes. If you change the artist name, the folder name for the artist may change — or the file may move to a new folder by that name. iTunes organizes the files based on the song information.

To make changes to song information *without* changing the files on your hard drive, choose Preferences (from the iTunes menu on a Mac or from the Edit menu on PCs) and click Advanced; in the Advanced pane, deselect the check mark next to Keep iTunes Music Folder Organized.

Keep your iTunes music folder organized — leave the option turned on — if you plan on copying the music files to an iPod that will then be used with a car installation. (We describe car installations in Chapter 15.) Most iPod interfaces for car stereos provide a way to navigate the iPod with the car stereo's controls, but won't display the proper artist, album, and song titles unless the music folder is organized by the default method.

Maybe you don't want to store copies of songs in the library — especially if you already have copies stored on your hard drive in another location and need to conserve space. If you want to add music to your iTunes library without copying the files into the iTunes Music folder, choose Preferences, click the Advanced button, and *turn off* the "Copy files to iTunes Music folder when adding to library" option. The next time you drag a song file into the iTunes window, it stores only a reference in your iTunes Music folder to the file, specifying its actual location. The file itself is not copied or moved.

Locating a song file

No matter where you store your iTunes library or your song files, you can find the location of any song by selecting the song and choosing File⇨Get Info and then clicking the Summary tab in the Song Information dialog. Look in the Kind section of the Summary. The Where section tells you where the song is, as shown in Figure 11-2.

If you access shared libraries on a network, you probably have music in your library that's not actually *in* your library at all, but rather part of a shared library or playlist on a network, as we describe in Chapter 6. When you look at the Summary tab of the Song Information dialog for a song in a shared library, the Where section doesn't appear.

Consolidating the iTunes Library

If you have song files stored on different hard drives connected to the same computer, you can have iTunes consolidate your music library by copying everything into the iTunes Music folder. By consolidating your library first, you make sure that your backup is complete.

To consolidate your music library, choose Advanced⇨Consolidate Library. The original songs remain where they are, but copies are made in your Music folder.

The Consolidate Library command copies any file ending in `.aac`, `.m4a`, `.m4p`, or `.mp3` into the Music directory and adds it to the iTunes library — including any `.mp3` sound files used in games, such as Quake. You might want to move files associated with games to another hard drive or backup disc before consolidating.

Exporting iTunes Playlists

With iTunes, you can export a playlist and import it into a different computer to have the same playlist in both places.

You must also copy the songs (or better yet, copy the entire artist folder containing the songs, to keep the songs organized) in order for the playlists on the other computer to work. Exporting a playlist does *not* copy the songs in the playlist. You get a list of songs in the XML (eXtensible Markup Language) format but not the songs themselves — you still need to copy the actual song files to the other computer.

To export a single playlist, select the playlist and choose File⇨Export Song List. On a Mac, choose the XML option from the Format pop-up menu in the Save: iTunes dialog, and click the Save button. On a Windows PC, choose the XML option from the Files drop-down menu in the Save window.

After exporting a playlist and copying it to another computer, you can import the playlist into iTunes on the other computer by choosing File⇨Import on that computer, selecting the XML file, and clicking the Choose button. You can also export all the playlists in your library at the same time by choosing File⇨Export Library; then import them into iTunes on the other computer by choosing File⇨Import and selecting the exported XML file.

You can also import playlist files exported from other applications as `.m3u` files. The `.m3u` format is supported by applications such as WinAmp for managing playlists.

Backing Up the iTunes Library

If you're like us, your iTunes library is huge. We've nearly filled the internal hard drives of two modern computers, each sporting 80GB of space. And you thought 80GB would be enough? What about the backup?

Yes, don't think twice: Backing up can be inconvenient, and it can eat up the capacity of all your external hard drives — but it must be done. Fortunately, it's easy to do. With iTunes, you can copy your library to another hard drive on your computer or to another computer. You can even copy a library from a Mac to a PC and vice versa.

Backing up on the same type of computer

To copy your entire music library to another hard drive, locate the iTunes folder on your computer. Drag this entire folder to another hard drive or backup device, and you're all set. This action copies everything, including the playlists in your library.

The copy operation can take some time if the library is huge. Although you can stop the operation anytime, the newly copied library might not be complete. Allowing the copy operation to finish is always best.

If you restore the backup copy to the same computer with the same names for its hard drive, the backup copy's playlists should work fine. Playlists are essentially XML lists of songs with pathnames to the song files — if the hard drive name is different, the pathnames won't work. However, you can import the playlists into iTunes by choosing File➪Import, which realigns the playlist pathnames to the new hard drive. Alternatively, you can use the method described in "Backing up from Mac to PC or PC to Mac."

If you copy just the iTunes Music folder and not the entire iTunes folder, you are copying the music itself but not your playlists. You still have to export your playlists — see "Exporting iTunes Playlists," earlier in this chapter.

If you use a Mac and subscribe to the Apple .Mac service, you can download and use the free Backup software, which allows you to save the latest versions of your files regularly and automatically so you never have to worry about losing important files. With Backup, you can quickly and easily store files on your iDisk (a portion of an Internet hard disk hosted by .Mac), or on CD or DVD as data files (not as CD songs — see Chapter 12 to read how to burn an audio or MP3 CD). The iDisk is perhaps the least convenient, even though you do get free space with a .Mac membership. It offers up to 250MB (barely enough for a few albums), and copying to the iDisk is slow with a modem connection. We use iDisk to transfer individual songs and other large files to other people and to back up very important documents, but you're better off using a CD-ROM or DVD-ROM (or a DVD-RW) as a backup medium for data, as well as an audio CD for your songs and albums.

Backing up from Mac to PC or PC to Mac

Maybe you use a Mac but you want to transfer your iTunes library to a PC running iTunes, or the other way around. Or perhaps you want a foolproof method of copying your entire music library to another computer, whether it's a Mac or a PC running Windows, or just a computer that uses a different name for its hard drive (or a different path to the Home folder or user folder).

To back up your iTunes music library no matter what the situation, follow these steps:

1. **Locate your iTunes Music folder on your "old" computer.**

   Locate your iTunes Music folder as described in "Finding the iTunes Library," earlier in this chapter. Consider the first computer the "old" computer and the one to receive the copied library the "new" computer.

2. **Download and install iTunes on the new computer.**

   See Chapter 2 for instructions on installing iTunes. If the new computer already has an iTunes Music folder with music that you want to pre- serve, move that iTunes Music folder to another folder on the hard drive, or copy it to another hard drive or storage medium.

3. **Copy the iTunes Music folder from the old computer to the newly installed iTunes folder of the new computer.**

   If you have multiple users on the new computer, make sure that you choose the appropriate user folder for a Windows PC or Home folder for a Mac. The copy operation for a large music library takes a while.

4. **Choose File⇨Export Library on the old computer, browse to a location on your hard drive or network, and click the Save button.**

   When you export your entire library, iTunes creates an XML file called `iTunes Music Library.xml` that links to music files and stores all your playlists.

5. **Start iTunes on the new computer.**

6. **Choose File⇨Import on the new computer and import the `iTunes Music Library.xml` file.**

   The music library is now available on the new computer.

The iTunes Music Library file (`iTunes Music Library.xml`) must be located within the iTunes folder where iTunes can find it.

Chapter 12

Feeling the iTunes Burn

*O*nce upon a time, when vinyl records were popular, rock radio disk jockeys that didn't like disco held *disco meltdown* parties. People were encouraged to throw their disco records into a pile to be burned or steam-rolled into a vinyl glob. This chapter isn't about that; neither is it about anything involving fire nor heat.

Rather, *burning* a CD refers to the process in which the CD drive recorder's laser heats up points on an interior layer of the disc, simulating the pits pressed into commercial CDs that represent digital information.

People burn CDs for a lot of reasons — reason numero uno is to make a backup of songs on your computer. Perhaps having your 12 favorite love songs on one CD for your next romantic encounter is convenient, or perhaps you want to burn a few CDs of obscure songs to impress your friends on your next big road trip. With iTunes you can even print CD jewel-case inserts with the list of songs and liner notes.

This chapter burns, er, boils everything down for you by telling you what kind of discs to use, which devices you can use to play the discs, how to get your playlist ready for burning, and what settings to use for burning. You find out what you need to know to make sure that your burns are not meltdowns — that the only melting is the music in your ears.

Selecting Recordable CDs

After importing music into your iTunes library, you can arrange any songs in your library into a playlist and burn a CD using that playlist (see Chapter 9 for more on creating playlists). If you have a CD-R, CD-RW, or DVD-R drive (such as the Apple SuperDrive for Macs), and a blank CD-R (R stands for *recordable*), you can create your own music CDs that play in most CD players.

Blank CD-Rs are available in most electronics and computer stores, and even supermarkets. You can also get them online from the Apple Store (not the music store — the store that sells computers and accessories). Choose iTunes➪Shop for iTunes Products on a Mac or the Help➪Shop for iTunes Products on a Windows PC to reach the Apple Store online.

The discs are called *CD-R* because they use a recordable format related to commercial audio CDs (which are not recordable, of course). You can also create a disc in the new MP3 format by creating a CD-R with data rather than music, which is useful for backing up a music library.

CD-Rs play just like regular audio CDs in most CD players, including car players and portable CD players. The CD-R format is the most universal and compatible with older players.

Many CD burners, such as the Apple SuperDrive, also burn CD-RWs (recordable, read-write discs) that you can erase and reuse, but CD players don't always recognize them as music CDs. Some burners can create data DVD-Rs and DVD-RWs also, which are useful for holding data files, but you can only use these discs with computers that have DVD drives. Most commercial DVD players won't read a data DVD-R or DVD-RW.

You can play MP3 files burned on a CD-R in the MP3 format on the new consumer MP3 disc players and combination CD/MP3 players as well as on many DVD players, and of course on computers that recognize MP3 CDs (including computers with iTunes).

What You Can Fit on a CD-R

You can fit up to 74 minutes of music on a high-quality CD-R; some can go as high as 80 minutes. The sound files on your hard drive might take up more space than 650 MB if they are uncompressed, but you can still fit 74 minutes (or 80 minutes, depending on the disc) because the CD format stores information without error-correction data.

The little Red Book that launched an industry

The typical audio CD and CD-R uses the CD-DA (Compact Disc-Digital Audio) format, which is known as *Red Book* — not something from Chairman Mao, but a document, published in 1980, that provides the specifications for the standard compact disc (CD) developed by Sony and Philips. According to legend, this document was in a binder with red covers.

Also according to legend, in 1979, Norio Ohga, honorary chairman and former CEO of Sony (who's also a maestro conductor), overruled his engineers and insisted that the CD format be able to hold Beethoven's *Ninth Symphony*

(which is 74 minutes and 42 seconds — now the standard length of a Red Book audio CD).

CD-DA defines audio data digitized at 44,100 samples per second (44.1 kHz) and in a range of 65,536 possible values (16 bits).

To import music into the computer from an audio CD, you have to convert the music to digital sound files by a program such as iTunes. When you burn an audio CD, iTunes converts the sound files back into the CD-DA format as it burns the disc.

If you burn music to a CD-R in the MP3 format, the disc can hold more than 12 hours worth of music. You read that right — 12 hours on one disc. Now you know why MP3 discs are popular. MP3 discs are essentially CD-Rs with MP3 files stored on them.

If you have a DVD burner, such as the Apple SuperDrive, you can burn data DVD-Rs or DVD-RWs to use with other computers. This approach is suitable for making backup copies of music files (or any data files). A DVD-R can hold about 4,700,000,000 bytes (about 4.38GB), which is enough to hold part of a music library.

To burn a CD-RW or DVD-RW that already has data on it, you must first erase it by reformatting it using the application supplied with the drive. CD-RWs and DVD-RWs work with computers but won't work with consumer players.

Creating a Burn Playlist

To burn a CD (actually a CD-R, but most people refer to the recordable CD-R discs as CDs), you must first define a playlist for the CD. See Chapter 9 to find out how to create a playlist. You can use songs encoded in any format that iTunes supports; however, you get higher quality music with the uncompressed AIFF and WAV formats, or with the Apple Lossless format.

To copy an album you already have in your iTunes library onto an audio CD, you can quickly create a playlist for the album by switching to Browse view in your iTunes library and dragging an album from the Album list (in the top-right section of the window in Browse view) to the white area below the items in your Source pane. iTunes automatically creates a playlist with the album name. You can then use that playlist to burn a CD.

If your playlist includes music purchased from the iTunes Music Store or other online stores in the protected AAC encoding format, some rules might apply. For example, the iTunes Music Store allows you to burn *seven copies* of the same playlist containing protected songs to an audio CD, but no more. You can get around this limitation by creating or using a different playlist and copying the protected songs to the other playlist, and then burning more CDs with the other playlist.

Calculating how much music to use

When you create a playlist, you find out how many songs can fit on the CD by totaling the durations of the songs, using time as your measure. You can see the size of a playlist by selecting it; the bottom of the iTunes window shows the number of songs, the amount in time, and the amount in megabytes for the currently selected playlist, as shown in Figure 12-1.

Figure 12-1:
Check the duration of the playlist below the song list.

In Figure 12-1, the selected playlist takes 1.1 hours (about 66 minutes) to play, so it fits on a standard audio CD. (The 13 songs take up only 65.3MB of hard drive space; they were purchased from the iTunes Music Store and encoded in the compressed and protected AAC format.)

A one-hour playlist of AIFF-encoded music, which might occupy over 600MB of hard drive space, would also fit on a standard audio CD. The amount you can fit on a standard audio CD depends on the duration, not the hard drive space occupied by the music files. Although a CD holds between 650MB and 700MB (depending on the disc), the music is stored in a special format known as CD-DA (or Red Book) that fills byte sectors without error-correction and checksum information. Thus, you can fit about 90MB more — 740MB — of AIFF-encoded music on a 650MB disc. We typically put 1.1 hours (66 minutes) of music on a 74-minute or 80-minute CD-R with many minutes to spare.

Always use the actual duration in hours, minutes, and seconds to calculate how much music you can fit on an audio CD — either 74 or 80 minutes for blank CD-Rs. Leave at least one extra minute to account for the gaps between songs.

You do the *opposite* for an MP3 CD — you use the actual megabytes to calculate how many songs can fit on a disc — up to 700MB for a blank CD-R. You can fit lots more music on an MP3 CD-R because you use MP3-encoded songs rather than uncompressed AIFF songs.

If you have too many songs in the playlist to fit on a CD, iTunes will burn as many songs in the playlist as will fit on the CD (either audio or MP3), and then it will ask you to insert another CD to continue burning the remaining songs in the playlist.

If you include in a burn playlist a very long song — longer than a CD — that you purchased from the iTunes Music Store, you see a dialog telling you to put the long song in its own playlist, and then burn that single-song playlist separately.

Importing music for an audio CD-R

Before you rip an audio CD of songs you want to burn to an audio CD-R, you might want to change the import settings. Check out Chapter 17 if you need to do so. Use AIFF, Apple Lossless, or WAV for songs from audio CDs if you want to burn your own audio CDs with music at its highest quality.

AIFF is the standard digital format for uncompressed sound on a Mac, and you can't go wrong with it. WAV is basically the same thing for Windows. The Apple Lossless encoder provides CD-quality sound in a file size that's about 55 to 60 percent of the size of an AIFF or WAV encoded file. Both the AIFF Encoder and the WAV Encoder offer the same Custom settings dialog, with settings for sample rate, sample size, and channels. You can choose the automatic settings, and iTunes automatically detects the proper sample rate, size, and channels from the source. Apple Lossless is always set to automatic.

Songs that you purchase from the iTunes Music Store come in the protected AAC format, which you can't convert to anything else, but you can still burn them onto CDs and the quality is acceptable. Audio books also come in a protected format that can't be converted, but you can burn them onto CDs with acceptable quality.

The AAC music file format is a higher-quality format than MP3 and acceptable to most CD listeners. We think it offers a decent trade-off of space and quality and is suitable (although not as good as AIFF or Apple Lossless) for burning to an audio CD.

Switching import encoders for MP3 CD-R

MP3 discs are essentially CD-Rs with MP3 files stored on them using the ISO 9660 file structure that is standard across computers and players. Consumer MP3 CD players are readily available in consumer electronics stores, including hybrid models that play both audio CDs and MP3 CDs.

You can fit an average of 12 hours of music on a CD using the MP3 format, although this amount can vary widely (along with audio quality) depending on the encoding options and settings you choose. For example, you might be able to fit up to 20 hours of mono (monaural) recordings because they use only one channel and carry less information. On the other hand, if you encode stereo recordings at high bit rates (above 192 bits per second), you will fit less than 12 hours. If you rip an audio CD, you can set the importing options to precisely the type of MP3 file you want; see Chapter 17.

You can use only MP3-encoded songs to burn an MP3 CD-R. Any songs not encoded in MP3 are skipped and not burned to the CD-R. Audible books and spoken-word titles are provided in an audio format that uses security technologies, including encryption, to protect purchased content. You can't burn an MP3 CD-R with Audible files; any Audible files in a burn playlist are skipped when you burn an MP3 CD-R.

Setting the Burning Preferences

Burning a CD is a simple process, and getting it right the first time is a good idea because when you burn a CD-R, it's done one time — right or wrong. You can't erase content on a CD-R like you can with a CD-RW. Because you can't play a CD-RW in as many CD players, if you want to burn an audio CD, we recommend using a CD-R. Fortunately, CD-Rs are inexpensive, so you won't be out more than a few cents if you burn a bad one — besides, they're good as coasters for coffee tables.

Setting the sound check and gaps

Musicians do a sound check before every performance to check the volume of microphones and instruments and their effect on the listening environment. The aptly named Sound Check option in iTunes allows you to do a sound check on your tunes to bring them all in line, volume-wise.

To have all the songs in your library play at the same volume level all the time, choose iTunes⇨Preferences on a Mac or Edit⇨Preferences on a Windows PC. In the Preferences dialog, click the Audio tab. Select the Sound Check check box, as shown in Figure 12-2, which sets all the songs to the current volume controlled by the iTunes volume slider.

Figure 12-2:
Adjust the song playback volume of all songs in the library to the same level.

After enabling Sound Check, you can burn your audio CD-R so that all the songs play back at the same volume, just like they do in iTunes. Choose iTunes⇨Preferences on a Mac/Edit⇨Preferences on a Windows PC, and then click the Burning button. Select the Use Sound Check option, as shown in Figure 12-3. *Note:* This option works whether or not you're already using the Sound Check option in the Audio preferences. You can select this option for burning without ever changing the preferences for your entire library.

Figure 12-3:
Select the
Use Sound
Check
option for
the CD-R
burn.

Consistent volume for all tracks makes the CD-R sound professional. Another professional touch is to add an appropriate gap between songs, just like commercial CDs. Follow these steps to control the length of the gap between the songs on your audio CD-R (not MP3 CD-R):

1. **Choose iTunes⇨Preferences on a Mac/Edit⇨Preferences on a Windows PC, and then click the Burning tab in the Preferences dialog.**

   The Burning Preferences appear; refer to Figure 12-3.

2. **Choose an amount from the Gap between Songs pop-up menu.**

   You can choose from a gap of 0 to 5 seconds. We recommend selecting a gap of 2 seconds, which is the default setting.

3. **Click OK.**

Setting the format and recording speed

Before burning a CD-R, you have to set the disc format and the recording speed. Choose Preferences (from the iTunes menu on a Mac/Edit menu on a Windows PC), and then click the Burning tab in the Preferences dialog.

The Disc Format setting in the Burning dialog (refer to Figure 12-3) offers three choices:

✔ **Audio CD:** Choose this to burn a normal audio CD of up to 74 or 80 minutes (depending on the type of blank CD-R) using any iTunes-supported music files, including songs bought from the iTunes Music Store. Although connoisseurs of music might use AIFF-encoded or WAV-encoded music to burn an audio CD, you can also use songs in the AAC and MP3 formats.

✔ **MP3 CD:** Choose this to burn an MP3 CD with songs encoded in the MP3 format. No other formats are supported for MP3 CD.

✔ **Data CD or DVD:** Choose this to burn a data CD-R, CD-RW, DVD-R, or DVD-RW with the music files. You can use any encoding formats for the songs. *Important:* Data discs won't play on most consumer CD players — they are meant for use with computers. However, data discs are good choices for storing backup copies of music bought from the iTunes Music Store.

Blank CD-Rs are rated for recording at certain speeds. iTunes typically detects the rating of a blank CD-R and adjusts the recording speed to fit. However, if your blank CD-Rs are rated for a slower speed than your burner, or you have problems creating CD-Rs, you can change the recording speed setting to match the CD's rating. Choose iTunes➪Preferences on a Mac/Edit➪Preferences on a Windows PC, and then click the Burning tab in the Preferences dialog. From the Preferred Speed pop-up menu or drop-down list in the Burning Preferences, choose a specific recording speed or choose the Maximum Possible option to set the recording speed to your burner's maximum speed.

Burning a Disc

After you set the burning preferences, you're ready to start burning. Follow these steps to burn a CD:

1. **Select the playlist designated for burning a disc and click the Burn Disc button.**

   A message appears telling you to insert a blank disc.

2. **Insert a blank disc (label side up).**

   iTunes immediately checks the media and displays a message in the status window that the disc is ready to burn.

3. **Click the Burn Disc button again.**

   This time, the button has a radiation symbol. The burn process begins. The "radioactive" button rotates while the burning takes place, and a progress bar appears with the names of the songs displayed as they burn to the disc.

   When iTunes has finished burning the CD, iTunes chimes, and the CD is mounted on the Desktop.

4. **Eject the newly burned disc from your CD drive and test it.**

Burning takes several minutes. You can cancel the operation at any time by clicking the X next to the progress bar, but canceling the operation isn't like undoing the burn. If the burn has already started, you can't use the CD-R or DVD-R again.

If the playlist has more music than can fit on the disc using the chosen format, iTunes burns as much as possible from the beginning of the playlist, and then asks you to insert another disc to burn the rest. To calculate the amount of music in a playlist, turn to the section, "Calculating how much music to use," earlier in this chapter.

Spoken word fans: Audible audio books with chapter markers are burned onto CD with each chapter as a separate track.

If you choose the MP3 CD format, iTunes skips over any songs in the playlist that are not in the MP3 format.

Printing Song and Album Information

Putting music on a blank CD-R doesn't change the disc's look in any way, so if you misplace it, how do you know it isn't just another blank? Put it inside a case and include something in print that identifies it.

Don't delete your burn playlist yet. You can print the CD jewel case insert, song list, and album notes for the CD you just burned from the playlist. You can even print the cover art that the iTunes Music Store provides with purchased songs (even artwork you added yourself, as described in Chapter 8). If you have a color printer, you can print gorgeous color inserts for your CDs. If you don't have a suitable printer, you can save the printed version as a Portable Document Format (PDF) file that can be printed at a Kinko's or similar copy shop.

Select the playlist and choose File⇨Print to see a dialog like that shown in Figure 12-4. You can see all the choices you have for CD jewel case inserts, song listings, and album notes, and a preview of how they look when printed.

Figure 12-4: Print a CD jewel case insert directly from iTunes that can include cover art provided with songs.

Printing CD jewel case inserts

Everyone calls the standard CD case a *jewel case* even though the only precious element in the package is the music. Jewel cases have slots for inserting a printed insert or booklet. You can print your own jewel case insert directly from iTunes using the burn playlist.

To print a CD jewel case, follow these steps:

1. **Choose File⇨Print.**

2. **In the dialog, select the "CD jewel case insert" option.**

   Figure 12-4 shows this dialog. After selecting that option, you have a choice of themes in the pop-up menu, such as Text Only (without song artwork), Mosaic (with artwork from songs arranged in a mosaic), Single Cover (with one song's artwork), and so on, as shown in Figure 12-5.

3. **Choose a theme.**

   Choose a theme such as Mosaic (Black & White) if you have songs with different cover art and you want to represent all the covers on a single page.

Figure 12-5:
Choose
a theme
for a CD
jewel case
insert —
Mosaic
(Black &
White) is
shown in
the preview.

iTunes offers a Page Setup button that takes you to the standard Page Setup dialog for Mac or Windows, where you can set page layout options such as landscape or portrait orientation. The CD jewel case themes automatically set the proper orientation, but you can change it by clicking the Page Setup button.

To print, click the Print button to activate the standard Print dialog box on the Mac or in Windows. Depending on your system, you may have multiple choices for printers, including choices for making electronic PDF files of printed output, such as PDFWriter on Windows. (The Mac offers a built-in PDF pop-up menu in the Print dialog.)

Printing song lists and album notes

Cover art for the jewel case is a nice decoration, but if you choose an art-based theme rather than one that lists the songs, you may still want another sheet with a song list to tell which track is which. You may also want a more detailed song list that includes information for each song, such as the composer, the duration, the original album, and perhaps even the rating you assigned it in iTunes.

To print a song listing, choose File➪Print. In the dialog, select the "Song listing" option shown in Figure 12-6. After choosing this option, the Theme pop-up menu changes to provide options for columns in the song list.

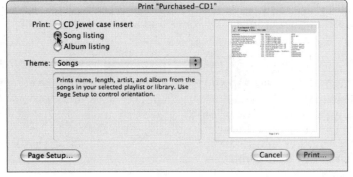

Figure 12-6:
Print a song listing with information about each song.

You can choose one of the following themes for the song listing:

- ✔ **Songs:** This theme prints a column each for the song name, duration, artist, and album title.

- ✔ **User ratings:** A bit wider, this theme prints the same columns as Songs and adds a ratings column with the ratings you've assigned in iTunes (as described in Chapter 8). This theme prints in a landscape orientation.

- ✔ **Dates played:** This theme prints the same columns as Songs and adds columns for the play count and the date last played, set by iTunes as you play songs. This theme prints in a landscape orientation.

- ✔ **Custom:** This theme prints the columns as they're currently set in the iTunes song list view — so you can print any piece of information about the songs that iTunes stores, such as Composer, Genre, and Year. See Chapter 7 to add or change the viewing options for columns in the song list view.

To print a catalog-style album listing, choose File➪Print. In the dialog, select the "Album listing" option shown in Figure 12-7. This option prints the album title, artist, album's song names, and song lengths.

Figure 12-7:
Print an
album listing
with
information
about the
songs in
each album.

You can use the Song listing or Album listing options to print a listing of all the songs in your iTunes library, rather than just a playlist. Select Library in the Source pane first, and then choose File➪Print and choose your printing options. If you want to save paper and create an electronic version, use the Macintosh or Windows Print dialog to create a PDF file.

If you want to print liner notes in a layout that iTunes doesn't offer in its printing themes, you can export the song information for all the songs in a playlist to a text file, and then edit that information in a word processor or page layout program to make liner notes for the CD. iTunes exports all the song information for a single song, a playlist, an album, songs by an artist, or songs in the library into a text file. Select the songs or playlist and choose File➪Export Song List. In the Export Song List dialog, make sure the Plain Text option is selected from the Format pop-up menu (unless you use a double-byte language, such as Japanese or Chinese, for which the Unicode option is the right choice).

Troubleshooting Burns

Murphy's Law applies to everything, even something as simple as burning a CD-R. Don't think for a moment that you are immune to the whims and treacheries of Murphy (no one really knows who Murphy is), who in all his infinite wisdom, pronounced that anything that *can* go wrong *will* go wrong. In this section, we cover some of the most common problems that you might encounter when burning CDs.

The best way to test your newly burned disc is to pop it right back into your computer's CD-ROM drive, or try it on a consumer CD player. On most CD players, an audio CD-R plays just like any commercial audio CD. MP3 CDs play fine on consumer MP3 CD players and also work in computers with CD-ROM and DVD drives.

If the CD works on the computer but not on a commercial CD player, you might have a compatibility problem with the commercial player and CD-R. We have a five-year-old CD player that doesn't play CD-Rs very well, and car players sometimes have trouble with them.

The following list gives some typical problems that you might run into when burning a CD, along with the solutions to those problems:

✔ **Problem:** The disc won't burn.

  Solution: Perhaps you have a bum disc. Hey, it happens. Try using another disc or burning at a slower speed.

✔ **Problem:** In a consumer CD player, the disc doesn't play, or it stutters when playing.

  Solution: This happens often with older consumer players that don't play CD-Rs well. Try the disc in your computer's CD-ROM drive. If it works there and you set the format to Audio CD, you probably have a compatibility problem with your consumer player.

✔ **Problem:** The disc doesn't show tracks on a consumer CD player, or it ejects immediately.

  Solution: Be sure to use the proper disc format — choose iTunes⇨ Preferences on a Mac/Edit⇨Preferences on a Windows PC, and click the Burning tab to see the Disc Format setting in the Burning dialog. The Audio CD format works in just about all consumer CD players that can play CD-Rs. MP3 CDs work in consumer MP3 CD players and computer CD-ROM and DVD drives. Data CDs or DVDs work only in computer drives.

✔ **Problem:** Some songs in my playlist were skipped and not burned onto the disc.

  Solution: Audio CD-Rs burn with songs encoded in any format, but you can use only MP3-encoded songs to burn an MP3 CD-R. Any songs not encoded in MP3 — including songs purchased from the iTunes Music Store in protected AAC format — are skipped when burning MP3 CDs. (Any Audible files are also skipped, which can't be put onto an MP3 CD.) If your playlist for an audio CD-R includes music purchased from the iTunes Music Store, some rules might apply — see the section, "Creating a Burn Playlist," earlier in this chapter.

Don't violate copyright law.

Part III
Playing Music

"I SAID, I THINK I FOUND YOUR iPOD!"

In this part . . .

*P*art III focuses on the many ways that you can use iTunes and an iPod to play music, and it covers the many different types of listening environments and accessories that accommodate them.

- ✔ Chapter 13 shows you how to locate and play songs on your iPod, create playlists on the fly, and adjust the iPod's volume.

- ✔ Chapter 14 is about playing music over home stereos, headphones, and portable speakers with your iPod, and it includes cool accessories for using your iPod at home.

- ✔ Chapter 15 shows you how you can use your iPod in planes, on trains, and in automobiles with cool travel accessories, and how to integrate your iPod with your car stereo.

- ✔ Chapter 16 shows you how to mix up your media in iTunes, including queuing up and cross-fading songs like a professional DJ, and playing videos. In this chapter, we also share how to play songs that reside on an iPod using iTunes on your computer or another computer.

Chapter 13

Playing Your iPod

For a music lover, nothing compares to the feeling of having so many song choices at your fingertips. Rather than sitting back like a couch potato and soaking up the preprogrammed sounds of radio or CDs, *you* control the iPod playback and can pick any song you want to hear at any time. Shuffle through songs randomly to get an idea of how wide your music choices are, or just to surprise yourself or others. Or follow a thread of musical ideas, such as the one that started with the Kingsmen's version of "Louie Louie" through "All Day and All of the Night" by the Kinks, "Dirty Water" by the Standells, "Little Bit of Soul" by the Music Explosion, and the Troggs' "Wild Thing," all the way to the version of "Wild Thing" by Jimi Hendrix.

You may have spent a few minutes creating playlists in iTunes that barely scratch the surface of the huge library you have in your hands. Now how do you switch songs or playlists while maintaining your jogging pace or avoiding wrecks on the freeway?

With all the current iPod models except the iPod shuffle, you can locate and play that music easily, browsing by artist and album, and even by composer. Selecting a playlist is simplicity itself, and if you don't have playlists from iTunes (or you don't want to hear those playlists), you can create a temporary On-The-Go playlist. This chapter shows you how to locate and play music on any iPod. If you have an iPod shuffle, you can skip to "Playing the iPod Shuffle" in this chapter.

Locating Songs

With so many songs on your iPod, finding a particular one can be hard — like finding a needle in a haystack, or trying to find "Needle in a Haystack" by the Velvelettes in the Motown catalog — even though you can narrow your search by genre, and also search by artist, composer, album, or playlist.

By artist

Your iPod organizes music by artist, and within each artist by album. Follow these steps to locate a song by artist and then album:

1. **Select the Music item from the iPod main menu.**

   Scroll the main menu until Music is highlighted, and then press the Select button. The Music menu appears.

2. **Select the Artists item.**

   The Artists item is second from the top of the Music menu. Scroll the menu until Artists is highlighted, and then press the Select button. The Artists menu appears.

   To browse by genre, select the Genres item, and then select a genre from the Genres menu to get a reduced list of artists that have songs in that genre (in alphabetical order by artist name).

3. **Select an artist from the Artists menu.**

   The artists' names are listed in alphabetical order by first word. *Note:* Any leading *The* is ignored so that *The Beatles* appears where *Beatles* would be in the list. Scroll the Artists menu until the artist name (such as *Radiohead* or *Bowie, David*) is highlighted, and then press the Select button. The artist's menu of albums appears. For example, the Radiohead menu in our iPod includes the selections All, *OK Computer,* and *The Bends;* the Bowie, David menu includes All, *Heroes, Space Oddity, Ziggy Stardust,* and many more).

4. **Select the All item or the name of an album from the artist's menu.**

   The All item is at the top of the artist's menu and should already be highlighted; you can press the Select button to select it or scroll until an album name is highlighted and then press the Select button. *Note:* Albums are listed in alphabetical order based on the first word. A leading *A* or *The* is *not* ignored, so the album *The Basement Tapes* is listed *after* the album *Stage Fright.* A song list appears after you select an album choice or All.

5. **Select the song from the list.**

   The songs in the album list are in album order (the order they appear on the album); in the All list, songs are listed in album order for each album. Scroll up or down the list to highlight the song.

By album

Follow these steps to locate a song by album directly:

1. **Select the Music item from the iPod main menu.**

   Scroll the main menu until Music is highlighted, and then press the Select button. The Music menu appears.

2. **Select the Albums item.**

   Scroll the Music menu until Albums is highlighted, and then press the Select button. The Albums menu appears.

   Select the Composers item to choose a composer, and then select a composer from the Composers menu to get a list of songs for that composer.

3. **Select an album from the Albums menu.**

   The albums are listed in alphabetical order (without any reference to artist, which might make identification difficult). The order is by first word (a leading *A, An,* or *The* is not ignored, so the album *The Natch'l Blues* is listed after *Taj's Blues* in the T section rather than the N section). Scroll the Albums menu until the album name is highlighted and then press the Select button. A song list appears.

4. **Select the song from the list.**

   The songs in the album list are in the order in which they appear on the album. Scroll the list to highlight the song name and press the Select button. The artist name and song name appear.

By playlist

When you update your iPod automatically from your entire iTunes library, all of your playlists in iTunes are copied to the iPod. You can choose to update your iPod with only specified playlists, as we describe in Chapter 11.

Playlists make playing a selection of songs or albums in a specific order easy. The playlist plays from the first song selected to the end of the playlist.

Follow these steps to locate a song by playlist on your iPod:

1. **Select the Music item from the iPod main menu.**

   Scroll the main menu until Music is highlighted, and then press the Select button. The Music menu appears.

2. **Select the Playlists item.**

   The Playlists item is at the top of the Music menu and might already be highlighted. If not, scroll the Music menu until Playlists is highlighted, and then press the Select button. The Playlists menu appears.

3. **Select a playlist.**

   The playlists are listed in alphabetical order. Scroll the Playlists menu to highlight the playlist name, and then press the Select button. A list of songs in the playlist appears.

4. **Select the song from the list.**

   The songs in the playlist are in *playlist order* (the order defined for the playlist in iTunes). Scroll up or down the list to highlight the song you want.

Playing a Song

After scrolling the song list until the song name is highlighted, press the Select button to play the selected song, or press the Play/Pause button — either button starts the song playing. When the song finishes, the iPod continues playing the next song in the song list.

While a song is playing, the artist name and song name appear, and you can use the scroll wheel to adjust the volume. See the section, "Adjusting the Volume," later in this chapter.

Press the Play/Pause button when a song is playing to pause the playback. Because the iPod is a hard drive, pause is the same as stop, and you won't find any delay in resuming playback.

Repeating Songs

If you want to drive yourself crazy repeating the same song over and over, the iPod is happy to oblige. (You might want to try this with "They're Coming to Take Me Away, Ha Ha" by Napoleon XIV, a favorite of Dr. Demento.) More than likely, you'll want to repeat a sequence of songs, which you can easily do.

You can set the iPod to repeat a single song automatically by following these steps:

1. **Locate and play a song.**

2. **As the song plays, press the Menu button repeatedly to return to the main menu, and then select the Settings item.**

   The Settings menu appears.

3. **Scroll the Settings menu until Repeat is highlighted.**

   The Repeat setting displays Off next to it.

4. **Press the Select button once (Off changes to One) to repeat one song.**

   If you press the button more than once, keep pressing until One appears.

You can also press the Previous/Rewind button to repeat a song.

To repeat all the songs in the selected album or playlist, follow these steps:

1. **Locate and play a song in the album or playlist.**

2. **As the song plays, press the Menu button repeatedly to return to the main menu, and then select the Settings item.**

   The Settings menu appears.

3. **Scroll the Settings menu until the Repeat item is highlighted.**

   The Repeat setting displays Off next to it.

4. **Press the Select button twice (Off changes to All) to repeat all the songs in the album or playlist.**

Shuffling the Song Order

Maybe you want your song selections to be surprising and unpredictable, and you want your iPod to read your mind, as the Apple ads suggest. You can *shuffle* the playback of songs so that they play in random order — like an automated radio station without a disk jockey or a program guide. With the shuffle feature you can mix up your song collection and play it back in a jumbled order — and see for yourself whether your iPod knows how to pick good tunes without your help.

To turn your iPod into a random song player so that you have no idea what comes next, choose Shuffle Songs from the main menu. Your iPod starts with a random song and continues to select songs randomly without ever repeating one, until it plays every song in your library.

Although it may seem that your iPod plays favorites, the shuffle algorithm is truly random, according to Apple. When an iPod does a shuffle, it reorders the songs much the way you would shuffle a deck of cards, then plays them back in the new order. If you keep listening for as long as it takes to complete the list, you will hear everything, just once.

You can also shuffle songs *within* an album or playlist, which gives you some control over random playback — for example, you could create a smart playlist for all jazz songs, and then shuffle the songs within the jazz playlist.

Follow these steps to shuffle songs in an album or playlist:

1. **Locate and play a song in the album or playlist.**

2. **As the song plays, press the Menu button repeatedly to return to the main menu, and then select the Settings item.**

   The Settings menu appears.

3. **Scroll the Settings menu until the Shuffle item is highlighted.**

   The Shuffle setting displays Off next to it.

4. **Press the Select button once (Off changes to Songs) to shuffle the songs in the selected album or playlist.**

You can set your iPod to repeat an entire album or playlist but still shuffle the playing order, so that the order is different each time you hear it.

What if you want to play albums randomly, but don't like when the songs in an album aren't played in proper album order? To shuffle all the albums in your iPod while still playing the songs in normal album order, follow these steps:

1. **Press the Menu button repeatedly to return to the main menu, and then select the Settings item.**

   The Settings menu appears.

2. **Scroll the Settings menu until the Shuffle item is highlighted.**

   The Shuffle setting displays Off next to it.

3. **Press the Select button twice (Off changes to Albums) to shuffle the albums without shuffling the songs within each album.**

When the iPod is set to shuffle, it won't repeat a song until it has played through the entire album, playlist, or library.

Creating On-The-Go Playlists

If you want to hear preprogrammed lists of songs but don't want to hear the iTunes playlists already in your iPod, or if you haven't created playlists yet, you can create temporary On-The-Go playlists in your iPod. (The On-The-Go playlist feature isn't available in first-generation and second-generation iPods.)You can create one or more lists of songs or entire albums to play in a certain order, queuing up the songs or albums on the iPod. This option is particularly useful for picking songs to play right before starting to drive a car. (Hel-*lo!* — you shouldn't be messing with your iPod while driving.)

Queued songs that you select appear automatically in a playlist called *On-The-Go* in the Playlists menu. (To use the Playlists menu, see the sections "Locating Songs" and "Playing a Song," earlier in this chapter.) The On-The-Go playlist remains defined in your iPod until you clear it (deleting the songs from the playlist), save it as a new iPod playlist, or update your iPod with new music and playlists — in which case it's copied to your iTunes library and cleared automatically. You can also save in your iTunes library any new playlist you create on your iPod.

Selecting songs for the playlist

To select songs or entire albums for an On-The-Go playlist, follow these steps:

1. **Locate and highlight a song or album title.**

2. **Press and hold the Select button until the title flashes.**

3. **Repeat Steps 1 and 2 in the order you want the songs or albums played.**

To play the On-The-Go playlist, scroll the Music menu until Playlists is highlighted, and then press the Select button. The Playlists menu appears. Scroll to the On-The-Go item, which you can always find at the very end of the list in the Playlists menu.

You can continue to add songs to the list of queued songs in the On-The-Go playlist at any time. Your iPod keeps track of the On-The-Go playlist until you clear it, save it, or update your iPod automatically.

Deleting songs from the playlist

To delete a song from the On-The-Go playlist in your iPod, follow these steps:

1. **Select the On-The-Go playlist.**

   If you don't see the iPod main menu, press the Menu button repeatedly to return to the main menu. Then choose Music from the main menu, and scroll the Music menu until Playlists is highlighted, and then press the Select button. The Playlists menu appears. Scroll to the On-The-Go item, which you can always find at the very end of the list in the Playlists menu. Press the Select button, and the list of songs in the playlist appears.

2. **Locate and highlight a song to delete.**

3. **Press and hold the Select button until the title flashes.**

4. **Repeat Steps 2 and 3 for each song you want to delete from the playlist.**

   As you delete songs, the songs disappear from the On-The-Go playlist one by one. The songs are still in your iPod, of course — only the playlist is cleared.

Clearing songs from the playlist

To clear the list of queued songs in the On-The-Go playlist, follow these steps:

1. **Select the On-The-Go playlist.**

   If you don't see the iPod main menu, press the Menu button repeatedly to return to the main menu. Then choose Music from the main menu, and scroll the Music menu until Playlists is highlighted, and then press the Select button. The Playlists menu appears. Scroll to the On-The-Go item, which you can always find at the very end of the list in the Playlists menu. Press the Select button, and the list of songs in the playlist appears.

2. **Scroll to the very end of the song list and select the Clear Playlist item.**

   The Clear menu appears, showing the Cancel and Clear Playlist items.

3. **Select the Clear Playlist item.**

   All of the songs disappear from the On-The-Go playlist. The songs are still in your iPod, of course — only the playlist is cleared. If you don't want to clear the playlist, select the Cancel item.

Saving the playlist in your iPod

You may want to create more than one On-The-Go playlist in your iPod, and save them temporarily for transferring to your iTunes library. To save your On-The-Go playlist in your iPod temporarily, follow these steps:

1. **Select the On-The-Go playlist.**

   Choose Music from the main menu and scroll the Music menu until Playlists is highlighted; then press the Select button. The Playlists menu appears. Scroll to the On-The-Go item. Press the Select button, and the list of songs in the playlist appears.

2. **Scroll to the very end of the song list and select the Save Playlist item.**

   The Save menu appears, showing the Cancel and Save Playlist items.

3. **Select the Save Playlist item.**

   The On-The-Go playlist is saved with the name *New Playlist 1* (and any subsequent playlists you save are named *New Playlist 2,* and so on). These appear at the very end of the Playlist menu, not in alphabetical order — they appear just above the On-The-Go Playlist item. If you don't want to save the playlist, select the Cancel item.

On-The-Go playlists saved as *New Playlist 1, New Playlist 2,* and so on, are stored temporarily in your iPod until you update the iPod automatically. The On-The-Go playlist is cleared each time you save it as a new playlist, so that you can start creating another On-The-Go playlist.

Transferring the playlists to iTunes

You can transfer the On-The-Go playlists to your iTunes library. Perhaps the songs you selected (or their order) inspired you somehow, and you want to repeat the experience.

When you update your iPod automatically (as we describe in Chapter 10), the current and other saved On-The-Go playlists (called *New Playlist 1, New Playlist 2,* and so on) are copied to your iTunes library, saved as regular playlists, and cleared from the iPod. The automatic update also places the newly created playlists back in your iPod in proper alphabetical location in the Playlist menu with the names *On-The-Go 1, On-The-Go 2,* and so on.

If you want to change your On-The-Go playlists to have a new name, rename them in your iTunes library, as shown in Figure 13-1. The next time you update your iPod automatically, the update changes the playlist names in your iPod to match your iTunes library.

iTunes

	Song Name	Time	Artist	Album	Track #
1	I Can't Make It Alone	3:30	Dylan, Bob	Blind Boy Grunt & the Hawk...	2 of 14
2	I'm Not There	5:00	Dylan, Bob	Blind Boy Grunt & the Hawk...	3 of 14
3	Hills of Mexico	2:56	Dylan, Bob	Blind Boy Grunt & the Hawk...	7 of 14
4	I'm Alright	0:57	Dylan, Bob	Blind Boy Grunt & the Hawk...	8 of 14
5	Frankie & Albert	3:50	Dylan, Bob	Good As I Been To You	1 of 13
6	Jim Jones	3:55	Dylan, Bob	Good As I Been To You	2 of 13
7	Black Jack Davey	5:49	Dylan, Bob	Good As I Been To You	3 of 13
8	Canadee-I-O	4:23	Dylan, Bob	Good As I Been To You	4 of 13
9	Sitting On The Top Of The World	4:30	Dylan, Bob	Good As I Been To You	5 of 13
10	Little Maggie	2:55	Dylan, Bob	Good As I Been To You	6 of 13
11	Hard Times	4:34	Dylan, Bob	Good As I Been To You	7 of 13
12	Step It Up And Go	2:57	Dylan, Bob	Good As I Been To You	8 of 13
13	Tomorrow Night	3:43	Dylan, Bob	Good As I Been To You	9 of 13
14	Arthur McBride	6:22	Dylan, Bob	Good As I Been To You	10 of 13
15	You're Gonna Quit Me	2:48	Dylan, Bob	Good As I Been To You	11 of 13
16	Diamond Joe	3:17	Dylan, Bob	Good As I Been To You	12 of 13
17	Froggie Went A-Courtin'	6:23	Dylan, Bob	Good As I Been To You	13 of 13
18	You Wanna Ramble	3:17	Dylan, Bob	Knocked Out Loaded	1 of 8
19	No More Auction Block	3:03	Dylan, Bob	The Bootleg Series, Vol. 1-...	4 of 22
20	House Carpenter	4:08	Dylan, Bob	The Bootleg Series, Vol. 1-...	5 of 22
21	Let Me Die In My Footsteps	3:33	Dylan, Bob	The Bootleg Series, Vol. 1-...	7 of 22
22	Quit Your Low Down Ways	2:39	Dylan, Bob	The Bootleg Series, Vol. 1-...	10 of 22
23	Walls Of Red Wing	5:05	Dylan, Bob	The Bootleg Series, Vol. 1-...	14 of 22
24	Walkin' Down The Line	2:52	Dylan, Bob	The Bootleg Series, Vol. 1-...	13 of 22
25	Who Killed Davey Moore?	3:09	Dylan, Bob	The Bootleg Series, Vol. 1-...	17 of 22
26	Only A Hobo	3:29	Dylan, Bob	The Bootleg Series, Vol. 1-...	18 of 22
27	When The Ship Comes In	2:55	Dylan, Bob	The Bootleg Series, Vol. 1-...	20 of 22
28	Subterranean Homesick Blues	2:56	Dylan, Bob	The Bootleg Series, Vol. 1-...	6 of 20
29	If You Gotta Go, Go Now (Or Else ...	2:56	Dylan, Bob	The Bootleg Series, Vol. 1-...	7 of 20
30	Sitting On A Barbed Wire Fence	3:54	Dylan, Bob	The Bootleg Series, Vol. 1-...	8 of 20
31	It Takes A Lot To Laugh, It Takes ...	3:22	Dylan, Bob	The Bootleg Series, Vol. 1-...	10 of 20
32	If Not For You	3:33	Dylan, Bob	The Bootleg Series, Vol. 1-...	15 of 20

Source: Jazz-impulse, Jigs_and_reels, Kinks-social satire, Last Fester Band set, Love-chrono, Lovelight list, Lovin' Spoonful-best, Mahal, Taj LPs, Mardi-Gras, Miller, Steve-chrono, New Riders_chrono, Newgrass, No Nukes, Nyro-best, O-Brother, On-The-Go 1, On-The-Go 2, On-The-Go 3, ONB8, Pentangle_set, Police-best, PPM_best, Procol Harum best, Purchased Music, Purchased-CD1, Purchased-CD2, Purchased-CD3, Purchased-CD4, Purchased-CD5, Purchased-CD6, Purchased-CD7

78 songs, 5 hours, 349.9 MB

Figure 13-1:
You can rename a saved On-The-Go playlist in iTunes.

TIP

When updating your iPod manually, as we describe in Chapter 10, you can drag the On-The-Go playlist and any saved playlists from your iPod library directly to the iTunes library.

Playing an iPod Shuffle

The iPod shuffle is a special model iPod with no display or any controls to select specific songs or albums. The idea behind the iPod shuffle is to load it with songs in the order you want them to play (like a long playlist), and then play the songs in that order or in shuffle (random) order. See Figure 13-2.

To set the iPod shuffle to play songs in the order they were copied, set the position switch to the *play in order* position (the middle position marked by the arrows pointing in a circle icon). To set it to play songs in random order, set the position switch to the *shuffle* position (the lower position marked by the arrows crossing icon).

To play the iPod shuffle songs, press the Play/Pause button. To stop (or pause) playback, press the Play/Pause button again. When you stop playback the iPod shuffle status light blinks green for a minute.

Off position

Play in order position

Shuffle songs position

Figure 13-2:
The iPod
shuffle has
a three-
position
switch on
the back for
playing
songs in
order, for
shuffling
songs, and
for turning
it off.

To navigate songs in the iPod shuffle, press the Previous/Rewind button to skip backward, or the Next/Fast-Forward button to skip forward. Press and hold these buttons to skip more than one song ahead or behind (as if you were fast-forwarding or rewinding a tape). You can start a song over by pressing Previous/Rewind while the song is playing.

If you set the position switch to the *play in order* position, the Previous/Rewind button skips backward and the Next/Fast-Forward button skips forward in the order the songs were copied to the iPod shuffle. However, if you set the position switch to the *shuffle* position, the playing order is randomized first — and then the Previous/Rewind button skips backward within the same shuffle order, and the Next/Fast-Forward button skips forward within the same shuffle order. For example, if your iPod shuffle, set in the *shuffle* position, played the 14th song, then the fifth song, and then the 20th song, pressing the Previous/Rewind button during the 20th song takes you back to the fifth song, and pressing it again takes you back to the 14th song; pressing the Next/Fast-Forward button skips through the songs in the same shuffle order again: the 14th song, the fifth song, and then the 20th song.

To go immediately to the beginning of an iPod shuffle playlist, press the Play/Pause button three times quickly (within a second).

Adjusting the Volume

The iPod is quite loud when set to its highest volume — you should turn it down before using headphones. To adjust the volume, follow these steps:

1. **Select and play a song on the iPod.**

2. **Change the volume with the scroll wheel.**

   A volume bar appears in the iPod display to guide you. Scroll with your thumb or finger clockwise to increase the volume, and counterclockwise to decrease the volume.

If you have the Apple iPod Remote — a handy controller that attaches by cable to the iPod headphone connection — you can use the volume button on the remote to adjust the volume. You can also use the remote controller to play or pause a song, fast-forward or rewind, and skip to the next or previous song. You can disable the buttons on the remote by setting the controller's Hold switch (similar to the iPod Hold switch).

To adjust the volume of an iPod shuffle, press the Volume Up (+) or Volume Down (-) buttons.

Bookmarking Audible Audio Books

Audible books, articles, and spoken-word titles are stored and played just like songs in iTunes and your iPod. (You can download titles from www.audible.com.) When you play an Audible title, you can automatically bookmark your place in the text with the iPod. Bookmarks work only with Audible titles. If you have an audio book or spoken-word file in any other format, such as MP3, bookmarks are not available.

When you use the Pause/Play button to pause an Audible file, the iPod automatically bookmarks that spot. When you press the Play button again, the Audible file starts playing from that spot.

Bookmarks synchronize when you copy an Audible title to your iPod — whichever bookmark is farther along in iPod or iTunes becomes the effective bookmark.

Chapter 14

Getting Wired for Sound

Sound studio engineers try to make recordings for typical listening environments, so they have to simulate the sound experience in those environments. Studios typically have home stereo speakers as monitors so that the engineers can hear what the music sounds like on a home stereo. In the 1950s and early 1960s, when AM radio was king, engineers working on potential AM radio hits purposely mixed the sound with low-fidelity monaural speakers so that they could hear what the mix would sound like on radio. Thank goodness those days are over, and cars offer higher-quality FM radio as well as very high quality audio systems.

The point is that the quality of the sound is no better than the weakest link in the audio system. Songs from older times that were mixed to a mono (single) channel for car radios don't sound as good even when played on a home stereo.

The audio CD bridges the gap between home stereos, car stereos, and portable CD players by enabling you to listen to high-quality music anywhere as long as you have a decent pair of headphones or good speakers. Music production changed considerably over the last few decades as more people listened to higher-quality FM radio; bought massive home stereos; and eventually bought CD players for their cars and boats and purchased portable players to use while flying and jogging. At each step, popular music was reissued in the new medium, such as audio CD, and remixed in the process for the new sound systems.

The iPod represents a major leap forward in bridging the gap between home stereos, car stereos, and portable players. Picking up where CDs left off, the iPod offers nearly as high quality sound as an audio CD in a convenient device that can hold several weeks' worth of music. What's more, you can tweak the sound not just for home stereos, but also for all your listening environments.

Making Connections

All iPod models enable you to connect headphones to your iPod, or connect your iPod to your home stereo with standard audio cables, or connect your iPod to your computer with either FireWire or USB cables. The connections are as follows. Refer to Figures 14-1 through 14-4.

FireWire/USB dock connector

Figure 14-1:
A fourth-
generation
color-
display iPod
with a dock
connector
cable.

Control socket   Headphone/line out

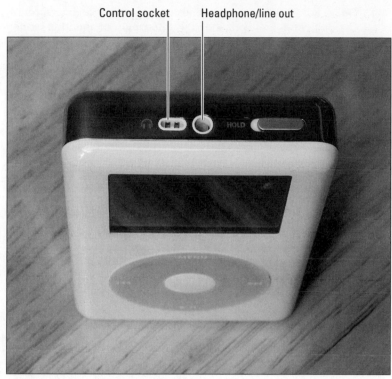

Figure 14-2:
A fourth-generation color-display iPod with connections on top.

✔ **FireWire/USB dock connector:** Current (fourth-generation) and third-generation models, including iPod mini, have a dock connection on the bottom for inserting into a dock connector or using with the dock connector cable. The dock connector cable has a dock connector on one end and a FireWire or USB connector (or both FireWire *and* USB connectors with a split cable) on the other.

✔ **FireWire (six pin):** First-generation and second-generation iPods have a six-pin FireWire-only connection on the top that works with any standard six-pin FireWire cable.

✔ **Headphone/line out and control socket:** You can connect headphones or a 3.5mm stereo mini-plug cable to the headphone/line-out connection. On a color-display iPod, the headphone/line-out connection also serves as an A/V (audio-video) connection for displaying slideshows and photos. The combination headphone and control socket connection on top of the iPod lets you plug in accessories such as remote control devices and voice recorders. (See Chapter 20 for information about voice recording.) The headphone/line-out connection on second-generation models includes an outer ring for connecting the Apple Remote supplied with those models.

✔ **Dock:** For current (fourth-generation) and third-generation iPod models, the dock supplied with the iPod offers two connections: one for the special cable to connect to a FireWire or USB connection, and a headphone/line-out connection for a stereo mini-plug cable (or headphones). For color-display models, the iPod docks include a third connection — S-Video Out for connecting to a television monitor and displaying photos and slideshows, as we describe in Chapter 24.

You can connect the FireWire or USB end of the dock connector cable to the computer (for synchronizing with iTunes and playing the iPod through iTunes, as we describe in Chapter 14) or to the power adapter to charge the iPod battery. The FireWire or USB connection to the computer provides power to the iPod as long as the computer's FireWire or USB hardware offers power to the device and the computer isn't in sleep mode. (See Chapter 1 for power information.)

FireWire/USB

Headphone/line out   Dock connector

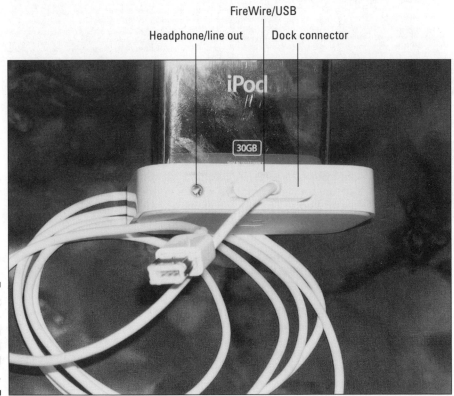

Figure 14-3:
A third-
generation
iPod
connected
to its dock.

Headphone/line out   FireWire

Connecting to a Home Stereo

Home stereo systems come in many shapes and sizes, from an audiophile's monster component racks to a kid's itty-bitty boom box. We're not talking about alarm-clock radios, but stereos with speakers that allow you to add another input device, such as a portable CD player.

Component-style stereo systems typically include a receiver (which offers a preamp/amplifier with a volume control, and a tuner to receive FM radio). Some separate these functions into separate components — such as a preamp, an amplifier, and a tuner. To find a place to connect your iPod or computer to a home stereo, look for RCA-type connections that are marked "AUX IN" (for auxiliary input), "CD IN" (for connecting a CD player), or "TAPE IN" (for tape deck input). All-in-one stereos and boom boxes that are all one piece typically don't have connections for audio input, although there are exceptions — look at the back and sides of the unit for any RCA-type connections.

You can connect a CD or tape player to most stereos with RCA-type cables — one (typically red or black) for the right channel, and one (typically white if the other is black, or white or black if the other is red) for the left channel. All you need is a cable with a stereo mini-plug on one end, and RCA-type connectors on the other, as shown in Figure 14-5. Stereo mini-plugs have two black bands on the plug, but a mono mini-plug has only one black band.

Figure 14-5:
RCA-type connectors (left) and a stereo mini-plug (right).

The Monster high-performance iCable for iPod (formerly called the Monster Cable) available in the Apple Store, looks cool and offers high-quality sound for the discerning listener with excellent stereo equipment.

Connect the stereo mini-plug to the iPod dock headphone/line-out connection (refer to Figure 14-3), or to the headphone/line-out connection on the top of the iPod (refer to Figure 14-2; see Figure 14-4 for second-generation models). Connect the left and right connectors to the stereo system's audio input — whatever connections are available, such as AUX IN (for auxiliary input); TAPE IN (for tape deck input); or CD IN (for CD player input).

Don't use the PHONO IN connection (for phonograph input) on most stereos. These connections are for phonographs (turntables) and aren't properly matched for other kinds of input devices. If you do this, you might get a loud buzzing sound that could damage your speakers.

You can control the volume from the iPod by using the scroll wheel, or from an iPod shuffle by using the volume control. (See Chapter 13 for volume controls.) This controls the volume of the signal from the iPod. Stereo systems typically have their own volume control to raise or lower the volume of the amplified speakers. For optimal sound quality when using a home stereo, set the iPod volume at less than half the maximum output and adjust your listening volume by using your stereo controls. By doing this, you prevent over-amplification, which can cause distortion and reduce audio quality.

Connecting Headphones and Portable Speakers

Apple designed the iPod to provide excellent sound through headphones, and with the headphone/line-out connection, the iPod can also play music through portable speaker systems. The speaker systems must be self-powered or able to work with very little power (like headphones) and allow audio to be input through a 3.5mm mini-plug stereo connection. Even the tiny iPod shuffle offers a standard headphone/line-out connection, as shown in Figure 14-6.

Figure 14-6:
An iPod shuffle with headphones connected to its headphone/line-out connection.

The iPod includes a small amplifier powerful enough to deliver audio through the headphone/line-out connection. All current models, including the iPod shuffle, have a frequency response of 20 Hz (hertz) to 20,000 Hz, which provides distortion-free music at the lowest or highest pitches. Hertz has nothing to do with rental cars — a hertz is a unit of frequency equal to one cycle per second. At pitches that produce frequencies of 20 cycles per second, or 20,000 cycles per second, the iPod responds with distortion-free sound.

Portable speaker systems typically include built-in amplifiers and a volume control, and offer a stereo mini-plug that you can attach directly to the iPod headphone/line-out connection or to the dock headphone/line-out connection. To place the external speakers farther away from the iPod, use a stereo mini-plug extension cable — available at most consumer electronics stores — which has a stereo mini-plug on one end and a stereo mini-socket on the other.

Portable speaker systems typically have volume controls to raise or lower the volume. Set your iPod volume to half and then raise or lower the volume of your speaker system.

When you travel, take an extra pair of headphones (or earbuds) and a splitter cable, such as the one in Figure 14-7, available in any consumer electronics store. The Monster iSplitter is available in the Apple Store. You can plug both headphones into the iPod and share the music with someone on the road.

Figure 14-7:
This headphone cable splits into two, allowing two sets of headphones to connect.

Accessories for the iHome

No home should be without an iPod on a pedestal, raising it above the desk clutter so that you can see its display and use its controls. Although you can play the music in your iTunes library from your computer, you might want to use the iPod in another room that has a stereo system, or you might want to play the iPod, freeing the computer to do other things.

Most of the accessories for the iPod (and hundreds of products are available) are designed for travel, and we describe the best in Chapter 15. However, companies also provide docks and stands for older iPods that don't have docks, as well as alternatives to the limited Apple Remote that connects by cable to the iPod.

The $30 iPodDock from Bookendz (www.bookendzdocks.com) supports the older iPod models in an upside down position on a desk or table and offers connection ports (audio and FireWire) for instant docking. The iPodCradle, also from Bookendz, supports the iPod in an upright position and is compatible with most cases on the market, so you can use your iPod in the cradle with or without the case. Bookendz also offers an iPodDock for third-generation iPods as an alternative to the standard Apple dock.

Need a blast of music for the barbecue out on your patio? The iBoom from Digital Lifestyle Outfitters (www.dlodirect.com) is a 20-watts-per-channel, four-speaker boombox system with a dock for a full-size iPod or iPod mini. It also includes a digital FM radio and auxiliary input jack for connecting another music source, and draws power either from an AC adapter or six D-size batteries (not included). While under AC power, the iBoom can recharge your iPod's battery.

If you don't want to remove your iPod from its dock to use its navigational controls, get a remote control. The Apple Remote, which is supplied with second-generation and some third-generation models, provides the usual CD player controls: Play/Pause, Next Track, Previous Track, and a volume button. It also has a Hold switch, just like the iPod, to render the controls useless and prevent accidental use. You connect the Apple Remote to the headphone/line out connection at the top of the iPod (not the dock). This connection has an outer ring for connecting remote control devices. The Apple Remote is tethered to the iPod by cable, so it isn't as useful in the home as it would be in a car — it has a clip for clipping the remote control to your shirt.

When your iPod is tethered to a dock and connected to your home stereo, you don't have to be within reach to control it remotely — you can control your iPod with a wireless remote control. For example, Ten Technology (www.tentechnology.com) offers the stylish $49.95 naviPod that provides wireless remote control of your iPod with standard Play/Pause, Next Track, Previous Track, and volume controls. The naviPod uses infrared wireless technology with a receiver unit that plugs directly into the control socket on top of the iPod. The receiver has FireWire and headphone connections on the bottom, which allow you to connect your headphones or hook up your iPod to your computer without removing the naviPod receiver.

Engineered Audio (www.engineeredaudio.com) offers the RemoteRemote for $34.95. Unlike infrared wireless controls, RemoteRemote is an RF (radio frequency) wireless remote control that works around corners and through walls. RemoteRemote offers standard Play/Pause, Next Track, Previous Track, and volume controls, and it operates in a range of up to 100 feet.

Chapter 15

Listening While on the Move

*Y*ou can truly go anywhere with an iPod. If you can't plug it into a power source while it's playing, you can use the battery for at least eight hours of playing time (and up to 15 hours for color-display models), before having to recharge. You can find all the accessories that you need to travel with an iPod in the Apple Store at www.apple.com.

Put on "Eight Miles High" by the Byrds while cruising in a plane at 40,000 feet. Ride the rails listening to "All Aboard" by Muddy Waters, followed by "Peavine" by John Lee Hooker. Or cruise on the Autobahn in Germany with Kraftwerk. Whatever. You have an entire music library with you wherever you go.

The iPod provides high-quality music no matter what the environment — even in an earthquake. With skip protection, you don't have to worry about turbulence, potholes, or strenuous exercise causing the music to skip. In addition to the hard drive, iPods also use a memory cache. The cache is made up of solid-state memory, with no mechanical or moving parts, so movement doesn't affect playback. Skip protection works by preloading up to 20 minutes of music to the cache at a time (depending on the iPod model). The iPod plays music from the memory cache rather than the hard drive.

Playing Car Tunes

We always wanted a car that we could fill up with music just as easily as filling it up with gasoline, without having to carry dozens of cassettes or CDs. With an iPod, an auto-charger to save on battery power, and a way to connect the iPod to your car's stereo system, you're ready to pump music. (Start your engine and queue up "Getting in Tune" and then "Going Mobile" by The Who.) Go one step further and get a new BMW or similar car that offers an iPod installed and integrated into the car's stereo system so that you can control it from your steering wheel.

There are three ways to link up your iPod with a car stereo:

- ✔ **Use a cassette player:** Use a standard cassette adapter and an iPod power adapter for your car's lighter socket. This works even with rental cars, as long as they are supplied with cassette players. For a semi-permanent installation you can add a car mount to keep your iPod secure. Cassette adapters offer medium quality that is usually better than wireless adapters.

- ✔ **Use your radio:** Use a wireless adapter that plays your iPod as if it were a station on your FM radio dial. Some car mounts offer built-in wireless adapters. This may be your only inexpensive choice if you don't have a cassette deck. Wireless adapters may not work well in cities where FM stations crowd the radio dial.

- ✔ **Install an iPod interface:** Install an iPod interface for your car stereo that offers high-quality line-in audio input and power. Once you have this interface installed, you simply plug your iPod into a cable and hide it in the glove box, as you can control the iPod from your car stereo's head unit. This method offers the best sound quality.

Unfortunately, not many car stereos offer a mini-socket for audio input, and as of this writing, the few accessories that integrate directly with car stereos require custom car installations. So far, there are no standard dock connectors for car stereos, which would be totally cool because the iPod is clearly designed for plugging into a "car dock" that offers both power and a connection to the car's stereo system. (Stay iTuned, because car docks are on the horizon.)

Getting in tune with cassette and power adapters

Until you can get a car with a mini-socket for stereo audio input (a.k.a. "stereo-in connection") or a FireWire connection — or get one installed — you can use a cassette-player adapter to connect with your car stereo or a wireless device that we describe later in this chapter, in the section "Connecting by Wireless Radio." These solutions provide lower sound quality than iPod interface installations or stereo-in connections but are inexpensive and work with most cars.

Many car stereos have a cassette player, and you can buy a cassette adapter from most consumer electronics stores or from the Apple Store (such as the Sony CPA-9C Car Cassette Adapter). The cassette-player adapter, shown in Figure 15-1, looks like a tape cassette with a mini-plug cable (which sticks out through the slot when you're using the adapter).

You can connect the mini-plug cable directly to the iPod, to the auto-charger if a mini-socket is offered, or to the Apple Remote that in turn is connected to the iPod. Then insert the adapter into the cassette player, being careful not to get the cable tangled up inside the player.

One inherent problem with this approach is that the cable that dangles from your cassette player looks unsightly. You also might have some trouble ejecting the adapter if the cable gets wedged in the door, but overall, this method is the best for most cars because it provides the best sound quality.

The Apple Remote, which is supplied with some models and optional with others, is more useful in a car than almost anywhere else — it provides the usual CD player controls: Play/Pause, Next Track, Previous Track, and a volume button (see Chapter 14), so you can pause a song, skip to the next or previous song, or adjust the volume without having to reach over to your iPod while driving. You can attach the Apple Remote to your shirt or the edge of something thin, such as an air-conditioner vent in your dashboard.

While some new vehicles (particularly SUVs and cars such as the Toyota Matrix mini-station wagon) offer 110-volt power outlets you can use with your Apple-supplied battery charger, most cars offer only a lighter/power socket that requires a power adapter to use with your iPod. Be careful to pick the right type of power adapter for your car's lighter/power socket. The automobile power adapters for first-generation and second-generation iPods provide a FireWire connector, but the adapters for the new dockable iPods use a dock connector cable. Some adapters, such as the Kensington Cassette Adapter/Charger for iPod (www.kensington.com), include a retractable power cord that doesn't dangle in front of the dashboard or tangle with other cords and cables.

Belkin (www.belkin.com) offers the Auto Kit for $49.95, and it includes a car power adapter with a convenient socket for a stereo mini-plug cable (which can connect directly to a car stereo if the stereo has a mini-socket for audio input). The adapter includes a volume-adjustable amplifier to boost the sound coming from the iPod before it goes into the cassette adapter or car stereo.

Even with a cassette adapter and power adapter, you have at best a clumsy solution that uses one cable (power) from a power adapter to the iPod, and another cable (audio) to your car stereo cassette adapter. Attached to these wires, your iPod needs a secure place to sit while your car moves — you don't want it bouncing around on the passenger seat.

You can fit your iPod securely in position in a car without getting a custom installation. The TuneDok ($29.95) from Belkin (www.belkin.com) holds your iPod securely and fits into your car's cup-holder; see Figure 15-2. The TuneDok's ratcheting neck and height-adjustment feature lets you reposition the iPod to your liking. The cable-management clip eliminates loose and tangled cables, and the large and small rubber base and cup fits most cup holders.

MARWARE (www.marware.com) offers an inexpensive solution for both car use and personal use. The $5.95 Car Holder, available when you select a MARWARE SportSuit case, attaches to the dashboard of your car, as shown in Figure 15-3, and lets you attach an iPod that's wearing one of the MARWARE SportSuit covering cases (see "Dressing Up Your iPod for Travel" later in this chapter). The clip on the back attaches to the Car Holder.

Figure 15-1: Inexpensive car accessories: cassette-player adapter (left); power adapter (upper right); and Apple Remote (lower right).

Figure 15-2:
The
TuneDok
mount for a
car cup
holder.

Figure 15-3:
Mounting
the
MARWARE
iPod holder
that works
with the
SportSuit
carrying
case.

ProClip (www.proclipusa.com) offers mounting brackets for clip-on devices. The brackets attach to the dashboard and can be installed in seconds. After you install the bracket, you can use different custom holders for the iPod models or for cell phones and other portable devices.

Going mobile . . . with car stereo integration

Premium car manufacturers are introducing new cars that are iPod-ready —
they include an iPod interface for the car stereo system. For example, BMW
offers an iPod-ready model with audio controls on the steering wheel.
Mercedes-Benz, Volvo, Mini-Cooper, Nissan, Alfa Romeo, and Ferrari all offer
iPod-ready models. In addition, car stereo manufacturers such as Alpine and
Clarion offer car audio systems with integrated iPod interfaces; see Figure 15-4.

Unless you can afford a new car that's iPod-ready, you can opt for a custom
installation of an iPod interface for your existing car stereo and car power
(such as using a custom cable interface for a CD changer, which can be
installed into your dashboard by a skilled car audio specialist). For example,
you can order a professional installation with the Dension ICE-Link ($149
to $239, depending on your car), which adds line-level audio output and
recharging capability to almost any vehicle. It uses the CD-changer connections in car CD players to directly connect your iPod into the car's audio
system. Dension (www.dension.com) assumes that the buyer is a professional installer, and although it's possible to install it yourself (especially if
you use a CD changer in your trunk), most installations require taking apart
the dashboard and installing the ICE-Link behind your CD stereo. ICE-Link can
be combined with almost any iPod mount.

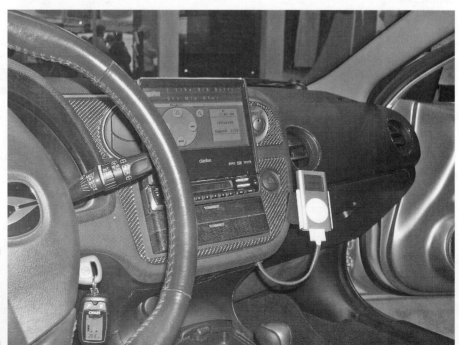

Figure 15-4:
An iPod-
integrated
car stereo
installation.

If your car stereo does not offer a CD changer interface, you may want to have a new car stereo professionally installed that offers a CD changer interface, such as the Alpine CDA-9835, which can be installed with the Alpine KCA-420i Interface Adapter for iPod (www.alpine-usa.com/driveyouripod/). Using this integrated iPod setup you can control the iPod from the Alpine head unit (which can be any Alpine head unit that is compatible with Ai-NET, Alpine's car network). The car stereo provides power to the iPod to keep it fully charged — in fact, the iPod is always charged up with power while the vehicle's ignition is on or in ACC mode (the car stereo itself does not have to be powered on). You can hide your iPod in the glove box while connected to the Alpine, and control the iPod as if it were the Alpine's CD changer, selecting songs by playlist, artist, or album — without having your iPod in view.

Connecting by Wireless Radio

A wireless music adapter lets you play music from your iPod on an FM radio, with no connection or cable, although the sound quality might suffer a bit due to interference. We always take a wireless adapter with us whenever we rent a car — even if a rental car has no cassette player (ruling out the use of our cassette adapter), the car probably has an FM radio.

You can use a wireless adapter in a car, on a boat, on the beach with a portable radio, or even in your home with a stereo system and tuner. We even use it in hotel rooms with a clock radio.

To use a wireless adapter, follow these steps:

1. **Set the wireless adapter to an unused FM radio frequency.**

   Some adapters offer you a choice of several frequencies — typically 88.1-, 88.3-, 88.5-, and 88.7 MHz — and others let you pick any FM frequency. You choose the frequency and set the adapter according to its instructions. Avoid FM stations at specific frequencies that would interfere with your iPod signal.

2. **Connect the wireless adapter to the iPod headphone/line-out connector or to the line-out connector on the iPod dock.**

   The wireless adapter acts like a miniature radio station, broadcasting to a nearby FM radio. (Sorry, you can't go much farther than a few feet, so no one else can hear your Wolfman Jack impersonation.)

3. **Tune to the appropriate frequency on the FM dial.**

   Tune any nearby radio to the same FM frequency that you chose in Step 1.

You need to set the adapter close enough to the radio's antenna to work, making it impractical for home stereos — you can get better quality sound by connecting to a home stereo with a cable.

Don't be surprised if the wireless adapter doesn't work as well in cities — other radio stations might cause too much interference.

Here are just a few wireless adapters that we recommend:

✔ For $29.99, the **irock 400FM Wireless Music Adapter** (`www.myirock.com`) from First International Digital requires standard replaceable batteries and offers a car power adapter.

✔ The **TuneCast II Mobile FM Transmitter** ($49.99) from Belkin (`www.belkin.com`) is particularly convenient in a car because it includes a 14-inch cable that delivers power when used with the Belkin Mobile Power Cord for iPod, so that you can preserve your batteries for times when you're away from an alternate source. It offers four programmable memory slots for saving the clearest radio frequency wherever you go.

✔ The **TransPod FM** ($99) from Digital Lifestyle Outfitters, available from Everything iPod (`www.everythingipod.com`), is an excellent all-in-one wireless FM transmitter, mounting system, and power adapter for using your iPod in a car, and it costs less than purchasing all three items separately.

Dressing Up Your iPod for Travel

The simple protective carrying case supplied with some iPod models is just not as stylin' as the myriad accessories that you can get for dressing up your iPod for travel. You can find different types of protective gear, from leather jackets to aluminum cases, in many different styles and colors — Apple offers access to hundreds of products from other suppliers on its accessories pages (`www.apple.com/ipod/accessories.html`). Some are designed primarily for protecting your iPod from harm; others are designed to provide some measure of protection while also providing access to controls.

On the extreme end of the spectrum are hardened cases that are ready for battlefields in deserts or jungles — the Humvees of iPod protective gear. The iPod Armor ($49.95) by Matias Corporation (`www.ipodarmor.com`) is a sturdy case that fits all models of iPod and offers possibly the best protection against physical trauma on the market. Your iPod rests within a hard, resilient metal exoskeleton that can withstand the abuse of bouncing down a flight of metal stairs without letting your iPod pop out. Of course, the very same feature that prevents your iPod from popping out also makes the iPod Armor difficult to open to get access to it — this is not a case to use while listening to music.

Business travelers can combine personal items into one carrying case. The iPod Leather Organizer from Belkin is made from fine-grain leather that even Ricardo Montalban would rave about. The case holds personal essentials, like business and credit cards, in four convenient slots. A handy mesh pocket keeps earphones easily accessible, and a billfold holds money and receipts.

On the sporty side, MARWARE (www.marware.com) offers the SportSuit Convertible case ($39.95) with a patented belt clip system offering inter-changeable clip options for use with the MARWARE Car Holder or with an armband or belt for jogging or working out. The neoprene case has vulcan-ized rubber grips on each side and bottom for a no-slip grip and plastic inserts for impact protection, offering full access to all iPod controls and con-nections while the iPod is in the case. There's even space inside the lid to store earbud headphones.

If you like to carry a backpack with everything in it, consider the very first backpack ever designed to control an iPod within it: The Burton Amp Pack ($199.95) (www.sidewaypeople.com/site/catalog/burton-amp-pack.htm) lets you switch songs on your iPod by pressing a button on the shoulder strap. Constructed from ballistic nylon, the Amp Pack offers a secure iPod storage pocket, a headphone port located on a shoulder strap, an easy-access side entry laptop compartment, and padded ergonomic shoulder straps with a soft, flexible control pad built into a strap. Perfect for listening to Lou Reed while hanging onto a pole in a subway car, or the Hollies while navigating your way to the back of the bus.

Using Power Accessories

If you want to charge your iPod battery when you travel abroad, you can't count on finding the same voltage as in your home country. However, you still need to plug your Apple power adapter into something to recharge your iPod. Fortunately, power adapters are available in most airports, but the worldly traveler might want to consider saving time and money by getting a travel kit of power accessories.

We found several varieties of power kits for world travel in our local interna-tional airport. Most kits include a set of AC plugs with prongs that fit different electrical outlets around the world. You can connect your iPod power adapter to these adapters. The AC plugs typically support outlets in North America, Japan, China, the United Kingdom, Continental Europe, Korea, Australia, and Hong Kong.

One way to mitigate the battery blues is to get an accessory that lets you use replaceable alkaline batteries — the kind that you can find in any convenience store. The Backup Battery Pack ($59.95) from Belkin (www.belkin.com) lets you power your iPod with four standard AA alkaline replaceable batteries — even when your internal iPod battery is drained. Discreet suction cups secure the unit to the back of your iPod without marring your iPod finish. A charge-level indicator tells you when your batteries are running low.

Another way to supply power to your iPod on the road is to use your FireWire-equipped or USB 2.0-equipped laptop to supply the power (make sure that you use FireWire or USB 2.0 hardware that provides power — see Chapter 1), and then use a power adapter with your laptop. You can use, for example, the Kensington Universal Car/Air Adapter from Apple to plug a Mac PowerBook or iBook into any car cigarette lighter or EmPower-equipped airline seat (the EmPower in-seat power system can provide either 110-volt AC or 15-volt DC power in an aircraft seat for passenger use). Then connect the iPod to the laptop with a FireWire cable.

If you fly often, the APC Travel Power ($79), available from the Apple Store, might be just the ticket. It includes an adapter that plugs into an airline seat power connection, as well as a car power adapter. The unit offers 75 watts of continuous power with built-in circuit protection. The flight attendant will still tell you to turn off your iPod before takeoff and landing, but you won't waste precious battery power during the flight.

Chapter 16

Spinning Tunes Like a DJ

*I*f you like to entertain folks by spinning tunes and playing movies at home or at parties, iTunes could easily become your media jockey console. You could set up a laptop that connects to a home stereo and connect the iPods that your friends bring over to augment your iTunes library. Imagine how much music you could choose from by connecting several 60GB iPods, each with 15,000 songs, to an iTunes library that already holds thousands of songs! But that's not all — you can keep track of video files using an iTunes playlist, and play your videos in full-screen mode.

Your computer is a mean multimedia machine with the ability to mix sounds and videos from different sources and play them through built-in displays and speakers, external displays and speakers, and headphones. Macs and PCs can play audio CDs, DVDs, and digital video files as well as iTunes music.

This chapter describes how you can play video files in iTunes, including music videos and movie trailers available in the iTunes Music Store. It also shows how to play music stored on your iPod through iTunes on your computer, so that the music comes through your computer's speakers. It also shows how you can use a wireless connection with AirPort Express and AirTunes to transmit iTunes songs to your home stereo or speakers without any wires. You could stroll through the party with your laptop, choosing songs, taking requests, and beaming the music directly to your stereo system.

Changing the Computer's Output Volume

You can control the volume and other characteristics of the sound coming out of your computer's speakers, headphones, or external speakers. Even if you connect your computer to a stereo amplifier with its own volume and equalizer controls, it's best to get the volume right at the source — your computer and iTunes — and then adjust the output volume as you please on your stereo or external speaker unit.

Volume is controlled by the computer system's audio controls. iTunes also controls the volume, but that control is within the range of the computer's volume setting. For example, if you set your computer's volume to half and set iTunes volume to full, you get half volume because the computer is limiting the volume to half. If you set your computer volume at half and also reduce the iTunes volume to half, you actually get *one-quarter* volume — half the computer' setting. The sound can be further adjusted after it leaves your computer by using the stereo system or external speakers with controls.

The appropriate volume depends entirely on your preferences for hearing music, but in general, the maximum level of output from your computer is preferable when connecting to a stereo system or speakers with volume controls. After setting your computer to the maximum volume, adjust the iTunes volume or your stereo or speaker volume (or both) to get the best sound. When using the computer's speakers or headphones, the computer's volume and the iTunes volume are the only volume controls that you have, so after adjusting the volume on your computer to the maximum level (or lower if you prefer), adjust the iTunes volume.

Adjusting the sound on a Mac

The Mac was built for sound from the very start. Making and playing music has been part of the Mac culture since day one, when Steve Jobs introduced the original Mac to an audience with sound coming from its small speaker. (It played synthesized speech and simple tones, but it was the first personal computer with built-in sound.)

Today's Mac comes with built-in or external speakers and at least one headphone/line-out connection that you can use to connect external speakers or a stereo system. Mac OS X lets you configure output speakers and control levels for stereo speakers and multichannel audio devices.

If you use external speakers, headphones, or a stereo system, make sure that you connect these devices properly before adjusting the volume. To adjust the volume on your Mac, follow these steps:

1. **Choose System Preferences from the Apple menu or the Dock, and then click the Sound icon.**

   Otherwise, press Option and a volume control key simultaneously as a shortcut. You can have iTunes open and playing music while you do this.

2. **In the Sound preferences window, click Output.**

If you have headphones attached, a Headphones option appears in the list of sound output devices; if not, an External Speakers or Internal Speakers option appears, as shown in Figure 16-1. If you have external speakers *and* a pair of headphones attached to your Mac, the external speakers disappear from the Sound preferences, but they're still enabled.

3. **Adjust the volume by dragging the Output volume slider.**

You can drag the slider to adjust the volume as you listen to music. You also have a Mute button in this window — click the Mute check box to silence your Mac. You can also adjust the stereo balance by dragging the Balance slider to put more music in the left or right channels.

4. **Close the Preferences window by choosing System Preferences⇨Quit System Preferences or by clicking the red button in the upper-left corner of the window.**

The Sound preferences window isn't like a dialog — when you change settings, you can hear the effect immediately without having to click an OK button. (There isn't an OK button, anyway.)

Figure 16-1:
Adjusting the sound output volume on a Mac PowerBook with internal speakers.

Adjusting the sound in Windows

Windows XP and Windows 2000 let you configure output speakers and control levels for stereo speakers and multichannel audio devices.

Use the Sounds and Audio Devices Properties dialog to change the volume. To open this window, choose Start⇨Control Panel, and click the Sounds and Audio Devices icon. Then click the Volume tab.

As shown in Figure 16-2, the Sounds and Audio Devices Properties dialog offers the Device volume slider — drag this slider to set the volume. You can also silence your PC by selecting the Mute check box.

Figure 16-2:
Adjusting
the sound
output
volume
on a PC.

If you select the Place Volume Icon in the Taskbar option, and your sound card supports changing the volume with software, a speaker icon appears in the notification area of Windows. You can then change the volume quickly without having to open the Sounds and Audio Devices Properties dialog — simply click the speaker icon and drag the slider that pops up. For more information about adjusting sound on a PC, see *PCs For Dummies*, 9th Edition by Dan Gookin (Wiley).

Spinning iTunes like a DJ

You can choose songs to play manually, but iTunes also provides several automated features so that you can spend less time prepping your music selection and more time enjoying it.

Queuing up tunes with Party Shuffle

Playlists are great for organizing music in the order that you want to play it, but you can have iTunes serve up songs at random by using Party Shuffle. It's not a dance step or pub game — *Party Shuffle* is a dynamic playlist that automatically generates a semi-random selection in a list that you can modify on the fly. With Party Shuffle at work, you might even find songs in your library you forgot about or rarely play — Party Shuffle always throws a few rarely played songs into the mix.

To use Party Shuffle, follow these steps:

1. **Click Party Shuffle in the Source pane.**

   The Song List pane and Browse pane are replaced with the Party Shuffle track list and settings at the bottom, as shown in Figure 16-3.

Figure 16-3:
Adjusting the settings for Party Shuffle.

2. **Select a source from the Source pop-up menu below the Party Shuffle track list.**

   You can select Library for the entire library, or select any playlist (including a smart playlist) as the source for music in the Party Shuffle. If you select a playlist, Party Shuffle limits its choices to songs from that playlist.

3. **Set the following options:**

   - *Recently played songs:* Choose how many songs should remain in the list after they are played. You can drag already-played songs (even though they are grayed out after playing) to a spot later in the list to play them again.

   - *Upcoming songs:* Choose how many songs should be listed as upcoming (not yet played). By displaying upcoming songs first, you can decide whether to rearrange the list or delete songs before they are played.

   - *Play higher rated songs more often:* Turn on this option to have iTunes add more high-rated songs to the random list. Using this option, you weight the randomness in favor of higher-rated songs. See Chapter 9 to learn how to add ratings to songs.

4. *Optional:* **If you don't like the order of songs, you can rearrange it; any songs you don't like you can eliminate.**

   You can rearrange the order of songs in the Party Shuffle by dragging songs to different positions in the Party Shuffle list. Eliminate songs by selecting them in the Party Shuffle list and pressing Delete/Backspace (or choosing Edit⇨Clear).

5. **Play the Party Shuffle by selecting the first song and clicking the Play button or pressing the Space bar.**

   You can start playing from the first song or from any song on the list. (When you pick a song in the middle to start playing, the songs before it are grayed out to show that they won't play.)

6. **Add, delete, or rearrange songs even while the Party Shuffle plays.**

   While the Party Shuffle list plays, you can add songs in one of two ways:

   - Open the Party Shuffle in a separate window by double-clicking the Party Shuffle item in the Source pane. You can then drag songs from the main iTunes window — either from the Library or from a playlist — directly into position in the Party Shuffle track list.

   - Without opening Party Shuffle in a separate window, you can switch to the library or a playlist, and drag the song to the Party Shuffle item in the Source pane, just like dragging a song to a playlist. When you add a song to the Party Shuffle, it shows up at the end of the track list. You can then drag it to a new position.

You can add one or more albums to the Party Shuffle track list by dragging the albums; the songs play in album order. You can also add all the songs by an artist by dragging the artist name. Party Shuffle acts just like a playlist, except dynamically — you add, delete, and change the order of songs on the fly.

Cool DJs mix the Party Shuffle window with other open playlist windows — just double-click the playlist item in the Source pane to open it in a separate window. You can then drag songs from different playlist windows to the Party Shuffle window while the Party Shuffle plays, adding songs in whatever order you want in real time.

Cross-fading song playback

You can often hear a song on the radio fade out as another song immediately fades in right over the first song's ending. This is a *cross-fade*, and with iTunes, you can smoothly transition from the ending of a song to the beginning of the next one. Ordinarily, iTunes is set to have a short cross-fade of one second — the amount of time between the end of the fade in the first song and the start of the fade in the second song.

What's totally cool about this is that you can cross-fade between two songs in iTunes even if they're from different sources — the songs could be in your library, in a shared library, on CD or DVD, or even on one (or more!) iPods connected to your computer and playing through iTunes (as we describe in "Playing an iPod through iTunes," later in this chapter). You could play DJ at a party with a massive music library on a laptop and still augment that library with one or more iPods and any number of CDs, and the songs cross-fade to the next just like on the radio or at a dance party with a professional DJ.

You can change the amount of the cross-fade by choosing Edit⇨Preferences in Windows or iTunes⇨Preferences on a Mac, and then clicking the Audio button. The Audio dialog appears, as shown in Figure 16-4.

Figure 16-4: Setting the cross-fade between songs.

In the Audio dialog, you select the Crossfade playback option, and then increase or decrease the amount of the cross-fade by dragging the slider. Each notch in the slider is one second. The maximum amount of cross-fade is 12 seconds. With a longer cross-fade you get a longer overlap from one song to the next — the second song starts before the first one ends. To turn off the cross-fade, deselect the check box.

Playing Videos in iTunes

Without any fanfare, Apple slipped a new feature into iTunes version 4.8 — the ability to play video files and track video files using playlists. Besides watching videos in the iTunes Music Store, you can now purchase videos for downloading into iTunes. You can also bring your own digital video files into iTunes. While today's iPod doesn't play videos, we bet that future iPods will.

Acquiring videos

You can watch QuickTime and MPEG-4 movies (files that end in .mov or .mp4) in iTunes. QuickTime, Apple's digital video file format, is installed on every Mac. It's also installed on PCs along with the Windows version of iTunes. QuickTime is used extensively in the digital video production world for making DVDs and movies for the Web. Music videos, movie trailers, and other videos you can buy on the iTunes Music Store are in the QuickTime format. MPEG-4 (Motion Picture Expert Group Version 4) is a standard format for digital video that works on just about any computer that can play video.

The iTunes Music Store offers music videos for sale. You can select and buy a music video, either as part of an album package or separately, and download the video into iTunes just like a song. The video file appears in your Purchased Music list just like any other song, as shown in Figure 16-5.

Video files are organized in folders and stored in the music library on your hard drive just like song files, as we describe in Chapter 11. You can find the video file's location on your hard drive and its type by choosing File➪Get Info, just as you would for a song file. (See Figure 16-6.) The Summary pane shows information about the video file, including its location and file type, in the Info pane.

 You can assign video files to playlists just like song files, but you can't copy them to an iPod (at least not until iPods can play video). You may want to create a playlist that consists solely of videos. Simply create the playlist as we describe in Chapter 9, and drag videos from Browse or List view into the playlist.

Figure 16-5:
Select a video purchased from the iTunes Music Store.

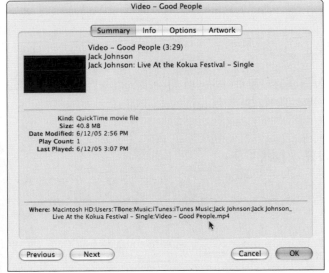

Figure 16-6:
The Get Info window shows the video file's location and file type.

If you have video files of your own, dragging them into iTunes makes it easier to find and play them. Drag each video file from the Windows desktop or Mac Finder to the Library or directly to a playlist in the iTunes Source pane, or to the Browse or song List view on the right side of the iTunes window, as shown in Figure 16-7.

Figure 16-7:
Bring a
video file
into iTunes.

You can create your own QuickTime or MPEG-4 video files with a suitable video editing application such as iMovie for the Mac (part of the iLife software suite that includes iTunes), or Apple's QuickTime Pro for Windows, available from the Apple Store.

Playing videos

To watch a video in iTunes, double-click it in your library or playlist. Use the iTunes Play/Pause, Forward/Next, and Previous/Rewind buttons to control playback, and the iTunes volume slider to control the volume, just like with songs.

The video appears in the Artwork pane in the lower-left corner of the iTunes window, as shown in Figure 16-8. If the Artwork pane isn't visible, click the Artwork button.

You can also fill your entire display with the video picture, or view it in a separate window. To watch the video full screen, click the full-screen video button underneath the Artwork pane; refer to Figure 16-8. This button is usually grayed out unless you have already selected and are playing a video. After clicking the full-screen video button, video fills your screen and plays. Pressing any key during playback stops full-screen video and returns you to the iTunes window.

Figure 16-8: Video appears in the Artwork pane; click the full-screen button to fill your display with the video picture.

To watch a video in a separate window, click the video as it plays in the Artwork pane. To make this setting more permanent, set your iTunes preferences to play video in a separate window. Open iTunes preferences by choosing Edit⇨Preferences in Windows or iTunes⇨Preferences on a Mac, and click the Advanced button. For the "Play video" option in the Advanced pane, choose "in a separate window" in the pop-up menu as shown in Figure 16-9. From that point on, videos in your library play in a separate window that offers QuickTime playback controls, as shown in Figure 16-10.

Figure 16-9: Change video playback to a separate window.

Figure 16-10:
Drag the
QuickTime
playback
slider to
move
forward or
backward
through a
video.

The QuickTime video buttons offer more control over playback in the separate window: Use the right-facing triangle on the bottom-left side of the window to play or pause, and drag the slider to move forward or backward through the video; refer to Figure 16-10. You can click the rewind or fast-forward buttons on the bottom-right side of the window to move backward or forward through a video.

The current video controls in iTunes seem crude, but we have no doubt that iTunes will be improved in the future to provide more video playback and organizational features, and that future iPods will be brimming with videos.

Playing an iPod through iTunes

You can't copy the songs from your iPod into your iTunes library using iTunes, but you can use iTunes on your computer to play the songs directly from the iPod. You can even bring your friend's iPod with you to a party, along with your laptop running iTunes, and include your friend's iPod songs in your Party Shuffle — include *anyone's* iPod songs in your Party Shuffle. Not only can you do that, but as you play songs from different iPods or from your library, you can cross-fade them, as we describe previously in "Cross-fading song playback," earlier in this chapter.

When you set your iPod to manually update and connect the iPod to your computer, the iPod name appears in the iTunes Source pane, and when you select it, the iPod's songs appear in the iTunes window. You can connect someone else's iPod this way, as we describe in the following section, "Connecting your iPod to another computer."

To play music on your iPod in iTunes, follow these steps:

 1. **Connect the iPod to your computer, holding down ⌘-Option on a Mac, or Ctrl-Alt on a PC, to prevent automatic updating.**

2. **Set the iPod to update manually.**

   To set the iPod to update manually, see Chapter 10. (The iPod updates automatically by default, but you can change that.)

3. **Select the iPod name in the iTunes Source pane.**

   After selecting the iPod in the iTunes Source pane, the list of songs on the iPod appears, as shown in Figure 16-11. You can scroll or browse the iPod's library just like the main iTunes library (as we describe in Chapter 7). Click the Browse button to browse the iPod's contents.

Figure 16-11: Select the iPod in the Source pane and play a song.

4. *Optional:* **View the iPod playlists.**

   After selecting the iPod in the iTunes Source pane, you can click the triangle next to its name to view the iPod's playlists.

5. **Click a song in the iPod song list, and then click the iTunes Play button.**

When an IPod song is playing in iTunes, it's just like playing a song from the iTunes library or a track on a CD. The Status pane above the list of songs tells you the name of the artist and song (if known) and the elapsed time.

Connecting your iPod to another computer

The previous section shows you how to connect your iPod to your computer. What if you want to connect your iPod to a computer other than your own? Or what if a friend arrives with an iPod filled with songs that you'd like to hear, and you want to hear them on your stereo system that's already connected to your computer?

You can connect your iPod to another computer, or connect someone else's iPod to your computer. Either way, iTunes starts up and recognizes that the iPod is not matched to the iTunes library (because it is matched to some other computer's iTunes library). iTunes displays a message asking whether you want to change the link to this iTunes music library and replace all existing songs and playlists. This is important: *click No.*

Unless you want to change the contents of your iPod to reflect this computer's music library, don't click Yes. *If you click the Yes button, iTunes erases the music library of your iPod* and then updates your iPod with the library on this computer. If you're using a public computer with no music in its iTunes library, you end up with an empty iPod. If you're using a friend's computer, your friend's library copies to your iPod, erasing whatever was on your iPod. So don't click Yes unless you really want to completely change the music on your iPod. You've been warned.

With color-display iPods, you also get a similar warning message about changing the link to the photo library and replacing all photos in the iPod. Again, click No to prevent this from happening.

After clicking No, the iPod appears in the iTunes Source pane. Set the iPod to update manually (see Chapter 9) to play songs from your iPod.

You can use a Windows-formatted iPod with a Mac, but you can't use a Mac-formatted iPod with Windows. When you install an iPod with Windows, the iPod is formatted for Windows; but you are still in luck with a Mac because Macs can read Windows drives. If you want to be a laptop DJ and use other people's iPods in the mix, use a Mac laptop because it can access both types of iPods.

If you connected a Mac-formatted iPod to a Windows computer, you get a warning message about reformatting it. *Don't do it!* Click Cancel — otherwise, you reformat the iPod and clear all music from it. Then click the Safely Remove Hardware icon on the Windows taskbar to open the Safely Remove Hardware window. Select the iPod and click Stop. Wait for the list of devices in the Safely Remove Hardware window to be cleared. Then wait for your iPod to display a message that it's okay to disconnect (or until the iPod main menu appears). You can then disconnect the iPod.

Using AirTunes for wireless stereo playback

You want to play the music in your iTunes library (or on your iPod connected to your computer), but your stereo system is in another room, and you don't want wires going from one room to the other. What you need is an AirPort in your home — specifically, AirPort Express with AirTunes, which lets you play your iTunes music through your stereo or powered speakers in virtually any room of your house, without wires — as long as your computer is within range of the AirPort Express Base Station.

AirPort is Apple's technology that provides Wi-Fi wireless networking for any AirPort-equipped Mac or PC that uses a Wi-Fi-certified IEEE 802.11b or 802.11g wireless card or offers built-in Wi-Fi. For more about AirPort, see *Mac OS X Tiger All-In-One Desk Reference For Dummies,* by Mark L. Chambers (Wiley).

AirPort Express uses the fast 802.11g wireless standard to deliver data rates up to 54 Mbps. It also works with the 802.11b wireless protocol, so that Macs and PCs with older Wi-Fi configurations can connect wirelessly.

To use a stereo system or powered speakers with AirTunes, connect the system or speakers to the audio port on the AirPort Express Base Station. iTunes automatically detects the connection.

If you already have a wireless network in place, you can add AirPort Express and AirTunes without changing anything. Connect the AirPort Express Base Station to the stereo system or powered speakers, and plug the Base Station into an electrical outlet. The AirPort Express Base Station wirelessly links to your existing wireless network without requiring any change to the network.

You can use several AirPort Express Base Stations — one for each stereo system or set of powered speakers, in different rooms — and then choose which stereo/speaker system to use in the pop-up menu.

To use AirTunes and the AirPort Express Base Station, follow these steps:

1. **Install the software supplied on CD-ROM, which includes support for AirTunes.**

2. **Connect your stereo or a set of powered speakers to the audio port of the AirPort Express Base Station.**

   You can use an optical digital or analog audio cable. (Both are included in the AirPort Express Stereo Connection Kit.) Which cable you use depends on whether your stereo or set of powered speakers has an optical digital or analog connection.

3. **Plug the AirPort Express Base Station into an electrical outlet.**

   Use the AC plug that came with the Base Station or the AirPort Express power extension cord included in the AirPort Express Stereo Connection Kit. The Base Station turns on automatically when connected to an electrical outlet. (The Base Station doesn't require a switch). The status light glows yellow while AirPort Express is starting up. When it starts up completely, the light turns green.

4. On your computer, use iTunes to set your preferences to look for speakers connected to your computer wirelessly using AirTunes.

Set your iTunes preferences to look for AirTunes speakers by choosing Edit➪Preferences in Windows or iTunes➪Preferences on a Mac, and click the Audio button. Select the "Look for remote speakers connected with AirTunes" option in the Audio pane, as shown in Figure 16-12.

In the Audio pane you can also disable the iTunes volume control for the remote speakers to control those speakers separately (such as using your amplifier's volume control); leaving this unchecked enables you to control the volume from iTunes.

Figure 16-12: Select the option to look for speakers connected wirelessly to your computer using AirTunes.

5. Use iTunes to select the AirTunes-equipped network.

After turning on the option to look for AirTunes-connected speakers, a Computer button appears in the lower-right corner of the iTunes window. Clicking this button displays a pop-up menu with any available wireless AirTunes networks, as shown in Figure 16-13. You can select the AirTunes network to play music ("Little Net Buddy" in Figure 16-13). From that point on, iTunes plays music through the AirTunes network rather than the computer. To play music through speakers connected to the computer (or through the computer's built-in speakers), choose Computer from the pop-up menu.

Figure 16-13:
Choosing
the AirTunes
network
"Little Net
Buddy" to
play music.

The AirPort Express Base Station is small enough to fit in the palm of your hand — and it travels well because all it needs is a power outlet. You can take your laptop and AirPort Express to a friend's house or a party, connect the Base Station to the stereo system, and then use your laptop anywhere in its vicinity to play DJ. You can even use portable powered speakers wirelessly in a hotel room, and use a hotel room's wired LAN-to-Internet access with an AirPort Express to connect your wireless computer and other wireless computers in the room to the Internet.

Part IV
Using Advanced Techniques

The 5th Wave   By Rich Tennant

"Margaret! Kyle's playing air bassoon the wrong way again! Doesn't iTunes have a help menu for this?"

In this part . . .

This part focuses on what you can do to improve the sound of your music.

✔ Chapter 17 gives you the info you need to make the right decisions for encoding and compressing sound files.

✔ Chapter 18 describes how to change your encoder and importing preferences to get the most out of the technology.

✔ Chapter 19 tells you about the iTunes and iPod equalizers and fine-tuning music playback in iTunes and on your iPod.

✔ Chapter 20 explains what you need to do to record sound from various analog sources (including vinyl LPs and tapes) for importing into iTunes.

✔ Chapter 21 covers other online music sources, how to play Web radio streams in iTunes, and how to acquire and play podcasts.

Chapter 17

Decoding Encoding

In This Chapter
▶ Finding out the quality and space tradeoffs with sound encoders
▶ Understanding how encoders use compression
▶ Choosing the appropriate encoder and import settings

A s you discover more about digital audio technology, you find that you have more decisions to make about your music library than you previously thought, and this chapter helps you make them. For example, you might be tempted to trade quality for space — import music at average-quality settings that allow you to put more songs on your hard drive and iPod than if you chose higher-quality settings. This might make you happy today, but what about tomorrow, when iPods and hard drives double or triple in capacity?

On the other hand, you might be very picky about the sound quality, and with an eye toward future generations of iPods and cheap hard drives, you might decide to trade space for quality, importing music at the highest possible quality settings and then converting copies to lower-quality, space-saving versions for iPods and other uses. Of course, you need more hard drive space to accommodate the higher-quality versions.

This chapter explains which music encoding and compression formats to use for higher quality and which to use for cramming more songs into your hard drive space.

Trading Quality for Space

The encoding format and settings that you choose for importing music when ripping a CD affect sound quality, iPod space, and hard drive space on your computer. The format and settings might also affect the music files' ability to play on other types of players and computers.

The audio compression methods that are good at reducing space have to throw away information. In technospeak, these methods are known as *lossy* (as opposed to lossless) compression algorithms. For example, the AAC and MP3 encoding formats compress the sound using lossy methods — the compression algorithms reduce the sound quality by throwing away information to make the file smaller, so you lose information and some quality in the process. On the other hand, the Apple Lossless encoder compresses the sound without any loss in quality or information, but the resulting file is only a bit smaller than the uncompressed version — the main reason to use Apple Lossless is to maintain quality for burning CDs while also playing the songs on iPods. The AIFF and WAV encoders do not compress the sound and are the best choices for burning CDs.

With lossy compression using MP3 or AAC, the amount of compression depends on the *bit rate* that you choose, as well as the encoding format and other options. The bit rate determines how many bits (of digital music information) can travel during playback in a given second. Measured in kilobits per second (Kbps), a higher bit rate, such as 320KB, offers higher quality than a bit rate of 192KB because the sound is not compressed as much — which means the resulting sound file is larger and takes up more iPod and hard drive space.

Using more compression (a lower bit rate) means that the files are smaller, and the sound quality is poorer. Using less compression (a higher bit rate) means that the sound is higher in quality, but the files are larger. You can trade quality for space and have more music of lower quality, or trade space for quality and have less music of higher quality.

Also, power is an issue with the iPod. Playing larger files takes more power because the hard drive inside the iPod has to refresh its memory buffers more frequently to process information as the song plays — you might even hear hiccups in the sound.

We prefer a higher-quality sound overall, and we typically don't use the lower-quality settings for encoders except for voice recordings and music recorded in ancient times — before 1960. (Ancient recordings are already low in quality, so you don't hear that much of a difference when compressed.) We can hear differences in music quality at the higher compression levels, and we prefer going out and buying another hard drive to store more music if necessary.

Choosing an iTunes Encoder

Your iPod's music software gives you a choice of encoders. This is perhaps the most important choice to make before starting to rip music CDs and build up your library. iTunes and MusicMatch Jukebox offer the same encoders — with some differences. Here we leapfrog years of technospeak about digital music file formats and get right to the ones that you need to know about. If you're using MusicMatch, visit the companion Web site at www.dummies.com/go/ipod.

Choose Preferences (from the iTunes menu on a Mac, or the Edit menu on a Windows PC) and click the Importing tab to see the Importing Preferences dialog. You can choose one of five encoders from the Import Using pop-up menu:

✔ **AAC Encoder:** All your purchased music from the iTunes Music store comes in this format. We recommend it for all uses except when ripping your own CDs to burn new audio CDs. Technically known as MPEG-4 Advanced Audio Coding, AAC is a higher quality format than MP3 at the same bit rate — meaning that AAC at 128 Kbps is higher quality than MP3 at 128 Kbps. (*MPEG* stands for Moving Picture Experts Group, a committee that recognizes compression standards for video and audio.) We think it offers the best tradeoff of space and quality for iPod users, and is especially useful for importing podcasts. (Read all about podcasts in Chapter 21.) It's suitable (though not as good as AIFF or Apple Lossless) for burning to an audio CD, and it's also excellent for playing on an iPod or from a hard drive. However, as of this writing, only Apple supports AAC.

✔ **AIFF Encoder:** The Audio Interchange File Format (AIFF) is the standard digital format for uncompressed sound on a Mac, and it provides the highest quality digital representation of the sound. Like the WAV encoder for Windows, the AIFF encoder uses a Mac-specific version of the original Pulse Code Modulation (PCM) algorithm required for compliance with audio CDs. Use AIFF if you plan to burn songs onto an audio CD or to edit the songs with a digital sound-editing program. Mac-based sound-editing programs import and export AIFF files, and you can edit and save in AIFF format repeatedly with absolutely no loss in quality. The downside is that AIFF files take up enormous amounts of hard drive and iPod space because they're uncompressed. Don't use AIFF for songs that you want to play on an iPod — use the Apple Lossless encoder instead.

✔ **Apple Lossless Encoder:** The Apple Lossless encoder is a compromise between the lower-quality encoding of AAC or MP3 (which results in lower file sizes) and the large file sizes of uncompressed, high-quality AIFF or WAV audio. The Apple Lossless encoder provides CD quality sound in a file size that's about 60 to 70 percent of the size of an AIFF or WAV encoded file. The virtue of this encoder is that you can use it for songs that you intend to burn onto audio CDs *and* for playing on iPods — the files are just small enough that they don't hiccup on playback, but are still much larger than their MP3 or AAC counterparts.

Using the Apple Lossless encoder is the most efficient method of storing the highest-quality versions of your songs. You can burn the songs to CDs without any quality loss and still play them on your iPod. You can't store as many songs on your iPod as with AAC or MP3, but the songs that you do store have the highest-possible quality.

✔ **MP3 Encoder:** The MPEG-1, Layer 3 format, also known as MP3, is supported by most computers and some CD players. Use the MP3 format for songs that you intend to use with other MP3 players besides your iPod (which also plays MP3 songs, obviously), or use with applications that support MP3, or to burn on an MP3 CD. (AIFF, WAV, or Apple Lossless formats are better for regular audio CDs.) The MP3 format offers quite a lot of different compression and quality settings, so you can fine-tune the format to get better quality, sacrificing hard drive (and iPod) space as you dial up the quality. Use the MP3 format for a song that you intend to use with MP3 players, MP3 CDs, and applications that support MP3.

✔ **WAV Encoder:** Waveform Audio File Format (WAV) is a digital audio standard that Windows PCs can understand and manipulate. Like AIFF, WAV is uncompressed and provides the highest quality digital representation of the sound. Like the AIFF encoder for the Mac, the WAV encoder uses a Windows-specific version of the original Pulse Code Modulation (PCM) algorithm required for compliance with audio CDs. Use WAV if you plan on burning the song to an audio CD or using the song with Windows-based digital sound-editing programs, which import and export WAV files (there is no difference between AIFF and WAV except that AIFF works with Mac applications and WAV works with Windows applications). WAV files take up enormous amounts of hard drive and iPod space because they're uncompressed. Don't use WAV for songs that you want to play on an iPod — use the Apple Lossless encoder instead.

If you want to share your music with someone who uses an MP3 player other than an iPod, you can import or convert songs with the MP3 encoder. As an iPod user, you can use the higher-quality AAC encoder to produce files that are either the same size as their MP3 counterparts but higher in quality, or at the same quality but smaller in size.

The past, present, and future of music

Our suggestions for encoders and importing preferences for ripping CDs are based on our own listening experiences and our preference of the highest quality and the best use of compression technology. You might be quite happy with the results of using these suggestions, but listening pleasure depends entirely on you and the way the song itself was recorded. Some people can hear qualitative differences that others don't hear or don't care about. Some people can also tolerate a lower-quality sound in exchange for the convenience of carrying more music on their iPods. And sometimes the recording is so primitive-sounding that you can get away with using lower-quality settings to gain more hard drive space.

Just a century ago, people gathered at *phonography parties* to rent a headset and listen to a new invention called a phonograph, the predecessor to the record player. Before records, radio, and jukeboxes, these parties and live performances were the only sources of music, and the quality of the sound must have been crude by today's standards, but still quite enjoyable.

The choices of formats for sound have changed considerably from the fragile 78 rpm records from the phonography parties of the early 1900s and the scratchy 45 rpm and 33 rpm records of the 1940s through the 1980s to today's CDs. Consumers had to be on the alert then, as you do now, for dead-end formats that could lock up music in a cul-de-sac of technology, never to be played again. You know what we're talking about — dead-end formats, such as the ill-fated 8-track cartridge or the legendary quadraphonic LP. You want your digital music to last forever and play at high quality — not get stuck with technology that doesn't evolve with the times.

Digital music has evolved beyond the commercial audio CD, and computers haven't yet caught up to some of the latest audio formats. For example, iTunes can't yet import sound from these formats:

- **DVD-audio:** DVD-audio is a relatively new digital audio format developed from the format for DVD video. DVD-audio is based on PCM recording technology but offers improved sound quality by using a higher sampling frequency and longer word lengths. Neither iTunes nor MusicMatch Jukebox support the DVD-audio format, but you can import a digital video file containing DVD-audio sound into iMovie, extract the sound, and export the sound in AIFF or WAV format, which you can use with iTunes. You can also use Toast 6 Titanium from Roxio (www.roxio.com) to import and burn DVD-audio.

- **Super Audio CD (SACD):** Super Audio CD is a new format developed from the past audio format for CDs. The SACD format is based on Direct Stream Digital (DSD) recording technology that closely reproduces the shape of the original analog waveforms to produce a more natural, higher quality sound. Originally developed for the digital archiving of priceless analog masters tapes, DSD is based on 1-bit sigma-delta modulation, and operates with a sampling frequency of 2.8224 MHz (64 times the 44.1 kHz used in audio CDs). Philips and Sony adopted DSD as the basis for SACD, and the format is growing in popularity among audiophiles. However, neither iTunes nor MusicMatch Jukebox support SACD. If you buy music in the SACD format, choose the hybrid format that offers a conventional CD layer and a high-density SACD layer. You can then import the music from the conventional CD layer.

You might also want to take advantage of the compression technology that squeezes more music onto your iPod. Although the Apple-supported AAC format offers far better compression and quality than the MP3 format does (at the same bit rates), the MP3 format is more universal, supported by other players and software programs, as well as the iPod and iTunes. Sticking with AAC or Apple Lossless as your encoder might make you feel like your songs are stuck inside iTunes with the MP3 blues again. However, with iTunes and your iPod, you can mix and match these formats as you please.

To have the best possible quality that you can get for future growth, and for music editing, consider not using compression at all (as with AIFF or WAV), or using Apple Lossless. You can import music at the highest possible quality — by using the AIFF or WAV encoders or the Apple Lossless encoder — and burn them to audio CDs; then convert the music files to a lesser-quality format for use in the iPod or other devices. If you use Apple Lossless for songs, you can use those songs on an iPod, but they take up much more space than AAC- or MP3-encoded songs. We describe how to convert music in Chapter 18.

Manic Compression Has Captured Your Song

Every person hears the effects of compression differently. You might not hear any problem with a compressed song that someone else says is tinny or lacking in depth.

Too much compression can be a bad thing. Further compressing an already-compressed music file — say, by converting a song — reduces the quality significantly. Not only that, but after your song is compressed, you can't uncompress the song back to its original quality. Your song is essentially locked into that quality.

The lossy-style compression used by MP3 and AAC loses information each time you use it, which means that if you compress something that has already been compressed, you lose even more information. This is bad. Don't compress something that's already compressed with a lossy method.

The Apple Lossless encoder doesn't use a lossy method, which is why it's called *lossless*. This is also why it reduces sound files to only two-thirds of their AIFF or WAV counterparts — which isn't as useful for saving space as the one-tenth compression that's common with MP3 or AAC.

MP3 and AAC use two basic lossy methods to compress audio:

✔ **Removing non-audible frequencies:** For non-audible frequencies, the compression removes what you supposedly can't hear (although this is a subject for eternal debate). For example, if a background singer's warble is totally drowned out by a rhythm guitar playing a chord, and you can't hear the singer due to the intensity of the guitar's sound, the compression algorithm loses the singer's sound while maintaining the guitar's sound.

✔ **Removing less important signals:** Within the spectrum of sound frequencies, some frequencies are considered to be less important in terms of rendering fidelity, and some frequencies most people can't hear at all. Removing specific frequencies is likely to be less damaging to your music than other types of compression, depending on how you hear things. In fact, your dog might stop getting agitated at songs that contain ultra-high frequencies that only dogs can hear (such as the ending of "Day in the Life" by the Beatles).

Selecting Import Settings

The AAC and MP3 formats compress sound at different quality settings. iTunes and MusicMatch Jukebox let you set the bit rate for importing, which determines the audio quality. You need to use a higher bit rate (such as 192 or 320 Kbps) for higher quality, which — all together now — increases the file size. Again, if you're using MusicMatch, visit the companion Web site at www.dummies.com/go/ipod.

Variable Bit Rate (VBR) encoding is a technique that varies the number of bits used to store the music depending on the complexity of the sound. Although the quality of VBR is endlessly debated, it's useful when set to the highest setting because VBR can encode at up to the maximum bit rate of 320 Kbps in those rare cases where the sound requires it, while keeping the majority of the sound at a lower bit rate.

iTunes and MusicMatch Jukebox also let you control the *sample rate* during importing, which is the number of times per second the sound waveform is captured digitally (or *sampled*). Higher sample rates yield higher quality sound and large file sizes. However, never use a higher sample rate than the rate used for the source. CDs use a 44.100 kHz rate, so choosing a higher rate is unnecessary unless you convert a song that was recorded from Digital Audio Tape (DAT) or directly into the computer at a high sample rate, and you want to keep that sample rate.

Another setting to consider during importing is the Channel choice. *Stereo,* which offers two channels of music for left and right speakers, is the norm for music. However, *mono* — monaural or single-channel — was the norm for pop records before the mid-1960s. (Phil Spector was known for his high-quality monaural recordings, and the early Rolling Stones records are in mono.) Monaural recordings take up half the space of stereo recordings when digitized. Most likely, you want to keep stereo recordings in stereo, and mono recordings in mono.

Chapter 18

Changing Encoders and Encoder Settings

In This Chapter

▶ Changing your importing preferences in iTunes

▶ Changing settings for the AAC, MP3, AIFF, and WAV encoders in iTunes

▶ Converting songs to a different encoding format in iTunes

*Y*ou might want to change your import settings before ripping CDs, depending on the type of music, the source of the recording, or other factors, such as whether you plan to copy the songs to your iPod or burn an audio or MP3 CD. The encoders offer general quality settings, but you can also customize the encoders and change those settings to your liking.

Whether you use iTunes or MusicMatch Jukebox, the software remembers your custom settings until you change them again. (If you're using MusicMatch, visit the companion Web site at www.dummies.com/go/ipod.)

This chapter provides the nuts-and-bolts details on changing your import settings to customize each type of encoder, importing sounds other than music, and converting songs from one format to another. With the choice of settings for music encoders, you can impress your audiophile friends — even ones who doubted that your computer could reproduce magnificent music.

You can also convert songs to another format as described in "Converting Songs to a Different Encoder in iTunes" later in this chapter. However, you can't convert songs that you buy from the iTunes Music Store to another file format because they're encoded as protected AAC files. If you could, they wouldn't be protected, would they? You also can't convert Audible books and spoken-word content to another format. (However, you can burn them to an audio CD and re-import them, which might cause a noticeable drop in quality.)

Customizing the Encoder Settings in iTunes

To change your encoder and quality settings and other importing preferences before ripping an audio CD or converting a file in iTunes, follow these steps:

1. **Choose iTunes⇨Preferences on a Mac, or Edit⇨Preferences on a Windows PC, and then click the Importing tab.**

   The Importing Preferences dialog appears, allowing you to make changes to the encoding format and its settings.

2. **Choose the encoding format that you want to convert the song into and select the settings for that format.**

   The pop-up menus help you make your changes. The Setting pop-up menu offers different settings depending on your choice of encoder in the Import Using pop-up menu. See the sections on each encoding format later in this chapter for details on settings.

3. **Click OK to accept changes.**

   After changing your importing preferences, and until you change them again, iTunes uses these preferences whenever it imports or converts songs.

The AAC, MP3, AIFF, and WAV encoders let you customize the settings for the encoders. The Apple Lossless encoder is automatic and offers no custom settings to change.

Changing AAC encoder settings

We recommend using the AAC encoder for everything except music that you intend to burn on an audio CD; AAC offers the best trade-off of space and quality for hard drives and iPods.

The Setting pop-up menu for the AAC encoder offers three choices: High Quality, Podcast, and Custom, as shown in Figure 18-1. The Podcast setting is useful for converting audio recordings exported from GarageBand or a similar audio editing application into iTunes. (For more information about podcasts, see Chapter 21.) We recommend using the High Quality setting for most music you rip from CDs, but for very intense music (such as complex jazz or classical music, recordings with lots of instruments, or your most favorite songs), you might want to fine-tune the settings. To customize your AAC encoder settings, select the Custom option from the Setting pop-up menu to see the AAC Encoder dialog, as shown in Figure 18-2.

Figure 18-1:
Customize
the settings
for the AAC
encoder.

The custom settings for AAC (see Figure 18-2) allow you to change the following:

- **Stereo Bit Rate:** This pop-up menu allows you to select the bit rate, which is measured in kilobits per second (Kbps). Use a higher bit rate for higher quality, which also increases the file size. 320 Kbps is the highest-quality setting for this format; 128 is considered high quality.

- **Sample Rate:** This pop-up menu enables you to select the *sample rate,* which is the number of times per second the sound waveform is captured digitally (or *sampled*). Higher sample rates yield higher quality sound and larger file sizes. However, never use a higher sample rate than the rate used for the source. CDs use a 44.100 kHz rate.

- **Channels:** This pop-up menu enables you to choose how you want the music to play through speakers — in stereo or mono. Stereo offers two channels of music for left and right speakers, and mono offers only one channel but takes up half the space of stereo recordings when digitized. If the recording is in stereo, don't choose mono because you will lose part of the sound (you might lose vocals or guitar riffs, depending on the recording). Select the Auto setting to have iTunes use the appropriate setting for the music.

- **Optimize for Voice:** This option filters the sound to favor the human voice. Podcasters can use this option, along with the AAC encoder, to convert audio recordings into a podcast format optimal for iTunes.

We recommend selecting the highest bit rate in the Stereo Bit Rate pop-up menu and leaving the other two pop-up menus set to Auto.

Figure 18-2:
Set the AAC encoder to import with the highest bit rate and with automatic detection of sample rate and channels.

Changing MP3 encoder settings

We prefer using the AAC encoder for music that we play on our iPods, but as of this writing, other MP3 players don't support AAC. The iPod supports both AAC and MP3 formats. You might want to use the MP3 encoder for other reasons, such as acquiring more control over the compression parameters and gaining compatibility with other applications and players that support MP3.

The MP3 encoder offers four choices for the Setting pop-up menu in the Importing Preferences dialog:

- ✔ **Good Quality (128 Kbps):** This is certainly fine for audio books, comedy records, and old scratchy records. You might even want to use a lower bit rate for voice recordings.

- ✔ **High Quality (160 Kbps):** Most people consider this high enough for most popular music, but we go higher with our music.

- ✔ **Higher Quality (192 Kbps):** This one's high enough for just about all types of music.

- ✔ **Custom:** To fine-tune the MP3 encoder settings, select the Custom setting. Customizing your MP3 settings increases the quality of the sound and keeps file size low.

The MP3 encoder offers a bunch of choices in its custom settings dialog (see Figure 18-3):

- ✔ **Stereo Bit Rate:** This pop-up menu's choices are measured in kilobits per second; select a higher bit rate for higher quality, which increases the file size. The most common bit rate for MP3 files you find on the Web is 128 Kbps. Lower bit rates are more appropriate for voice recordings or sound effects.

We recommend at least 192 Kbps for most music, and we use 320 Kbps, the maximum setting, for songs that we play on our iPods.

✔ **Use Variable Bit Rate Encoding (VBR):** This option helps keep file size down, but quality might be affected. VBR varies the number of bits used to store the music depending on the complexity of the sound. If you select the Highest setting from the Quality pop-up menu for VBR, iTunes encodes at up to the maximum bit rate of 320 Kbps in sections of songs where the sound is complex enough to require a high bit rate. Meanwhile, iTunes keeps the rest of the song at a lower bit rate to save file space. The lower limit is set by the rate that you select in the Stereo Bit Rate pop-up menu.

Some audiophiles swear by VBR, but others don't ever use it. We use it only when importing at low bit rates, and we set VBR to its highest quality setting.

Although your iPod plays VBR-encoded MP3 music, other MP3 players might not support VBR.

✔ **Sample Rate:** This pop-up menu enables you to select the *sample rate* (the number of times per second that the sound waveform is captured digitally). Higher sample rates yield higher quality sound and larger file sizes. However, never use a higher sample rate than the rate used for the source — CDs use a 44.100 kHz rate.

✔ **Channels:** This pop-up menu enables you to choose how you want the music to play through speakers; in stereo or mono. Stereo, which offers two channels of music for left and right speakers, is the norm for music. Monaural (mono) recordings take up half the space of stereo recordings when digitized. Choose the Auto setting to have iTunes use the appropriate setting for the music.

✔ **Stereo mode:** This pop-up menu enables you to select Normal or Joint Stereo. Normal mode is just what you think it is — normal stereo. Select the Joint Stereo setting to make the file smaller by removing information that's identical in both channels of a stereo recording, using only one channel for that information while the other channel carries unique information. At bit rates of 128 Kbps and below, this mode can actually improve the sound quality. However, we typically don't use the Joint Stereo mode when using a high-quality bit rate.

✔ **Smart Encoding Adjustments:** This option, when selected, tells iTunes to analyze your MP3 encoding settings and music source and to change your settings as needed to maximize the quality of the encoded files.

✔ **Filter Frequencies Below 10 Hz:** This option, when selected, filters out low frequency sounds. Frequencies below 10 Hz are hard to hear, and most people don't notice if they're missing. Filtering inaudible frequencies helps reduce the file size with little or no perceived loss in quality. However, we think selecting this option and removing the low-frequency sounds detracts from the overall feeling of the music, and we prefer not to filter frequencies.

```
                    MP3 Encoder
    Stereo Bit Rate: [ 192 kbps       ◆]
              □ Use Variable Bit Rate Encoding (VBR)
         Quality: [ Medium           ]
    (With VBR enabled, bit rate settings are used for a guaranteed minimum bit rate.)
    Sample Rate: [ Auto              ◆]
       Channels: [ Auto              ◆]
    Stereo Mode: [ Normal            ◆]
         ☑ Smart Encoding Adjustments
         ☑ Filter Frequencies Below 10 Hz

    ( Use Default Settings )          ( Cancel )  ( OK )
```

Figure 18-3:
Customize
the settings
for the MP3
encoder.

Changing AIFF and WAV encoder settings

We recommend that you use the AIFF, WAV, or Apple Lossless encoders for songs from audio CDs if you intend to burn your own audio CDs with the music. You get the best possible quality with these encoders because the music isn't compressed with a lossy algorithm. The Apple Lossless encoder (which is automatic and offers no settings to change) reduces file size to about 60–70 percent of the size of AIFF or WAV versions. However, AIFF or WAV files are preferable for use with digital sound-editing programs, and they offer settings that you can change, such as the number of channels (Stereo or Mono) and the sampling rate.

The AIFF and WAV formats have technical differences, but the only major difference in storing and playing music is that AIFF is the standard for Mac applications and computers, and WAV is the standard for PC applications and computers.

You can import music with AIFF or WAV at the highest possible quality and then convert the music files to a lesser-quality format for use in your iPod.

AIFF and WAV files take up huge amounts of hard drive space (about 10MB per minute), and although you can play them on your iPod, they take up way too much space and battery power to be convenient for anyone but the most discerning audiophile who can afford multiple iPods. You can handle these large files by adding another hard drive or by backing up portions of your music library onto other media, such as a DVD-R (which can hold 4.7GB). However, if multiple hard drives and backup scenarios sound like unwanted hassles, use the AAC or MP3 encoders to compress files so that they take up less space on your hard drive.

The AIFF encoder and the WAV encoder offer similar custom settings dialogs; the AIFF Encoder dialog is shown in Figure 18-4. The pop-up menus offer settings for Sample Rate, Sample Size, and Channels. You can select the Auto setting for all three pop-up menus, and iTunes automatically detects the proper sample rate, size, and channels from the source. If you select a specific setting, such as the Stereo setting in the Channels pop-up menu, iTunes imports the music in stereo, regardless of the source. Audio CDs typically sample at a rate of 44.1000 kHz, with a sample size of 16 bits, and with stereo channels.

Figure 18-4:
The
Channels
pop-up
menu in the
AIFF
encoder
custom
settings
allows you
to import
regardless
of the
source.

The Sample Rate pop-up menu for AIFF and WAV offers more choices than for AAC, down to a very low sample rate of 8.000 kHz, which is suitable only for voice recordings.

Importing Audio Books and Voice Recordings in iTunes

Audio books are available from Audible (www.audible.com) and from the iTunes store in a special format that doesn't require any further compression, but you can also import audio books, spoken-word titles, comedy CDs, and other voice recordings in the MP3 format.

If the recording has any music at all or requires close listening to stereo channels (such as a Firesign Theatre or Monty Python CD), treat the entire recording as music and skip this section. ("Nudge-nudge, wink-wink. Sorry! Everything you know is wrong!")

By fine-tuning the import settings for voice recordings and sound effects, you can save a significant amount of space without reducing quality. We recommend the following settings depending on your choice of encoder:

✔ **AAC encoder:** AAC allows you to get away with an even lower bit rate than MP3 to achieve the same quality, thereby saving more space. We recommend a bit rate as low as 80 Kbps for sound effects and voice recordings. Use the Optimize for Voice option to filter the sound to favor the human voice.

✔ **MP3 encoder:** Use a low bit rate (such as 96 Kbps). You might also want to reduce the sample rate to 22.050 kHz for voice recordings. Filter frequencies below 10 Hz because voice recordings don't need such frequencies.

Converting Songs to a Different Encoder Format in iTunes

Converting a song from one format to another is useful if you want to use one format for one purpose, such as burning a CD, and a second format for another task, such as playing on your iPod. It's also useful for converting uncompressed songs or podcasts that were created in GarageBand (or a similar audio editing application) and exported or copied to iTunes.

Converting a song from one compressed format to another is possible (say from AAC to MP3), but you might not like the results. When you convert a compressed file to another compressed format, iTunes compresses the music *twice,* reducing the quality of the sound. You get the best results by starting with an uncompressed song that was imported using either the AIFF or WAV format, and then converting that song to the compressed AAC or MP3 format.

You can tell what format a song is in by selecting it and choosing File⇨Get Info. Then click the Summary tab to see the song's format. You might want to keep track of formats by creating CD-AIFF-version and iPod-MP3-version playlists for different formats.

To convert a song to another encoding format, follow these steps:

1. **Choose iTunes⇨Preferences on a Mac, or choose Edit⇨Preferences on a Windows PC, and then click the Importing tab.**

   The Importing Preferences dialog appears, allowing you to make changes to the encoding format and its settings.

2. **Select the encoding format that you want to convert the song into from the Import Using pop-up menu; in the custom settings dialog that appears, select the settings for that encoder.**

   For example, if you're converting songs in the AIFF format to the MP3 format, choose MP3 Encoder from the Import Using pop-up menu, and then select the settings that you want in the MP3 Encoder dialog that appears.

3. **Click OK to accept the settings for your chosen format.**

4. **In the iTunes window, select the song(s) that you want to convert, and then choose Advanced⇨Convert Selection.**

   The encoding format that you chose in Step 2 appears on the menu: Convert Selection to MP3, Convert Selection to AAC, Convert Selection to AIFF, or Convert Selection to WAV. Choose the appropriate menu operation to perform the conversion. When the conversion is complete, the newly converted version of the song appears in your iTunes library (with the same artist name and song name, so it's easy to find). iTunes doesn't delete the original version — both are stored in your music library.

If you convert songs obtained from the Internet, you may find MP3 songs with bit rates as low as 128 Kbps, and choosing a higher stereo bit rate doesn't improve the quality — it only wastes space.

The automatic copy-and-convert operation can be useful for converting an entire music library to another format — hold down the Option key on a Mac, or the Alt key in Windows, and choose Advanced⇨Convert Selection, and all the songs copy and convert automatically. If you have a library of AIFF tunes, you can quickly copy and convert them to AAC or MP3 in one step, and then assign the AIFF songs to the AIFF-associated playlists for burning CDs, and MP3 or AAC songs to MP3 or AAC playlists that you intend to copy to your iPod.

Chapter 19

Fine-Tuning the Sound

. . . .

. . . .

Sound is difficult to describe. Harder still to describe is how to adjust sound to your liking. Maybe you want more oomph in the lows, or you prefer highs that are as clear as a bell. Even if you've never mastered a stereo system beyond adjusting the bass and treble controls, the volume control, and the loudness button, you can use this limited knowledge of sound to quickly fine-tune the sound in iTunes, as we show in this chapter.

If you are a discerning listener, you might want to change the equalizer settings in iTunes and perhaps even use different settings for different songs. With iTunes, you have to change those settings only once. This chapter shows you how to make presets for each song in your library so that iTunes remembers them. What's more, you can use the iTunes settings on your iPod, which also offers an equalizer. This chapter shows you how.

Adjusting the Sound in iTunes

Some songs are just too loud. We don't mean too loud stylistically, as in thrash metal with screeching guitars; we mean too loud for your ears when you're wearing headphones or so loud that the music sounds distorted in your speakers. And some songs are just too soft, and you have to turn up the volume to hear them, then turn it down to hear other songs. Is there a way to set the volume in advance for a certain song or album?

Of course there is — you can set the overall volume in advance in the song information dialog by choosing File⇨Get Info. You can also make all the songs in your library play at the same volume by leveling the volume with the Sound Check option.

You can change the volume level at any time by sliding the volume slider in the upper-left section of the iTunes window. The maximum volume of the iTunes volume slider is the maximum set for the computer's sound in the Sound pane of System Preferences, as we describe in Chapter 16.

Setting the volume in advance for songs

With songs that you already know are too loud (or too soft), consider setting the volume for those songs (or certain albums) in advance, so that they always play with that volume adjustment.

To adjust the overall volume of a particular song in advance, so that it always plays at that setting, perform the following steps:

1. **Click a song to select it.**

2. **Choose File⇨Get Info.**

   The song information dialog appears.

3. **Click the Options tab.**

   Drag the Volume Adjustment slider left or right to adjust the volume lower or higher, as shown in Figure 19-1. You can do this while playing the song.

Figure 19-1:
Adjust the volume setting for a song here.

To set the volume for more than one song at once, you can select an entire album in iTunes Browse view or select multiple songs; then choose Get Info to open the Multiple Song Information dialog. The Volume Adjustment slider appears on the bottom-right corner of the dialog. Drag the slider as described earlier to set the volume adjustment for the entire album of songs or the selected songs.

Enhancing the sound

Audiophiles and sound purists frown on it, but many of you probably use the loudness button on home or car stereos to enhance the sound. iTunes offers a similar option — *Sound Enhancer* — that improves the depth of the sound by enhancing the high and low frequencies. Audiophiles and sound purists would most likely use the equalizer to boost frequencies, but you can use this brute force method to enhance the sound.

To turn on Sound Enhancer, choose Preferences (from the iTunes menu on a Mac/Edit menu on a Windows PC). Click the Audio button to show the Audio dialog, as shown in Figure 19-2.

Figure 19-2: Use Sound Enhancer and Sound Check options in the Audio preferences.

To increase the sound enhancement (boosting the high and low frequencies), drag the Sound Enhancer slider to the right toward the High setting. This is similar to pressing the loudness button on a stereo or the equivalent of boosting the treble (high) and bass (low) frequencies in the equalizer (described in

"Equalize It in iTunes," later in this chapter). To decrease the high and low frequencies, drag the slider to the left toward the Low setting. The middle setting is neutral, adding no enhancement — the same as turning off the Sound Enhancer by clearing its check box.

Sound-checking the iTunes volume

Because music CDs are mastered differently, there can be discrepancies in volume between them. Some CDs play more loudly than others; occasionally, individual tracks within a CD are louder than others.

You can standardize the volume level of all the songs in your iTunes music library with the Sound Check option. Hey, musicians do a sound check before every performance to check the volume of microphones and instruments and its effect on the listening environment. The aptly named Sound Check option in iTunes allows you to do a sound check on your tunes to bring them all in line, volume-wise. This option has the added benefit of applying the same volume adjustment when you play the songs back on your iPod, as described in the upcoming section, "Sound-checking the iPod volume." However, be prepared for the sound check operation to take a bit of time, perhaps even several hours for a very large music library.

To ensure that all the songs in your library ripped from CDs play at the same volume level, follow these steps:

1. **Drag the iTunes volume slider to set the overall volume for iTunes.**

   The volume slider is in the top-left corner of the iTunes window, under the Play button.

2. **Choose iTunes⇨Preferences on a Mac/Edit⇨Preferences on a Windows PC.**

   The Preferences dialog appears.

3. **Click the Audio button.**

   The Audio preferences dialog appears; refer to Figure 19-2.

4. **Select the Sound Check check box.**

   iTunes sets the volume level for all songs according to the level of the iTunes volume slider.

5. **Click OK.**

   The Sound Check option sets a volume adjustment based on the volume slider on all the songs so that they play at approximately the same volume.

Sound-checking the iPod volume

You can take advantage of volume leveling in your iTunes music library with the Sound Check option, and then turn Sound Check on or off on your iPod by choosing Sound Check in the iPod Settings menu.

This is useful especially when using your iPod in a car (or when jogging while listening to headphones) because you don't want to have to reach for the volume on the iPod or on the car stereo every time a song comes on that's too loud. However, the Sound Check option on your iPod works only if you've also set the Sound Check option in your iTunes library. (Audio purists frown on volume leveling as much as they frown on sound enhancement, preferring to adjust the volume only when they need to.)

In iTunes, select the Sound Check option as described in the preceding section, "Sound-checking the iTunes volume." Then, on the iPod, choose Settings⇨ Sound Check⇨On from the main menu to turn on the Sound Check feature. To turn it off, choose Settings⇨Sound Check⇨Off.

Equalize It in iTunes

The iTunes equalizer (EQ) allows you to fine-tune the specific sound spectrum frequencies in a more precise way than with the typical bass and treble controls you find on home stereos and powered speakers. (See the sidebar on equalizers, later in this chapter.) You can use the equalizer to improve or enhance the sound coming through a particular stereo system and speakers. With the equalizer settings, you can customize playback for different musical genres, listening environments, or speakers.

You might want to pick entirely different equalizer settings for car speakers, home speakers, and headphones. Fortunately, you can save your settings, as described in the upcoming "Saving your own presets" section.

To see the iTunes equalizer, click the Equalizer button, which is the icon with three mixer faders on the bottom-right side of the iTunes window. (On a Mac, you can also choose Window⇨Equalizer.)

Adjusting the preamp volume

The *preamp* in your stereo is the component that offers a volume control that applies to all frequencies equally.

What's the frequency, Kenneth? The Equalizer opportunity

The Beach Boys were right when they sang "Good Vibrations" because that's what music is — the sensation of hearing audible vibrations conveyed to the ear by a medium such as air. The *frequency* of vibrations per second is how we measure pitch. The waves can oscillate slowly and produce low-pitched sounds, or they can oscillate rapidly and produce high-pitched sounds. The *amplitude* is a measurement of the amount of fluctuation in air pressure — therefore, amplitude is perceived as loudness.

When you turn up the bass or treble on a stereo system, you are actually increasing the volume, or intensity, of certain frequencies while the music is playing. The equalizer lets you fine-tune the sound spectrum frequencies in a more precise way than with bass and treble controls. It increases or decreases specific frequencies of the sound to raise or lower highs, lows, and midrange tones. The equalizer does this with several band-pass filters all centered at different frequencies, and each filter offers controllable *gain* (the ability to boost the volume).

On more sophisticated stereo systems, an equalizer with a bar graph display replaces the bass and treble controls. An equalizer (*EQ* in audio-speak) enables you to fine-tune the specific sound spectrum frequencies, which gives you far greater control than merely adjusting the bass or treble controls.

Volume knobs generally go up to 10 — except, of course, for Spinal Tap's preamps, which go to 11.

The iTunes equalizer, as shown in Figure 19-3, offers a Preamp slider on the far-left side. You can increase or decrease the volume in 3-decibel (dB) increments up to 12 dB. *Decibels* are units that measure the intensity (or volume) of the frequencies. You can adjust the volume while playing the music to hear the result right away.

Figure 19-3: Use the Preamp slider to adjust the volume across all frequencies.

You might want to increase the preamp volume for songs recorded too softly, or decrease it for songs that are so loud you can hear distortion. If you want to make any adjustments to frequencies, you might need to adjust the preamp volume first if volume adjustment is needed, and then move on to the specific frequencies.

Adjusting frequencies

You can adjust frequencies in the iTunes equalizer by clicking and dragging sliders that look like mixing-board faders.

The horizontal values across the equalizer represent the spectrum of human hearing. The deepest frequency ("Daddy sang bass") is 32 hertz (Hz); the midrange frequencies are 250 Hz and 500 Hz, and the higher frequencies go from 1 kilohertz (kHz) to 16 kHz (treble).

The vertical values on each bar represent decibels, which measure the intensity of each frequency. Increase or decrease the frequencies at 3 dB increments by clicking and dragging the sliders up and down. You can drag the sliders to adjust the frequencies while the music is playing, to hear the effect immediately.

Using iTunes' presets

iTunes offers *presets,* which are equalizer settings made in advance and saved by name. You can quickly switch settings without having to make changes to each frequency slider. iTunes comes with more than 20 presets of the most commonly used equalizer settings, for each musical genre from classical to rock. You can then assign the equalizer settings to a specific song or set of songs in your iTunes library.

These settings copy to your iPod along with the songs when you update your iPod.

To use an equalizer preset, click the pop-up menu in the Equalizer window at the top of the equalizer, as shown in Figure 19-4, to select a preset. If a song is playing, you hear the effect in the sound immediately after choosing the preset.

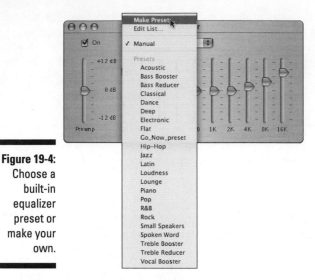

Figure 19-4:
Choose a
built-in
equalizer
preset or
make your
own.

Saving your own presets

Don't settle for Apple's presets — you can create your own equalizer presets.
When you make the changes that you want to the frequencies, the pop-up
menu automatically switches to Manual when you drag the sliders to change
the frequencies. Then choose the Make Preset option from the pop-up menu
(refer to Figure 19-4) to save your changes. The Make Preset dialog appears,
as shown in Figure 19-5. Give your new preset a descriptive name. The name
appears in the pop-up menu from that point on — your very own preset.

Figure 19-5:
Save your
adjustments
as your own
preset.

| Make Preset |
| New Preset Name: |
| Car stereo |
| Cancel   OK |

You can rename or delete the presets by choosing the Edit List option from
the pop-up menu, which displays the Edit Presets dialog for renaming or
deleting presets, as shown in Figure 19-6. Click Rename to rename a preset,
click Delete to delete a preset, and click Done when you're finished editing
the list.

Figure 19-6:
Rename or
delete
presets.

You can rename or delete any preset, including the ones supplied with iTunes (which is useful if you want to recall a preset by another name).

Assigning equalizer presets to songs

One reason why you go to the trouble of setting equalizer presets is to assign the presets to individual songs. The next time you play the song, it will use the equalizer preset that you assigned.

When you transfer the songs to your iPod, the preset assignments stay assigned to them, and you can choose whether to use the preset assignments when playing the songs on your iPod.

Assign an equalizer preset to a song or set of songs by following these steps:

1. **Choose Edit➪View Options.**

   The View Options dialog appears, as shown in Figure 19-7.

Figure 19-7:
Show the
equalizer
column to
assign
presets to
songs.

2. **Select the Equalizer check box and then click OK.**

    The Equalizer column appears in the song list in the iTunes window.

    You can combine Steps 1 and 2 by Control-clicking any song list column heading on a Mac (or right-clicking on a Windows PC), and then choosing Equalizer from the shortcut menu that appears.

3. **Locate a song in the song list and scroll the song list horizontally to see the Equalizer column, as shown in Figure 19-8.**

4. **Choose a preset from the pop-up menu in the Equalizer column.**

    The Equalizer column has a tiny pop-up menu that allows you to assign any preset to a song.

Figure 19-8: Select a song and scroll the iTunes song list to see the Equalizer column.

When you transfer songs with presets to the iPod, the presets can be used for song playback using the iPod equalizer.

Equalize It in Your iPod

You leave the back-road bliss of the country to get on the freeway, and now the music in your car doesn't have enough bass to give you that thumping rhythm you need to dodge other cars. What can you do? Without endangering anybody, you can pull over and select one of the iPod equalizer presets, such as Bass Booster.

Yes, your iPod also has a built-in equalizer. Like the iTunes equalizer, the iPod built-in equalizer modifies the volume of the frequencies of the sound. And although you don't have sliders for faders like the iTunes equalizer, you do get the same long list of presets to suit the type of music or the type of environment. You can use the iPod equalizer for on-the-fly adjustments.

The iPod equalizer uses a bit more battery power when it is turned on, so you might have less playing time on your iPod battery.

You can also use the iTunes equalizer to improve or enhance the sound, assigning presets to each song and then updating your iPod.

Choosing an EQ preset on your iPod

To select an iPod equalizer preset, choose Settings from the main menu and then choose EQ from the Settings menu. The EQ is set to Off until you select one of the presets.

Each EQ preset offers a different balance of frequencies designed to enhance the sound in certain ways. For example, Bass Booster increases the volume of the low (bass) frequencies; Treble Booster does the same to the high (treble) frequencies.

To see what a preset actually does to the frequencies, open the iTunes equalizer and select the same preset. The faders in the equalizer display show you exactly what the preset does.

The Off setting turns off the iPod equalizer — no presets are used, not even one you assigned in iTunes. You have to choose an EQ preset to turn on the iPod equalizer.

Applying the iTunes EQ presets

When you assign a preset to the song using iTunes, the iPod uses the assigned EQ preset from iTunes even when you choose an EQ preset on the iPod. That's right — the assigned EQ preset from iTunes takes precedence over the preset in the iPod.

Here's a workaround, though. If you know in advance that you need to use specific presets for certain songs, assign presets to the songs in iTunes before copying the songs to the iPod. If, on the other hand, you don't want the songs fixed to use a certain preset, *don't* assign presets to the songs in iTunes. You can then experiment with the presets in the iPod to get better playback in different listening environments.

To assign built-in or custom presets to songs with the iTunes equalizer, see "Assigning equalizer presets to songs," earlier in this chapter.

After assigning a preset to a song in iTunes, you turn on the iPod equalizer by choosing any EQ setting (other than Off), and the iPod uses the song's preset for playback.

Chapter 20

Recording and Editing Sound

*Y*ou can find millions of songs on the Internet, and some digital recordings of songs might even be good enough to please audiophiles. With so many songs available in the iTunes Music Store, you might not want to spend a lot of time recording and digitizing the hits from your record collection, or even the B-sides and album cuts. Most likely those songs are also available from the online store in digital form, ready to play.

However, you might have sounds that were never released on CD or made available to the public. Rare record collectors and tape archivists — you know who you are — have recordings that you just can't find on the Internet or on CD, and if you create your own music, how do you get that stuff into your iTunes library so that you can burn a CD or include the songs on your iPod?

This chapter explains what you need to record and digitize sounds from other sources, such as tape players and turntables, and store the digital recordings in your iTunes library. It also shows you how to set the start and stop times of songs in your iTunes library, which is a trick you can use to edit the beginnings and endings of songs.

All the applications described in this chapter are commercially available for downloading from the Internet. Some are free to use, some are free for a limited time before you have to pay, and some require cash up front. Nevertheless, all are worth checking out if you have sounds you want to put into iTunes.

Recording Records, Tapes, and Analog Sources

Sound can be brought directly into your computer from a sound system or home stereo that offers a stereo audio output connection (such as Tape Out), or even directly from a cassette player or microphone. If you have old vinyl records with music that can't be found anymore, on CD or otherwise, you can convert the music to digital by using a phonograph connected to a stereo system with a Tape Out connection.

Songs already converted to digital can be copied into iTunes directly without any recording procedure. For example, MP3 CDs are easy to import. Because they're essentially data CDs, simply insert them into your CD-ROM drive, open the CD in Windows or the Mac Finder, and drag and drop the MP3 song files into the iTunes window, as we describe in Chapter 5. Downloaded song files are even easier — just drag and drop the files into iTunes. If you drag a folder or CD icon, all the audio files that it contains are added to your iTunes library.

Before recording sound into your computer, be sure that you have enough disk space to record the audio in an uncompressed form (which is best for highest quality). If you're recording an hour of high-quality music, you need about 600MB of disk space to record it.

Connecting and setting up audio input

Most computers offer a Line In connection that accepts a cable with a stereo mini-plug. You can connect any kind of mono or stereo audio source, such as an amplifier or preamp, a CD or DVD player, or an all-in-one stereo system that offers recording through a Tape Out or similar connection.

Find the Line Out or Tape Out connection in your stereo system, and connect a cable that uses RCA-type left and right stereo plugs or a stereo mini-plug to this connection. See Chapter 14 for more information about audio cables. Connect the stereo mini-plug to your computer's Line In connection. You can then record anything that plays on your home stereo into your computer.

If your computer doesn't offer a Line In connection, you can purchase a Universal Serial Bus (USB) audio input device, such as the Griffin iMic (www. griffintechnology.com).

When recording from a phonograph (turntable for vinyl records), the phonograph must either include an amplifier or be connected to an amplifier in order to raise the signal to line levels and apply proper equalization curves.

After connecting the audio source to your computer, set the audio input for your computer and adjust the volume for recording.

On a Mac, follow these steps:

1. **Choose System Preferences from the Apple menu or the Dock, and then click the Sound icon.**

2. **Click the Input tab.**

   The Input tab displays the sound input preferences, as shown in Figure 20-1.

3. **Choose Line In from the list of input devices.**

   Use Line In to record into your computer. The alternative is to use the built-in microphone, which is useful for recording live performances — but not for records or tapes because it also picks up any noise in the room.

Figure 20-1: Set audio input to Line In and adjust the input volume.

4. **Adjust the volume for the Line In input.**

   To set the volume level for sound input, start playing the record, tape, or source of sound. As it plays, watch the input level meter. As the volume gets louder, the oblong purple dots seem to light up with highlights, from left to right. To adjust the volume, drag the slider underneath the input level meter. If all the dots are highlighted all the time, you're way too *hot* (studio tech talk for being too loud). If the dots are not highlighted at all, you're way too *low*. (For some reason, the studio techs don't say *cool* or *cold* — just *low*.) You want the dots to be highlighted about three-fourths of the way across from left to right for optimal input volume.

5. **Quit System Preferences by choosing System Preferences⇨Quit System Preferences, or by clicking the red button in the top-left corner of the window.**

On a Windows PC, you must have a Line In connection and an audio card driver that controls it. Some PCs are equipped only with microphone-controlling drivers, and some offer both Line In and microphone input. If you have the appropriate hardware, follow these steps:

1. **Open the sound properties control panel.**

   In Windows XP, select Control Panel from the Start menu, and click the Sounds and Audio Devices icon. The Sounds and Audio Devices Properties window appears. Depending on your version of Windows, you might have a Control Panel specific for the audio driver and hardware, or Windows Mixer, or the Sound and Audio Devices control panel. You can open the appropriate control program by right-clicking the small speaker icon in your system tray, and choosing Adjust Audio Properties. In Windows Mixer, choose Options⇨Properties.

2. **Click the Audio tab in the row of tabs along the top of the window.**

   As shown in Figure 20-2, the Sounds and Audio Devices Properties window offers sections for sound playback, sound recording, and MIDI (Musical Instrument Digital Interface) music playback.

3. **Choose the input device for sound recording.**

   Use the drop-down list in the Sound recording section to choose the input device, which is the hardware for controlling the Line In connection or microphone. In Windows Mixer, select Recording under Adjust volume and then turn on the option for Line-In or Microphone to get to the Recording Control panel.

4. **Click the Volume button in the Sound recording section to set the input volume.**

   The Volume window offers a volume slider. Drag this slider to set the input volume (to the left is low, to the right is high).

5. **Click OK to finish and save your settings.**

After setting up the audio input and adjusting the volume, you need to launch an application that records sound.

Figure 20-2:
Set audio
input and
adjust the
volume of
input for a
Windows
PC.

Choosing a sound editing application

The Sound Studio application lets you record and digitize directly to your hard disk on a Mac running OS X. You can download a copy free from Felt Tip Software (www.felttip.com/products/soundstudio). You can then use it for two weeks before having to pay $49.99 for it.

Toast 6 Titanium from Roxio (www.roxio.com) for Mac OS X includes the CD Spin Doctor 2 application for recording sounds. CD Spin Doctor offers a Noise Reducer option to select filters for noise reduction: *de-click* removes loud distortions, which occur frequently with vinyl records; *de-crackle* removes surface crackling, which happens often with well-played vinyl records; and *de-hiss* removes the hissing noise that occurs with many different analog sources, including records and tapes. Roxio also offers a Windows application, Easy Media Creator 7.5, which includes the LP and Tape Assistant for streamlining the process of converting classic analog recordings. You can apply similar cleaning effects as CD Spin Doctor to easily remove noise, pops, and clicks from old recordings.

Modifying Songs in iTunes

Although iTunes was never meant to be a song editing application, it offers a simple control over the starting and stopping points for playing back a song. You can use this feature to cut out unwanted *intros* and *outros* of a song, such as announcers and audience applause. You can also use it in conjunction with the Convert feature to split a track into multiple tracks.

To do more significant modifications or editing, use the applications described in "Recording Records, Tapes, and Analog Sources," earlier in this chapter, or use GarageBand on a Mac.

Setting the start and stop points in a song

iTunes will play only a portion of a song if you specify start and stop times within the song. To set the start and/or stop points in a song, select the song and choose File⇨Get Info; then click Options to show the dialog that lets you specify the start and stop times, as shown in Figure 20-3.

Try (Just A Little Bit Harder) (Live)

| Summary | Info | **Options** | Artwork |

Volume Adjustment: ——————⬤——————
         −100%   None   +100%

Equalizer Preset: None ▢

My Rating: ★★★★★

☑ Start Time: 0:30

☐ Stop Time: 8:15.978

Previous   Next   Cancel   OK

Figure 20-3: Set the start time for a song.

Click inside the Start Time field to set the start time; for example, in Figure 20-3, we set the Start Time to 0:30 (30 seconds). Click inside the Stop Time field to set the stop time. The time is in minutes, seconds, and hundredths of a second (decimal) — 8:15.978 is 8 minutes and 15.978 seconds.

To determine with accuracy the time for the start and stop points, play the song and look in the Status pane at the top-center part of the iTunes window for the Elapsed Time. You can drag the slider in the Status pane to move quickly through the song and find the exact times for the start and stop points you want to set. *Note:* If you click Elapsed Time in the Status pane, it toggles to Remaining Time; click it again for Total Time, and click it once more to see Elapsed Time again.

iTunes plays only the part of the song between the start and stop times. You can use this feature to your advantage because when you convert the song, iTunes converts only the part of the song between the start and stop times.

Splitting a track into multiple tracks

You might have a CD that was created with all the songs combined into one track, or you might have recorded an entire side of a vinyl record or cassette tape into one sound file. Either way, you probably want to separate the songs into separate tracks in iTunes.

The best way to split a long track into smaller tracks is to open the sound file in a sound editing program that lets you select sections and save them separately, as we describe in "Recording Records, Tapes, and Analog Sources," earlier in this chapter.

However, you can also separate a track into smaller tracks in iTunes, as long as you use the AIFF format at first. Follow these steps:

1. **Before ripping a CD or importing a sound file, set the encoder in your importing preferences to AIFF.**

   Choose iTunes⇨Preferences on a Mac/Edit⇨Preferences on a Windows PC. Click Importing, and set your Importing encoder to AIFF (full quality).

2. **Rip the CD track into iTunes or import an AIFF sound file into iTunes.**

   Because you set the importing preferences to AIFF, the CD track is imported into iTunes as AIFF at full quality. You want to do this because you're going to convert it in iTunes later, and you need the uncompressed version to convert. Use a song name to identify this track as a long track with multiple tracks — for example, call it *side one* or something like that.

3. **Change your Importing preferences to AAC or MP3. (We use AAC mostly.)**

   Choose iTunes⇨Preferences on a Mac/Edit⇨Preferences on a Windows PC. Click Importing, and set your Importing encoder to AAC or MP3. Now you're ready to convert the song segments from the long track.

4. **Select the song in iTunes and choose File⇨Get Info.**

   The song information dialog appears.

5. **Click Options to show the Start Time and Stop Time fields.**

   You can set the start and stop times for the song (refer to Figure 20-3).

6. **Define the Start Time and Stop Time for the first song in the long track, and click OK.**

   Play the song and look in the Status pane at the top-center part of the iTunes window for the Elapsed Time. You can drag the slider in the Status pane to move quickly through the song and find the exact times for the start and stop points you want to set. For example, if the first song were exactly 3 minutes and 12 seconds, you would define the first section to start at 0:00 and play to 3:12. After setting the start and stop times, click OK to close the song information window.

7. **Convert the defined segment of the long track from AIFF to AAC or MP3.**

   Select the long track *(side one)* and choose Advanced⇨Convert Selection to AAC (or Advanced⇨Convert Selection to MP3 if you chose the MP3 encoder in Step 6). iTunes converts only the section of the song defined by the Start Time and Stop Time fields that you set in Step 5, and creates a new song track in the AAC or MP3 format (depending on your choice in Step 3). iTunes converts the uncompressed AIFF segment into the compressed AAC or MP3 format.

8. **Change the song name of the newly converted track to the actual song name.**

   The converted section of the long track still has the same name *(side one)*. Change its name by clicking inside the song name in the iTunes song list, or by choosing File⇨Get Info, clicking the Info tab, and clicking inside the Name field. You can also enter a track number in the Track field. The converted song starts and stops as you specified in Step 5; because it's also converted to AAC or MP3, it's ready for use in your iTunes library and in your iPod.

9. **Repeat Steps 4–8 for each song segment.**

   Repeat these steps, selecting the long track *(side one)* each time and setting a new start and stop time for each new song, and then changing each newly converted song's name.

10. **When finished, delete the long track in AIFF format.**

    Delete the long track *(side one)* by selecting it and pressing Delete/Backspace. You don't need it anymore if you converted all the segments to separate songs.

Chapter 21

Enhancing Your Music Library

....

....

*Y*our music library is the center of your iPod and iTunes world — your control console for playing Master DJ at the party, your basement studio for burning CDs, and your archive of the most important music in the universe. Of course you would want to enhance it in any way possible.

In this chapter, we cover ways to enhance your iTunes library. We cover downloading music from online sources other than the iTunes Music Store as well as playing Web radio streams on your computer using iTunes. We also describe how to get *podcasts,* which are similar to syndicated radio shows but can be downloaded into iTunes and listened to at your convenience via computer and iPod.

Downloading Music from Other Sources

The iTunes Music Store isn't the only place to get music online for your iPod. Other digital music services such as Napster 2.0, Rhapsody, BuyMusic.com, MusicNow, and MusicMatch also offer music you can purchase.

iTunes can store MP3, AIFF, Apple Lossless, and WAV audio files as well as AAC audio files. If you have Windows Media Player version 9 or newer installed on your PC, iTunes can also convert unprotected Windows Media audio (WMA) files, but not the copy-protected music available for purchase from online services. See Chapter 5 for details on how to import music files into iTunes.

If you buy copy-protected music in the Windows Media format or other protected format, you can always burn a CD of the music and then rip the CD into iTunes. It's a good practice to burn a CD of music that you buy online to have a backup copy in mint condition.

Music sources for iTunes and MusicMatch Jukebox

You can find music in the following types of places online:

✔ **From the source:** New artists and musicians, and even legendary bands, are increasingly offering a bit of music on their own Web sites for free. This is the best source of free music because it's legal and benefits the artists directly — they want you to listen and tell your friends. Examples include The Zen Tricksters (www.zentricksters.com/home.html), Little Feat (www.littlefeat.net), and the Flying Other Brothers (www.flyingotherbros.com).

✔ **Protected music:** Online music stores and services offer protected music for sale. Windows Media-protected songs and other protected formats can't be imported into iTunes because they're tied to the computer and player used for the format. However, you can burn a CD with the music (using a different player, such as Windows Media Player) and then rip the CD into iTunes. You lose no quality because burning a CD doesn't reduce the music's quality, and ripping the CD in iTunes doesn't reduce the music's quality if you use the AIFF format or the Apple Lossless encoder (or reduces quality only slightly if you use the AAC or MP3 encoders with the same or higher bit rate — see Chapter 18 for information about setting the AAC or MP3 encoder bit rate). You can also rip the CD into MusicMatch Jukebox using the WAV or MP3 encoders.

✔ **Unprotected music:** Some online services and Web sites offer unprotected music for sale or for free downloading as part of a promotion for artists. These sites and services typically offer MP3 or Windows Media (WMA) unprotected files that you can import directly into iTunes or MusicMatch Jukebox. For example, Warp Records (a prominent electronic music label) hosts Bleep.com (www.warprecords.com/bleep), which offers downloads of ordinary MP3s from several independent labels, without copy protection, for about $1.35 a song.

✔ **Swapped music:** Free and "pirate" networks using peer-to-peer technology allow users to "swap" music for free. That is, people can trade music, but the network essentially allows them to download music from others on the network for free. Some networks require registration for (cough) joining them so that they maintain the semblance of privacy. Others operate outside the legal jurisdiction of the U.S. copyright law and the laws of other countries. We don't like to recommend these networks for two reasons. One, the music might be pirated (and we believe copyright owners deserve to have some control over distribution, even free distribution). Two, the music might not be the highest quality because of compromises (such as lower bit rates for MP3 files, which make for poorer quality music).

If you have a choice of music formats to download, choose the highest quality format that you can download (depending on the bandwidth of your Internet connection) — typically MP3 at the highest bit rate offered. iTunes can import AIFF, WAV, AAC, Apple Lossless, and MP3 files, and the Windows version of iTunes can also import WMA (unprotected) files if you have Windows Media Player version 9 installed on your PC. MusicMatch Jukebox can import WAV, MP3, or WMA (unprotected) files. You can use AIFF, WAV, AAC, Apple Lossless, or MP3 files in your iPod, and convert files from other formats into these formats as we describe in Chapter 18. If you're using MusicMatch, visit the companion Web site at www.dummies.com/go/ipod.

Playing Streaming Radio in iTunes

Radio stations from nearly every part of the world are broadcasting on the Internet. You can tune into Japan-A-Radio for the top 40 hits in Japan, or Cable Radio UK from the south coast of England, or Radio Darvish for Persian traditional music. You can also check out the local news and sports from your hometown, no matter where you are. You can listen to talk radio and music shows from all over the country and the world.

By *radio,* we really mean a *streaming broadcast;* of course, real radio stations make use of this technology to broadcast their programs over the Internet. A streaming broadcast sends audio to your computer in a protected stream of bits over the Internet. Your computer starts playing the stream as soon as the first set of bits arrive, and more sections are transferred while you listen, so that you hear it as a continual stream. Broadcasters can use this technology to continually transmit new content (like a radio station).

In addition, thousands of Web sites offer temporary streaming audio broadcasts all the time. A rock group on tour can offer a broadcast of a special concert, available for only one day. You might want to tune in weekly or monthly broadcasts such as high-tech talk shows, news programs, documentaries, or sporting events . . . the list is endless. You can even have access to private broadcasts such as corporate board meetings.

You can't record or save a song from a streamed broadcast without special software. Nor can you play a streaming broadcast on your iPod, except as a podcast. (See "Adding Podcasts" later in this chapter.) But you *can* add your favorite stations to your iTunes music library to tune in quickly and easily. You can also tune in any MP3 streaming broadcast if you know the Web address.

iTunes offers a set of links to radio stations on the Internet, so you might want to try these first. Follow these steps:

1. **Select the Radio option in the Source pane.**

   The iTunes window displays a list of categories of radio stations.

2. **Click the Refresh button to retrieve the latest radio stations.**

   More Web radio stations are added all the time. The Refresh button in the top-right corner of the iTunes window (taking the place of the Browse button) connects iTunes to the Internet to retrieve the latest list of radio stations for each category.

3. **Open a category to see a list of stations in that category.**

   Click the triangle next to a category name to open the list of radio streams in that category, as shown in Figure 21-1. Some large radio stations offer more than one stream.

4. **Select a stream and click the Play button.**

   To select a stream, click its name in the iTunes song list (actually, radio station list because you selected Radio in the Source pane). Then click the iTunes Play button. Within seconds, you hear live radio off the Web.

Figure 21-1:
Opening a list of radio streams in the International category.

If you use a dial-up modem connection to the Internet, you might want to choose a stream with a bit rate of less than 56 Kbps for best results. The Bit Rate column (refer to Figure 21-3) shows the bit rate for each stream.

iTunes creates a buffer for the audio stream so that you hear continuous playback with fewer Internet-related hiccups than most Web radio software. The buffer temporarily stores as much of the stream as possible, adding more of the stream to the end of the buffer as you play the audio in the buffer. If you hear stutters, gaps, or hiccups when playing a stream, set your buffer to a larger size by choosing iTunes⇨Preferences on a Mac/Edit⇨Preferences on a Windows PC. In the Preferences dialog, click the Advanced button and then choose a size from the Streaming Buffer Size pop-up menu. Your choices are Small, Medium, or Large (sorry, no X-Large).

Car radios offer preset stations activated by you pressing a button. Of course, you first need to tune into the station of your choice to set that button. You can save your radio station choices in an iTunes playlist, and the process is just as easy:

1. **Select a radio station stream.**

2. **Create a playlist or scroll the Source pane to an existing playlist.**

   See Chapter 9 to discover how to create a playlist.

3. **Drag the stream name over the playlist name.**

   iTunes places the stream name in the playlist with a broadcast icon next to it. You can click the playlist name and rearrange the playlist as you want, dragging stream names as you would drag song names.

Drag as many steams as you like to as many playlists as you like. Radio streams in your playlists play only if you are connected to the Internet.

To quickly create a playlist from selected radio streams, first select the streams just as you would select multiple songs, and then choose File⇨New Playlist from Selection.

You can tune into any broadcast on the Internet. All you need to know is the Web address, also known as the *URL* (Uniform Resource Locator), which is the global address of documents and other resources on the Web. You can find most URLs from a Web site or e-mail about a broadcast.

Follow these steps to add a Web broadcast to a playlist:

1. **Choose Advanced⇨Open Stream.**

   The Open Stream dialog appears, with a URL text field for typing a Web address.

2. **Type the exact, full URL of the stream.**

   Include the `http://` prefix, as in `http://64.236.34.141:80/stream/1014`.

   If you're connected to the Internet, iTunes automatically retrieves the broadcast and places it at the end of your song list.

3. **Click OK.**

As of this writing, iTunes supports only MP3 broadcasts. You can find lots of MP3 broadcasts from SHOUTcast (`www.shoutcast.com`) and Live365.com (`http://live365.com`).

Adding Podcasts

Podcasting is a popular method of publishing audio files to the Internet, enabling people to subscribe to a feed and receive new audio files automatically. Similar to a tape of a radio broadcast, a podcast can be saved and played back at your convenience, both in iTunes on your computer and on your iPod.

A podcast can be anything from a single song to a commentary-hosted radio show. Podcasts are saved in the MP3 format and can be used with any media player, device, or application that supports MP3, including your iPod. The podcast producer uses technology called *Real Simple Syndication (RSS)* to publish the podcast. RSS is widely used by the Weblog community to publish the latest blog headlines with links to the full stories. It's now common to find RSS feeds on major Web sites. RSS feeds are typically linked to with an orange rectangle with the letters RSS or *XML* (for *eXtended Markup Language,* the language of RSS). With a feed reader or aggregator application or browser plug-in, you can automatically check RSS-enabled Web pages and display updated stories and podcasts. RSS is supported directly by some Web browsers, including Apple's Safari 2.0 for Mac OS X 10.4, or newer versions.

You can use iTunes to subscribe to podcasts (available on the iTunes Music Store) and to automatically update your iPod with podcasts. You can play the podcast, incorporate it into playlists, and make copies and burn CDs as much as you like. If you don't like the podcast, simply delete it from your iTunes library and update your iPod. You can listen to most common podcast file formats in iTunes, including MP3, AAC, WAV, and .M4B.

If you prefer to use a podcast receiver application that supports the *OPML* (*Outline Processor Markup Language,* a format for storing outlines in XML) standard for importing and exporting podcast subscription lists, use iPodder (from `www.ipodder.org`) for either Mac or Windows. iPodder searches for your specified show and alerts you that a new show is downloadable. It then downloads the show directly into iTunes and, if your iPod is connected, automatically copies it to your iPod.

Selecting and subscribing to podcasts in iTunes

The iTunes Podcast page on the iTunes Music Store lets you browse, find, preview, and subscribe to over 3,000 podcasts, all of which are free of charge. To use iTunes to select and play podcasts, visit the iTunes Music Store. Click Music in the Source pane to select the iTunes Music Store and visit its home page, as described in Chapter 4. You don't need an account to browse the store and subscribe to podcasts. The Music Store home page replaces the iTunes Song List and Browse panes.

To select a podcast from the store's home page, click the Podcast link in the column on the left side. This link opens the Podcasts page shown in Figure 21-2.

You can also get to Podcast page by clicking Podcasts in the Source pane, then clicking Podcast Directory at the bottom of the song list view for Podcasts.

Figure 21-2: Select an advertised podcast from the Podcasts page in the iTunes Music Store.

You don't have to settle for the podcasts advertised on the iTunes Music Store's Podcasts page — thousands of podcasts are available for free, and Apple can't possibly highlight them all. To find a podcast more to your liking, click the Browse button, which displays a browse view of the podcasts as shown in Figure 21-3. iTunes lets you browse podcasts by Genre, Categories within each genre, and Subcategories within each category — just like browsing songs in the store.

Figure 21-3:
Browse
thousands
of podcasts
in the iTunes
Music
Store.

You can also search the iTunes Music Store specifically for podcasts. Click inside the search field above the Search all podcasts pop-up button in the left column of the Podcasts page, as shown in Figure 21-4. Use the pop-up menu to narrow your search to just podcast titles or authors.

To select, play, and subscribe to a podcast, follow these steps:

1. **Click a podcast feed link to select a podcast.**

   iTunes takes you to the podcast's page in the store, as shown in Figure 21-5, which offers a description, a Subscribe button to receive new podcasts, and a link to the podcast's Web site for more information. The page also lists the most recent podcast. Some podcasters offer several podcasts in one feed.

2. **Select a podcast in the list; either click the Play button or press the spacebar.**

   You can play any podcast in the list. (Some podcasts are not free and provide only previews.) iTunes plays the podcast just like a Web radio station, streaming to your computer. To jump ahead in a podcast or play random sections, you must first subscribe to it. By subscribing, you download the podcast to your computer.

Figure 21-4:
Search for a specific podcast in the iTunes Music Store.

Figure 21-5:
Play a podcast before subscribing to it.

3. Click the Subscribe button to subscribe to the podcast.

In typical Apple fashion, iTunes first displays an alert, as shown in Figure 21-6, to confirm that you want to subscribe to the podcast.

4. Click OK to confirm.

iTunes downloads the podcast to your computer and switches to the Podcasts selection in the Source pane. It displays your newly subscribed podcast in the song list, as shown in Figure 21-7. You can click the lower-case "i" icon on the far-right podcast listing margin to display separate information about the podcast.

5. Select a podcast and click the Play button.

You can now play the podcast just like any other song in your iTunes library. The podcast may be long, but it's still just a song. You can use the iTunes playback controls to fast-forward or rewind the podcast or play it from any point. The blue dot next to a podcast means you haven't yet played it. As soon as you start listening to a podcast, the dot disappears.

Podcasts only show up in the song list that appears when you select Podcasts in the Source pane. They won't show up in Party Shuffle unless you drag them into the Party Shuffle playlist. Podcasts can't be shared over a network, and you can't include podcasts with Autofill when updating an iPod shuffle.

When you play a podcast, iTunes remembers your place when you stop listening to it, just like a bookmark in an audio book. iTunes resumes playing from the bookmark when you return to the podcast to play it.

Some podcasts are enhanced to include chapter marks and photos. When you play an enhanced podcast in iTunes, a bookmark menu icon appears to the top left of the iTunes window display, as shown in Figure 21-8. Click this icon to display a pop-up menu offering the podcast's chapter marks, artwork, and chapter start times, as shown in Figure 21-9.

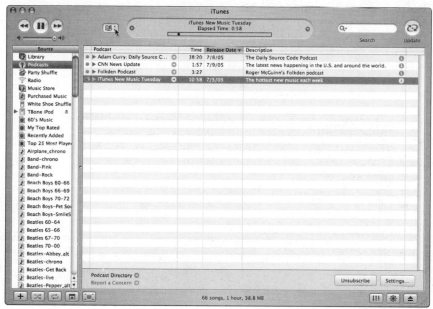

Figure 21-8:
Enhanced podcasts include a bookmark menu.

You can drag a podcast to the Source pane to create a new playlist, as shown in Figure 21-10, which takes on the name of the podcast. (For example, dragging the Folkden Podcast podcast to the Source pane in Figure 21-10 creates the Folkden Podcast playlist.)

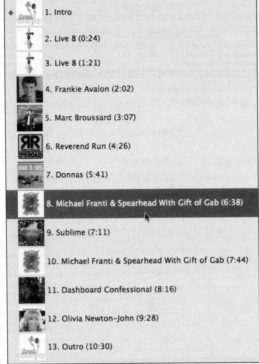

Figure 21-9:
Selecting a
chapter
within an
enhanced
podcast
using the
bookmark
menu.

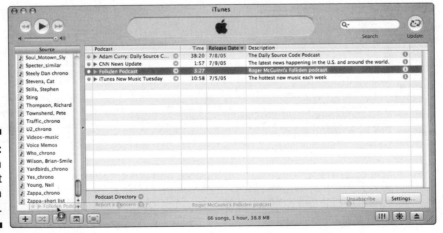

Figure 21-10:
Creating a
new playlist
with a
podcast.

Like any playlist, the new playlist can be burned on CD or copied to an iPod. You can also add multiple podcasts to playlists and burn them to CDs or include them in your iPod. What you can't do, as of this writing, is create a Smart Playlist that includes podcasts.

If the podcaster embedded a photo in an audio podcast file or included a link to a video from the file, the photo or video content appears in the Artwork pane.

Updating podcasts in iTunes

Many podcast feeds provide new material on a regular schedule, and iTunes can check these feeds automatically and update your library with new podcast downloads. You can, for example, schedule iTunes to check for new podcasts — such as news, weather, and traffic reports, and morning talk shows — before you wake up and automatically update your iPod. When you get up, you have new podcasts to listen to in your iPod.

To check for updates manually, select Podcasts in the Source pane and click the Update button. That button replaces the usual Browse button in the upper-left corner of the iTunes window whenever you select Podcasts in the Source pane. All subscribed podcast feeds are updated immediately when you click Update, and iTunes downloads the most recent (or all) episodes, depending on how you've set your Podcasts preferences.

To set your Podcasts preferences so iTunes can check for new podcasts automatically, choose iTunes⇨Preferences on a Mac or Edit⇨Preferences on a Windows PC. In the Preferences dialog, click the Podcasts button to display the Podcasts preferences, as shown in Figure 21-11.

You can set the "Check for new episodes" pop-up menu to every hour, every day, every week, or manually. You can also decide what to do when a new episode (podcast) is available — set the pop-up menu to download the most recent one, download them all, or do nothing. You can also set the Keep pop-up menu to keep all episodes, all unplayed episodes, the most recent episodes, or previous episodes.

If syncing podcasts automatically to your iPod, don't set iTunes to keep only your unplayed episodes. If you listen to part of a podcast on your iPod, and then update your iPod, the podcast disappears from iTunes.

Figure 21-11:
Set your
Podcasts
preferences
to auto-
matically
check for
new
updates.

Using iTunes to synchronize podcasts on your iPod

While you can listen to Web radio or a podcast at any time on your computer, a podcast's real value is that you can take it with you in your iPod. You can keep your iPod synchronized with the most recent podcasts automatically. You can also drag podcasts directly to your iPod just like any song, as long as your iPod is set to be updated manually, as we describe in Chapter 9.

To update your iPod with podcasts automatically, follow these steps:

1. **Connect your iPod to your computer. Wait for iTunes to start and for your iPod to be ready in the Source pane.**

   If the iPod is set for automatic updating, wait for the iPod to finish its usual updating of songs, calendar information, and contacts.

2. **Choose iTunes⇨Preferences on a Mac or Edit⇨Preferences on a Windows PC.**

3. **Click the iPod button.**

   iTunes displays the iPod preferences dialog.

4. **Click the Podcasts button in the iPod preferences dialog.**

   iTunes displays the iPod Podcasts preferences, as shown in Figure 21-12.

   You can also display the iPod preferences by clicking the iPod Preferences button in the Podcasts preferences dialog. Refer to Figure 21-13.

5. **Set your iPod to update all podcasts, selected podcasts, or no podcasts.**

6. **Click OK.**

If you choose to update only selected podcasts, select each podcast in the list box that you want copied in the update, as shown in Figure 21-14. You can also set the Update pop-up menu to update all episodes, only the most recent episode, or only unplayed episodes; refer to Figure 21-14.

Figure 21-12:
Set your iPod to be automatically updated with new podcasts.

After updating your iPod with podcasts, the Podcasts menu selection appears in your iPod's Music menu. Select Podcasts from the Music menu to see a podcasts menu on your iPod. Select a podcast to play it. On an iPod, podcasts aren't included when you select Shuffle Songs or Music Quiz.

You can synchronize podcasts with filenames ending with .m4b to any iPod and never lose your bookmarked place, whether you listen on your iPod or on your computer.

When you play an enhanced podcast on an iPod, your iPod displays the name of the chapter you're listening to above the playback position in the episode. To see this, press the Select button during play to make a diamond appear in the bar. You can then scroll the wheel right to scrub forward, or left to scrub backwards.

To play podcasts on your iPod when it's connected via a car stereo interface and controlled by the car's audio head unit, create a podcasts playlist first. You can then select that playlist using the audio head unit navigation controls and play the podcast.

Figure 21-13:
Set your
iPod to be
updated
with only
the recent
episodes of
selected
podcasts.

Using iPodder to select and play podcasts

To use iPodder to acquire podcasts, download iPodder from www.ipodder.org and double-click the iPodder installer to install the application. After installing, follow these steps:

1. **Double-click the iPodder icon to launch it.**

2. **Click the Status button to display the Status pane, and click the select feed button.**

   Click the "Select feeds from the podcast directory" button as shown in Figure 21-14. A list of podcast folders appears in a directory format.

3. **Open a category and select a podcast.**

   Click the triangle to the left of a podcast folder, as shown in Figure 21-15, to open the folder. Some folders contain subfolders. Podcast feeds have a globe icon next to them. After selecting a feed, its Web address (URL) appears at the bottom of the window.

4. *Optional:* **Click "Open in browser" to open the podcast's Web page and read information about it.**

   Most have associated Web sites that provide information.

Figure 21-14:
Select
podcasts in
iPodder.

5. **In iPodder, click the "Add selected feed" button to add the podcast feed, and close the Select Podcast Feeds window.**

   A message tells you that iPodder added the feed.

6. **Click OK.**

   To close the Select podcast feeds window, click the red button in the top-left corner. After adding a feed, it shows up in the Status pane as `newly-subscribed`.

Figure 21-15:
Add a
podcast to
iPodder for
automatic
updating.

7. **Select the podcast feed in the Status pane, and click the "Check selected feed" button.**

   iPodder checks the selected feed for any new podcasts and automatically downloads them into an iTunes playlist named after the feed. For example, the podcast from the Coverville feed appears in your iTunes library in the newly created Coverville playlist.

You can play the podcast directly in iTunes, just like any other song in the iTunes library, and assign the podcast to other playlists. If your iPod is connected to your computer when iPodder downloads the podcast into iTunes, iTunes automatically updates your iPod with the playlist containing the podcast. You can also connect your iPod later and update it automatically by playlist, as described in Chapter 9.

You can also add a podcast feed directly to iPodder by copying the URL for the podcast feed into the text input box in the Status pane and clicking the Add button.

Scheduling podcast updates in iPodder

One iPodder benefit is the ability to schedule automatic updating with new podcast downloads. To set up iPodder with an update schedule, launch iPodder and follow these steps:

1. **Click the Scheduler button to display the Scheduler pane.**

2. **Click the "Check for new podcasts automatically" option in the Scheduler pane.**

3. **Click the "Check at these specific times" option and enter specific times, or click the "Check at regular intervals" option and choose an interval.**

   To enter specific times, use military time (for example, 16:30 is 4:30 PM). Type the time into the time field as shown in Figure 21-16, and click the check box next to the time field to make it active. The alternative to scheduling specific times is to set the update to occur at regular intervals. Choose an interval of hours or minutes from the "Repeat every" pop-up menu.

4. **Click "Apply scheduler settings" to apply the settings in the Scheduler pane.**

5. **Hide or minimize the iPodder window but leave it running.**

   iPodder must be running to automatically keep its schedule of checking and downloading podcasts. To minimize the iPodder window, click the minimizer button (yellow button in the top left corner in Mac OS X, or dash button in the top right corner in Windows). Minimizing a window shrinks the window to an icon on the Windows Taskbar or Mac Dock.

Based on your scheduler settings, iPodder will check for and download new podcasts and transfer them to your iTunes library in playlists named after the podcast feeds.

Figure 21-16:
Setting a schedule for iPodder to automatic-ally check for and download new podcasts.

Part V
Have iPod, Will Travel

The 5th Wave   By Rich Tennant

"Why can't you just bring your iPod like everyone else?"

In this part . . .

This part explains how you can use your iPod to take care of personal business the way people often use PDAs — especially on the road. It also covers how to troubleshoot problems with your iPod.

- Chapter 22 covers managing your life on the road — waking up with the alarm clock, playing games, sorting your contacts, recording voice memos, and customizing the iPod menu and display settings.

- Chapter 23 is about using your iPod as a hard drive, and it includes saving files, storing notes and text, and even saving a copy of the Mac system on your iPod.

- Chapter 24 explains how to use photos with your color-display iPod and create slideshows for viewing on televisions. it also details how to copy photos from a digital camera to an iPod.

- Chapter 25 shows you how to use both Apple and Microsoft applications to enter personal contact and calendar information in preparation for iPod synchronization.

- Chapter 26 describes automatically synchronizing your iPod with personal information. Here you can also find out about adding information manually to your iPod so that you don't miss any of your appointments or forget anybody's name.

- Chapter 27 gets into the nitty-gritty of trouble-shooting iPod problems, including how to use the iPod Updater to update or restore your iPod.

Chapter 22

Sleeping with Your iPod

. . . .

In This Chapter

▶ Setting the time, date, and sleep functions

▶ Setting up your iPod as an alarm clock

▶ Changing the iPod display settings

▶ Checking your calendar and sorting your contacts

▶ Recording voice memos on your iPod

▶ Customizing your iPod menus and settings

. . . .

You might have purchased an iPod simply to listen to music, but those thoughtful engineers at Apple who get to travel a lot with their iPods put a lot more into this device.

As we show in this chapter, your iPod keeps time, and you can use it as an alarm clock to awaken you to your favorite music (or just a beep). In particular, you can alleviate the boredom of travel with games, and check the time, date, and month (in case you're stranded for a long time). You can also check your calendar and To-Do list, and look up contact names, addresses, and phone numbers. You can even speak into your iPod and record dictation, conversations, or notes. You can also make your iPod more convenient to use while traveling by customizing the iPod menu.

Setting Date, Time, and Sleep Functions

All iPods running iPod software version 2.0 or newer have a digital clock that doubles as an alarm clock and a sleep timer. To access the clock, choose Extras⇨Clock from the main menu.

To set the date and time, follow these steps:

1. **Press the Menu button.**

2. **Choose Extras⇨Clock.**

   The clock appears with menu selections underneath (except in older models).

   You can also set the date and time by choosing Settings⇨Date & Time from the main menu.

3. **Select the Date & Time option.**

   The Date & Time menu appears.

4. **Select the Set Time Zone option.**

   A list of time zones appears in alphabetical order.

5. **Scroll the Time Zone list and select a time zone.**

   The Date & Time menu appears again.

6. **Select the Set Date & Time option.**

   The Date & Time display appears with up and down arrow indicators over the hour field, which is now highlighted.

7. **Change the field setting using the scroll wheel.**

   Scroll clockwise to go forward and counterclockwise to go backward.

8. **Press the Select button after scrolling to the appropriate setting.**

   The up and down arrow indicators move over to the minutes field, which is now highlighted.

9. **Repeat Steps 7 and 8 for each field of the date and time: minutes, AM/PM, the calendar date, calendar month, and year.**

When you finish setting the year by pressing the Select button, the Date & Time menu appears again.

You can change the time display to show the number of hours from 1 to 24 (military style). In the Date & Time menu, scroll to the Time option and press the Select button. The option changes from *12-hour* to *24-hour* (military style). With 24-hour display, 11 p.m. is displayed as 23:00:00 rather than 11:00:00. To switch back to *12-hour,* click the Select button again with the Time option.

To display the time in the menu title for all iPod menus, scroll to the Time in Title option in the Date & Time menu, and press the Select button to turn this option On. Press the Select button again to switch it back to Off to stop showing the time in the menu title.

Just like a clock radio, you can set your iPod to play music for a while before going to sleep. To set the sleep timer, select the Sleep Timer option from the Clock menu. A list of intervals appears from 0 (Off) up to 120 minutes (2 hours). You can select a time amount or the Off setting (at the top of the list) to turn off the sleep timer. After the iPod shuts itself off (after you hold down the pause button, or it remains idle for a few minutes and shuts itself off), the preference for the Sleep Timer is reset to the default status, Off.

Setting the Alarm Clock

Time is on your side with the iPod Alarm Clock function, which is located in the iPod Clock menu (found only in third- and fourth-generation models). To set the Alarm Clock, follow these steps:

1. **Choose Extras➪Clock➪Alarm Clock from the main menu.**

   The Alarm Clock menu appears.

2. **Highlight the Alarm option and press the Select button (Off changes to On).**

3. **Select the Time option.**

   The Alarm Time menu appears with up and down arrow indicators.

4. **Change the time using the scroll wheel.**

   Scroll clockwise to go forward and counterclockwise to go backward.

5. **Press the Select button after scrolling to the appropriate alarm time.**

   The Alarm Clock menu appears again.

6. **Select the Sound option in the Alarm Clock menu.**

   A list appears, with the Beep option at the top of the list, followed by playlists on your iPod in alphabetical order.

7. **Choose an option as the alarm sound, and then press the Select button.**

   If you choose Beep, the alarm beeps without the need for any headphones or speakers. If you choose a playlist, when the alarm goes off, the playlist plays until you stop it by pressing the Play/Pause button. Of course, you need speakers or headphones to hear the music.

8. **You can return to the main menu by pressing Menu until you see the main menu.**

   When the alarm goes off, the playlist (or beep tone) plays until you stop the alarm by pressing the Play/Pause button.

Choosing Display Settings

Your future may be so bright that you got to wear shades, but your iPod black-and-white display might need a bit of an adjustment so you can see it better in bright sunlight or the dark of night. With the iPod Settings menu, you can change the timer for the backlight and also set the contrast of black-and-white displays for better visibility. (The contrast setting for color-display iPod models is not adjustable.) Choose the Settings menu from the iPod main menu.

Backlight timer

Ordinarily, your iPod display's backlight turns on when you press a button or use the scroll wheel, and then it turns off after a short amount of time. On third-generation iPods, the backlight also lights up the iPod buttons.

You can set the backlight to remain on for a certain interval of time. Choose Settings from the iPod main menu and then select Backlight Timer. A menu appears — 2 seconds, 5 seconds, 10 seconds, and so on. Select one by scrolling to highlight the selection, and then press the Select button.

The backlight drains the iPod battery; the longer you set the interval, the more frequently you need to recharge the battery.

You can turn off the backlight (and the iPod itself) by pressing down and holding the Play/Pause button. The backlight turns on when you press any button or use the scroll wheel. You can also turn on the backlight by selecting Backlight from the iPod main menu.

You can set the backlight to *always* be on or *always* be off. If you set it to always be off, the backlight doesn't turn on automatically when you press any button or use the scroll wheel. You can still turn it on, however, by selecting Backlight from the main menu.

The backlight isn't that useful when the display is tilted toward direct sunlight. As we discuss in the next section, it's better to adjust the contrast to get better visibility in bright lighting conditions.

Don't be alarmed if your backlight turns itself on at midnight for a brief flash. The iPod is just setting its internal clock. If you find this annoying, turn the Backlight Timer to off.

Contrast for better visibility

You can set the contrast of black-and-white iPod displays to make the black characters appear sharper against the display background. (This feature isn't provided in color-display iPod models.) You might need to adjust the contrast after a sharp temperature difference freezes or bakes your iPod. If you keep your iPod in your car overnight in the cold, or even in direct sunlight for a time, the contrast can change so much that you can't see your iPod display. Allow the iPod to warm up (slowly — don't use the oven or microwave) if it's cold, or cool down if the display is hot, and then adjust the contrast.

To adjust the contrast, choose Settings from the iPod main menu, and then choose Contrast from the Settings menu. The Contrast screen appears with a slider that shows the contrast setting, which ranges from low contrast (a black-and-white dot) to high contrast (a full black dot). Scroll clockwise to increase the contrast (toward the black dot) and counterclockwise to decrease the contrast (toward the black-and-white dot).

If you accidentally set the contrast too dark or too light, you can reset it to the halfway point between too dark and too light by pressing and holding down the Menu button for at least four seconds.

Playing Games

The games that come with the iPod — Brick, Parachute, and Solitaire — are a bit dorky for the information age, but hey, they're extras. Music Quiz, on the other hand, is a cool way to test your knowledge of your music library.

To find the games, choose Extras⇨Games. (On older iPods choose Extras⇨ Game). And of course you can listen to music while you play — in fact, with Music Quiz, you have to.

Brick and Parachute

Brick is like the original version of Breakout for the Atari. To access this game, choose Extras⇨Games⇨Brick (Extras⇨Game on older iPods), and press the Select button to start the game. Move the paddle from side to side along the bottom of the display by scrolling with the scroll wheel. You get a point for each brick you knock out. If you break out — knock out all the bricks — you move up a level in the game, and the game starts again.

Parachute is a crude shoot-'em-up game where you play the role of an antiaircraft gunner. Choose Extras⇨Games⇨Parachute, and press the Select button to start the game. You pivot the gun at the bottom with the scroll wheel. Press the Select button to fire on helicopters and paratroopers. Don't let the paratroopers reach the ground, or else they'll heave grenades at you. War is hell.

Solitaire

Rather than playing the card game *'til one, with a deck of 51,* try the iPod version of Solitaire (also known as "Klondike"). Choose Extras⇨Games⇨Solitaire, and press the Select button to start the game. To move cards, place the hand pointer over a card by scrolling the scroll wheel, and press the Select button to select the card. Then scroll again to move the hand pointer to the new location for the card, and press Select to place the card at that position. To deal out another round of three cards, move the hand pointer over the card deck in the top-left corner of the display, and press the Select button. After going through an entire deck, the game places the remaining cards into a new deck so that you can continue dealing cards. The game improves considerably in a smoke-filled room with take-out pizza nearby; gangsters are optional.

Music Quiz

Music Quiz tests your knowledge of your music library and is probably the greatest time-waster of them all. The game plays the first few seconds of a song picked at random from your iPod. Choose Extras⇨Games⇨Music Quiz, put on your headphones or connect your iPod to speakers, and press the Select button to start the game. As the song plays, you have ten seconds to pick the song title from a list of five titles. If you choose the wrong title, the game displays Incorrect! and moves on to the next one. If you choose the right title, you gain points and move on to the next one. ("Life's a Long Song" by Jethro Tull would be appropriate.)

Checking Your Calendar

Imagine a musician going backstage after a performance and meeting a promoter who says he can get him ten more gigs if he can confirm the dates *right now.* This musician happens to carry around an iPod, and amid the backstage craziness, he scrolls through his calendar for the entire year, finding all the details he needs about gigs and recording sessions, right down to the minute, including travel directions to each gig. "No problem," the musician says.

Your iPod accepts calendars from calendar applications such as iCal on Mac or Outlook on Windows, as described in Chapter 25. You can view these calendars (or a blank calendar, if you haven't updated your iPod with your calendar files) by choosing Extras⇨Calendars and then selecting a specific calendar by name, or All for a merged view of all your calendars. Select a calendar and then use the scroll wheel to go through the days of the calendar. Select an event to see its details. Press the Next and Previous buttons to skip to the next or previous month. To see your To-Do list, choose Extras⇨Calendars⇨To Do.

If your calendar events use alarms, you can turn on the iPod's calendar alarms. Choose Extras⇨Calendars⇨Alarms. Select Alarms once to set the alarm to Beep, or once again to set it to Silent (so that only the message for the alarm appears), or one more time to set it to Off. (The Alarms choices cycle from Beep to Silent to Off and then back to Beep.)

Calendars are far more useful if you enter your personal information as we describe in Chapter 25.

Sorting Your Contacts

The most likely bits of information that you might need on the road are someone's phone number or address (or both). The iPod stores up to 1,000 contacts right alongside your music. To see how to put your personal contacts into your iPod, see Chapter 25.

The iPod contact list is sorted automatically, and the iPod displays contact names in alphabetical order when you select Extras⇨Contacts. You can choose whether to display contacts by last or first name. Choose Settings⇨Contacts⇨Display; then press the Select button in the scrolling pad for each option:

- **First Last:** Displays the contacts list by first name and the last name, as in *Ringo Starr.*
- **Last, First:** Displays the contacts list by last name followed by a comma and the first name, as in *McCartney, Paul.*

You can also change how the contacts sort so that you don't have to look up people by their first names (which can be time-consuming with so many friends named Elvis). The sort operation uses the entire name, but you decide whether to use the first name or the surname first. Choose Settings⇨Contacts⇨Sort. Press the Select button in the scrolling pad for each option:

- **First Last:** Sorts the contact list by first name, followed by the last name, so that *Mick Jagger* sorts under *Mick* (after *Mick Abrahams* but before *Mick Taylor*).
- **Last, First:** Sorts the contacts by last name, followed by the first name, so that *Brian Jones* sorts under *Jones.* (*Jones, Brian* appears after *Jones, Alice* but before *Jones, Norah.*)

Speaking into Your iPod

Do you record conversations and interviews on the road? Throw out that tape recorder. A full-size third- or fourth-generation iPod can record hundreds of hours of voice-quality memos, meetings, notes, and interviews with a touch of a button. All you need is an accessory that includes a microphone, such as the tiny Belkin iPod Voice Recorder (www.belkin.com), about $30, or the Griffin iTalk Voice Recorder (www.griffintechnology.com), about $40. Either accessory fits right on top of your iPod. The voice memos are stored on your iPod, where you can review them immediately using the built-in speaker of the accessory or your headphones or speakers. Even better, the voice memos are automatically transferred to your iTunes library for archiving or reviewing on your computer.

The voice recorder (such as the Belkin iPod Voice Recorder or the Griffin iTalk Voice Recorder) attaches to the remote connector on the top of full-size third-generation and fourth-generation iPods (updated by version 2.1 of the iPod software or newer). Sorry, you can't use them with the iPod mini, iPod nano, or iPod shuffle.

Recording voice memos

To record voice memos, connect the voice recorder to the iPod and choose Extras⇨Voice Memos⇨Record Now. The iPod displays the Record screen. Press the Play/Pause button to begin recording, and hold the iPod as you would a microphone, with the voice recorder pointing at the sound source (or your mouth for your voice). With the Belkin iPod Voice Recorder, a green LED turns on when recording. You can pause the recording by pressing the Play/Pause button again.

When you finish recording, press the Menu button. The audio files for voice memos are stored on your iPod in the Recordings folder, using the date and time of the recording as the filename.

Playing back voice memos

To play back a voice memo, choose Extras⇨Voice Memos and choose the voice memo from the list. (The Voice Memos menu doesn't appear unless you have already connected the voice recorder at least once.) Then select Play (or press the Play/Pause button).

The voice memo plays just like any other song on your iPod — you can press Play/Pause to pause playback, and press it again to resume. You can hear the playback in the voice recorder's tiny speaker, attach headphones to your iPod, or connect your iPod to a home stereo, car stereo, or self-powered speakers.

You can play music through the speaker of either the Belkin Voice Recorder or the Griffin iTalk Voice Recorder by connecting the accessory to your iPod and playing. This comes in handy if you set your iPod as an alarm clock to play a music playlist; you can hear music when you wake up without having to connect the iPod to speakers. See the earlier section, "Setting the Alarm Clock."

Managing voice memos in iTunes

Just like your music, your voice memos synchronize automatically with your iTunes library if you set your iPod to update automatically. (See Chapter 9 to discover how to set your iPod to update automatically.) iTunes stores the voice memos in the library and creates a playlist named Voice Memos, as shown in Figure 22-1, so that you can find them easily.

Figure 22-1:
The Voice
Memos
playlist in
iTunes.

If you update your iPod manually, you can drag voice memo files directly from the Recordings folder to your hard drive, or drag and drop them over the iTunes window. *Note:* The iPod must already be enabled as a hard drive. (Read Chapter 23 to see how to enable your iPod as a hard drive.)

Voice memos are stored as WAV files. If you want to archive them in a format that takes up less hard drive space, convert them by using the AAC or MP3 encoder, as we describe in Chapter 18.

Customizing the Menu and Settings

When traveling or using your iPod in situations or environments where portability is important, you might want to customize your iPod menu and display to make doing things easier, such as selecting certain albums, displaying the time, displaying menus with backlighting turned on longer than usual, and so on.

The Settings menu in the iPod main menu offers ways to customize your iPod experience by changing the main menu to have more choices. Choose the Settings menu from the main menu, and then choose Main Menu. The iPod displays a list of menus; each menu is set to either On or Off. On means the menu appears in the iPod main menu; Off means the menu does not appear in the main menu. (Don't worry; the menus are still where they are supposed to be. Turning one to On simply adds it to the main menu as well.)

Other ways to customize your experience include setting the clicker sound and setting the language to use for the menus. The options in the Settings menu include:

✔ **About:** This displays information about the iPod, including number of songs (and number of photos in a color-display iPod), how much space is used, how much space is available, the software version in use, and the serial number.

✔ **Main Menu:** This allows you to customize the main menu on iPods that use iPod software 2.0 or newer. For example, you can add items from other menus, such as Artists or Songs from the Music menu (Browse menu in older iPods), to the main menu.

✔ **Backlight Timer:** You can set the backlight to remain on for a certain amount of time by pressing a button or using the scroll wheel. Specify two seconds, five seconds, and so on. You can also set it to always be on.

The backlight drains the iPod battery; the longer you set the interval, the more you need to recharge the battery.

✔ **Compilations:** This option, available in the color-display models, works with the "Group compilations when browsing" setting in iTunes. It removes from the Artists (but not Albums) menu the artists and songs designated as compilation albums in iTunes. It groups them into a new entry in the Music menu called Compilations. Using this option you can reduce the number of artists in the Artists menu to just those artists with songs that aren't part of compilations.

✔ **Contrast:** With black-and-white iPod displays you can set the contrast by using the scroll wheel to increase or decrease the slider in the Contrast screen. If you accidentally set the contrast too dark, you can reset it by holding down the Menu button for at least four seconds. This option isn't offered in the color-display iPod.

✔ **Clicker:** When this setting is on, you hear a click when you press a button; when it's off, you don't hear a click. With color-display iPod models, the Clicker can be set to Speaker (the iPod speaker), Headphones, Both, or Off.

✔ **Language:** This sets the language used in all the menus. See Chapter 1 for how to set the language.

✔ **Legal:** This displays the legal message that accompanies Apple products.

✔ **Reset All Settings:** This resets all the Settings menu settings in your iPod, returning them to the state they were in originally. However, your music and data files on the iPod are not disturbed. This is not the same as resetting (and restarting) the iPod software itself; Reset All Settings simply returns all settings to their defaults. See Chapter 1 for how to reset the iPod itself.

Chapter 23

Using the iPod as a Hard Drive

*Y*ou have a device in your pocket that can play weeks of music, sort your contacts, remind you of events, wake you up in the morning, and tuck you in at night. Did you also know that you can use your iPod to keep a safe backup of your most important files?

You read that right. Windows and Mac users can put their most important files on an iPod and use it just like a hard drive. Mac users can even put a version of the Mac system on the iPod in case of emergencies. (Unfortunately, you can't do this with Windows.) Apple doesn't recommend putting the Mac system on the iPod because using the iPod as a startup hard drive might make your iPod too hot from overuse, but you can do it. You can also copy applications and utility programs that you might need on the road or even copy your entire User folder to the iPod if you have room after putting music on it.

But that's not all. You can use software, such as Pod2Go, that offers synchronized feeds that supply your iPod with news, weather forecasts, and even sections of Web pages for reading on the iPod screen. The handy iPod shuffle, which plugs directly into a USB connection, can double as a USB flash memory drive for portable file storage.

If you format an iPod for Windows first, you can transfer files to and from Mac and Windows computers. An iPod shuffle, which fits in the palm of your hand and draws its power from the computer, is especially useful for transferring files back and forth.

The key to these capabilities is the fact that the iPod serves as an external hard drive. After you mount the iPod on your Mac or Windows desktop, you can use it as a hard drive, but do so sparingly.

We don't recommend using the iPod regularly as a hard drive to launch applications. The iPod is designed more for sustained playback of music, and you can eventually burn out the device by using it to launch applications all the time. Instead, use it as an external hard drive for backing up and copying files, and use it in emergency situations for starting up the system.

Enabling the iPod as a Hard Drive

You can use any iPod, including an iPod shuffle, as an external hard drive (or in the case of an iPod shuffle, a flash memory drive). And like any hard drive, you can transfer files and applications from your computer to your iPod and take them with you wherever you go. The iPod is smart enough to keep your files separate from your music collection so that you don't accidentally erase them when you update your music. And because your iPod is *with you,* it's as safe as you are.

The iPod, as shipped, is formatted as a Macintosh hard drive and can be connected to any Mac. When you connect it to Windows, the iPod is reformatted as a Windows hard drive. You can then connect it to any Windows PC or any Mac. (Macs can use hard drives formatted for Windows PCs, but can't start the system from them.)

Setting up the iPod hard drive on a Mac

To use your iPod as an external hard drive on a Mac, follow these steps:

1. **Connect your iPod to your Mac.**

2. **Select the iPod name in the iTunes Source pane.**

3. **Click the iPod Options button on the bottom-right side of the iTunes window, or click the iPod button in the iTunes Preferences dialog.**

   The iPod Options button appears only when an iPod is connected and selected in the Source pane. You can also choose iTunes⇨Preferences and click the iPod button — whether or not the iPod is selected in the Source pane (although it has to be connected). The iPod preferences dialog appears.

4. **Click the Music button in the iPod preferences dialog if it's not already selected.**

   When you first open iPod preferences, the Music button is already selected and displays the iPod music updating preferences, as shown in Figure 23-1.

5. **Select the "Enable disk use" option and click OK.**

   The "Enable disk use" option is available if your iPod is set to automatically update. If you already set your iPod to manual updating (as we describe in Chapter 10), this option is grayed out because it isn't needed — setting the iPod to update manually automatically enables you to use it as a hard drive.

6. **Open the iPod icon in the Finder to see its contents.**

Figure 23-1:
Enable the
iPod as a
Mac hard
drive.

The iPod hard drive opens up to show at least three folders — Calendars, Contacts, and Notes. You may also have other folders depending on the iPod model; for example, a color-display iPod includes the folders shown in Figure 23-2. You can add new folders, rename your new folders, and generally use the iPod as a hard drive, but don't rename the folders already provided on the iPod. They link directly to functions on the iPod — for example, the Calendars folder links directly to the Calendar menu on the iPod.

Figure 23-2:
The iPod opens as a hard drive on the Mac and its icon appears on the desktop.

7. *Optional:* **Drag files or folders to the iPod window.**

   To keep data organized, create new folders on the iPod, and then drag files and folders that you want to copy to the newly created folders.

8. **Before disconnecting the iPod, eject the iPod from the system.**

   Click the Eject button next to the iPod name in the Finder, or drag the iPod icon to the Trash icon, which turns into an Eject button as you drag the iPod icon into it.

After ejecting the iPod, its display shows the `OK to disconnect` message on older models, or the main menu on newer models. You can then disconnect the iPod from its dock or disconnect the dock from the computer. Don't ever disconnect an iPod before ejecting it. You might have to reset your iPod. (If you do, head to Chapter 1.)

To delete files and folders from the iPod, drag them to the Trash just like an external hard drive.

Don't use a hard drive utility program, such as Disk Utility or Drive Setup, to erase or format the iPod's hard drive. If you erase your iPod's hard drive in this way, it might be unable to play music.

To see how much free space is left on the iPod, you can use the Finder. Select the iPod icon on the desktop, and then choose File⇨Show Info. You can also choose Settings⇨About from the iPod's main menu.

Setting up the iPod hard drive on a Windows PC with iTunes

You can set up your iPod to use as an external hard drive on a Windows PC by using iTunes. If you use iTunes, follow these steps:

1. **Connect your iPod to your computer.**

2. **Select the iPod name in the iTunes Source pane.**

3. **Click the iPod Options button on the bottom-right side of the iTunes window, or click the iPod button in the iTunes Preferences dialog.**

   The iPod Options button appears only when an iPod is connected and selected in the Source pane. You can also choose Edit⇨Preferences and click the iPod button — whether or not the iPod is selected in the Source pane (although it has to be connected). The iPod pane appears in the iTunes preferences dialog.

4. **Click the Music button in the iPod pane of the preferences dialog if it's not already selected.**

   When you first open the iTunes preferences iPod pane, the Music button is already selected. It displays the iPod music updating preferences, as shown in Figure 23-3.

5. **Select the "Enable disk use" option and click OK.**

   The "Enable disk use" option is available if your iPod is set to automatically update. You must select this option to use your iPod as a hard drive. If you already set your iPod to manual updating (as we describe in Chapter 10), this option is grayed out because it isn't needed — setting the iPod to update manually automatically enables you to use it as a hard drive.

Figure 23-3:
Enable the
iPod as a
Windows
hard drive.

6. **Double-click the iPod icon in the My Computer or Windows Explorer window to see its contents.**

If you open the My Computer window, the iPod appears as an external hard drive, as shown in Figure 23-4. The iPod in the figure is named *Journeyman* and assigned to drive "E:". Windows automatically assigns the iPod hard drive to a Windows drive letter.

Figure 23-4:
Selecting the iPod hard drive in the My Computer window.

The iPod hard drive opens up to show at least three folders — Calendars, Contacts, and Notes. You may also have other folders depending on the iPod model; for example, the color-display iPods include the folders shown in Figure 23-2. You can add new folders, rename your new folders, and generally use the iPod as a hard drive, but don't rename the folders already provided on the iPod. They link directly to functions on the iPod — for example, the Calendars folder links directly to the Calendar menu on the iPod.

7. *Optional:* **Copy files or folders to the iPod.**

To keep data organized, create new folders on the iPod, and then copy files and folders to the newly created folders by using the drag-and-drop method in the My Computer window or Windows Explorer, or by copying and pasting.

8. **Before disconnecting the iPod, eject the iPod from Windows.**

Right-click the iPod name or icon and choose Eject from the shortcut menu. You can do this from within iTunes by clicking the Eject button next to the iPod's name in the Source pane.

After ejecting the iPod, it displays the OK to disconnect message on older models, or the main menu on newer models. You can then disconnect the iPod from its dock or disconnect the dock from the computer. Don't ever disconnect an iPod before ejecting it. You might have to reset your iPod. (If you do, head to Chapter 1.)

To delete files and folders from the iPod, select the filename and press Backspace, or choose File⇨Delete from the Windows Explorer menu, just like you do on your internal hard drive.

Don't use the Windows formatting utility or another company's hard drive utility program to erase or format the iPod's hard drive. If you erase the hard drive in your iPod in this way, it may be unable to play music.

To see how much free space is left on the iPod, select the iPod icon in My Computer and choose File⇨Properties. You can also choose Settings⇨About from the iPod's main menu.

Setting up the iPod shuffle as a flash memory drive

The iPod shuffle makes a really convenient flash memory drive, which is like a hard drive except that it uses flash memory rather than a disk drive. *Flash memory* is a rewritable memory chip that holds its content without power. The name "flash memory" was coined by Toshiba to express how much faster it could be erased (in a flash, you see). Flash memory is widely used for external storage devices such as USB keychain-sized drives and digital camera memory cards. The iPod software makes the flash memory look like a hard drive to the operating system.

To enable your iPod shuffle to act as a flash memory drive to transfer folders and data files, follow these steps:

1. **Connect the iPod shuffle and select it in the Source pane.**

2. **Click the iPod Options button or click the iPod button in the iTunes Preferences dialog.**

   The iPod Options button appears only when an iPod is connected and selected in the Source pane. You can also choose iTunes⇨Preferences on a Mac or Edit⇨Preferences on a Windows PC, and click the iPod button.

3. **Click the Music button in the iPod preferences dialog if it's not already selected.**

   When you first open iPod preferences, the Music button is already selected and displays the iPod music updating preferences, as shown in Figure 23-5.

Figure 23-5:
Enable the
iPod shuffle
as a flash
memory
drive that
looks like a
hard drive.

4. **Select the "Enable disk use" option.**

   The "Enable disk use" option in the iPod preferences pane enables the iPod shuffle to act as a hard drive.

5. **Drag the slider to the right to enable more space for data.**

   The iPod preferences pane for the iPod shuffle (refer to Figure 23-5) includes a storage allocation slider with More Songs on the left side and More Data on the right side. Drag the slider to the right to open up more space for data.

6. **Click OK to close the Preferences dialog.**

   If you set the storage allocation slider to allocate more space for data, and you have music stored on the iPod shuffle that takes up more space than what you've just allocated, iTunes asks if you want to delete music from the iPod shuffle to make room for data. You can click Yes to delete music or No to leave the music alone — in which case you have less room for data.

7. **Eject the iPod shuffle before disconnecting it.**

   Click the iPod Eject button, which appears in the bottom-right side of the iTunes window, or click the eject icon next to the iPod shuffle name in the Source pane. When the iPod shuffle's status light stops blinking and stays on, you can disconnect the iPod shuffle.

On a Mac, you can also eject the iPod shuffle by dragging the iPod shuffle icon to the Trash. On a Windows PC, you can eject the iPod shuffle by clicking the Safely Remove Hardware icon in the Windows system tray and selecting the iPod shuffle.

The Mac can use Windows-formatted hard drives, but Windows can't use Mac-formatted hard drives. If you want to transfer data files to and from Mac and Windows computers, set up the iPod shuffle on a Windows computer to format as a Windows hard drive.

Adding Notes and Text

You can add text notes to your iPod so that you can view them on the iPod display — all sorts of notes, such as driving directions, weather information, or even news items. If you just use your iPod for music, you might want notes about the music. This feature works with iPods that run iPod software 2.0 or newer (including iPod mini and all iPods that use the dock connector).

Using the Notes folder

In a perfect world you could rip audio CDs and also capture all the information in the liner notes — the descriptions of who played which instruments, where the CD was produced, and other minute detail. Then, while sharing your iPod music with others, you could view the liner notes on the iPod screen whenever a question arises about the music.

You can almost achieve the same result by typing some of the liner notes or any text you want (or copy or export song information from iTunes, as we describe in Chapter 12) into a word processing program, such as TextEdit on a Mac or NotePad on a Windows PC. You can then save the document as a text-only file (with the filename extension ".txt") and drag it to the Notes folder of the iPod.

Documents must be saved as text-only files to be viewed on the iPod display. If you use a word processor, such as Microsoft Word, choose File➪Save As, and select the Text Only option (or the Text Only with Line Breaks option) from the Save As Type drop-down list in Windows or the Format pop-up menu on a Mac. Notes text files can be up to 4K in length — that's roughly 2 or 3 printed pages of information.

Text files in the Notes folder are organized by filename. You can view these notes files by choosing Extras➪Notes. Make sure that you name your notes with descriptive filenames so that you can easily scroll the list of notes files to find the liner notes for the album you're listening to.

Your iPod can also display a folder hierarchy in the Notes folder, allowing you to organize your notes by creating folders (using the Finder with your iPod mounted as a hard drive) and putting notes files within the folders in the Notes folder. The size of any single note is limited to 4K; any text beyond 4K is truncated. You can transfer up to 1,000 notes.

Notes can include basic HTML tags (used on Web pages) such as paragraph markers (`<P>` and `</P>`) and line breaks (`<BR>`). The HTML tags can define links to other Notes text files and to audio files. Software companies such as Talking Panda (`http://talkingpanda.com/`) have created textual guides you can install in the iPod Notes folder that use these tags and links to present text on the iPod screen and play audio files. You can learn how to develop your own HTML tags by downloading Apple's iPod Note Reader User's Guide (`http://developer.apple.com/hardware/ipod/ipodnotereader.pdf`).

To navigate the Notes section of your iPod, use the iPod controls as follows:

- ✔ Use the select button to open a Note from its folder, just like playing a song in an album.

- ✔ Use the scroll wheel to scroll up and down the list of notes in a folder, and up and down the text in a Note.

- ✔ As you scroll through text, iPod jumps from link to link, highlighting each link. When a link is already highlighted, you can use the select button to follow the link. To go back to the previous link, use the Menu button.

- ✔ To go up to the folder that contains the Note text file, use the Menu button several times to back up through the links until the iPod displays the folder.

Adding guides, books, and news feeds

Do you want the latest news, weather, sports scores, or driving directions available at the touch of a button of your iPod? How about lessons on speaking French, German, Italian, Spanish, or other languages? Enterprising software entrepreneurs have moved in to fill the vacuum left by Apple with accessories that provide displayable text on your iPod screen, such as the following:

- ✔ **Pod2Go** (available at `www.kainjow.com/pod2go/`) for Mac OS X offers synchronized feeds for news, weather forecasts, movie listings, stock quotes, horoscopes, sections of Web pages, and driving directions.

- ✔ **NewsMac 3** (available at `www.thinkmac.co.uk/newsmac`), also for Mac OS X, lets you keep tabs on world news Web sites and lets you transfer entire Web pages.

- **iLingo** (available at `http://talkingpanda.com/ilingo.php`) offers language lessons, with over 400 essential words and phrases of your chosen language, organized as Notes folders and files. It also includes audio files, created by native speakers, that provide proper pronunciation for all included phrases.

- **iBar** (available at `http://talkingpanda.com/ibar.php`) offers drink recipes with ingredients, instructions for mixing and proper garnishing, and advice on which glass to use. Many recipes are linked to audio anecdotes about the origin of the cocktail as well as instructions on how to mix it.

- **EphPod** for Windows (available at `www.ephpod.com`) lets you update your iPod with news, weather, and other information updates.

- **Book2Pod** (available at `www.tomsci.com/book2pod`) is a shareware program for the Mac that allows you to read entire books on your iPod display. There's also a similar shareware program for Windows called **iPodLibrary** (available at `www25.brinkster.com/carmagt/ipodlibrary/iPodLibrary.htm`).

- You can also take advantage of the Notes folder and other iPod features by using some of the handy AppleScripts provided for iTunes and the iPod, which you can download from the Apple site (`www.apple.com/applescript/ipod`).

Taking Your Mac System on the Road

Although the iPod is the road warrior's dream weapon for combating road fatigue and boredom, if you update and maintain its hard drive contents wisely, it can also be invaluable as a tool for providing quick information and for saving your computer from disaster. Don't let hard drive space go to waste: Fill up your iPod and let the iPod be your road manager. You can put your most important applications, utilities, and files on the iPod hard drive as a backup.

You can even use your iPod to save your Mac in a system crisis. Although this operation isn't officially supported by Apple, you can load the iPod with a minimally configured Mac system and then use the iPod to start up your Mac. Depending on the size of your iPod, you should be able to fit both a minimal system and a considerable amount of music on the iPod.

Life on the road can be hazardous to your laptop's hard drive, and if any portion of the hard drive containing system files is damaged, your system might not start up. When this happens, you ordinarily use the installation CDs to start the Mac, scan and fix the hard drive trouble spots, and reinstall the Mac operating system. With your iPod, you can at least start the Mac and scan and fix the hard drive trouble spots, and you can also use any other files or applications that you previously put on your iPod.

Mac models introduced after January 2003 can't start up with Mac OS 9, so you need to save Mac OS X to your iPod unless you use an older Mac.

To get the most functionality from your iPod, make sure that you have the latest version of iPod software. To find out which version of software your iPod uses, choose Settings⇨About from the iPod main menu. To update your iPod software to the latest version, see Chapter 27.

To copy files and applications to your iPod, first enable the iPod as a hard drive, as we describe earlier in this chapter.

Installing Mac OS X

To install a custom version of OS X older than version 10.2 on your iPod (such as 10.0 or 10.1), connect your iPod as a hard drive, as we describe earlier in this chapter, and then follow these steps:

1. **Insert your Mac OS X installation CD into your Mac and follow the directions to start up the installation process.**

   You have to restart the Mac with the installation CD while holding down C to start the computer from the CD.

2. **When the installer asks you to select a destination, choose the iPod hard drive.**

   Don't use the option to erase and format the hard drive, because the hard drive of your iPod is specially formatted for playing music, and formatting it in this manner prevents it from playing music again. So *don't* format it! If you format or erase the iPod's hard drive by mistake, you must restore it to its factory condition, as we describe in Chapter 27.

3. **Specify a custom installation rather than a standard installation.**

   To make sure that you don't use up too much hard drive space on your iPod, choose a custom installation of OS X. In the custom installation section, choose only the languages that you need. These language options take up a lot of space, and you probably don't need them.

4. **After installation finishes and the Mac restarts from the iPod, continue through the setup procedure, and then use Software Update in System Preferences to update the Mac system on your iPod.**

   Most likely a lot of system updates are waiting for you — updates released after the date of your installation CDs. Take the time to update your system because these updates might make a difference in how your computer performs with certain applications.

To install a custom version of OS X version 10.2 (Jaguar) on your iPod, you can use Carbon Copy Cloner, a $5 shareware program (available from www.bombich.com/software/ccc.html). Although you could clone your system by using the Unix ditto command in the Terminal window of Mac OS X, this process is tedious and you could easily make a mistake. Carbon Copy Cloner lets you specify what parts of the system you don't need cloned, and you can use its Preferences dialog to make the "target disk" (your iPod) bootable. You can also install OS X version 10.2 on your iPod using SuperDuper! (www.shirt-pocket.com/SuperDuper/SuperDuperDescription.html), a $19.95 advanced disk-copying program.

To install a custom version of OS X version 10.3 (Panther) or version 10.4 (Tiger) on your iPod, connect your iPod as a hard drive, and then use the Disk Utility program supplied with OS X. (It's in the Utilities folder inside your Applications folder.) Using Disk Utility, drag the icon for a source hard drive with a version of OS X to the Source text box in the Disk Utility dialog, and then drag your iPod hard drive icon into the Destination text box. Then click Restore, and the program does everything for you.

To start up a Mac in an emergency situation from an iPod that runs Mac OS X, connect the iPod, hold down Option, and choose Restart from the Apple menu (or if your system is already hosed, use the Power button to reboot while holding down Option). Eventually, as the Mac resets itself and scans itself for any startup drives, all the startup drives appear as icons in a row, with a right-pointing arrow underneath the icons. Click the icon representing the iPod hard drive, and then click the right-pointing arrow to start the system from that drive.

While you're at it, copy the Disk Utility program to your iPod so that you can repair any Mac's hard drive by using your iPod as the startup drive.

Installing Mac OS 9

Macs sold since 2003 no longer use OS 9, and some older models can't use a FireWire drive (such as an iPod) as a startup drive. However, you can still install OS 9 on an iPod to use as a startup drive for a Mac that can run OS 9. To install a custom version of OS 9 on your iPod, connect your iPod as a hard drive, and then follow these steps:

1. **Insert your Mac OS 9 installation CD into your Mac and follow the directions to start up the installation process.**

   You have to restart the Mac with the installation CD while holding down C to start the computer from the CD.

2. **When the installer asks you to select a destination, select the iPod hard drive.**

3. **After the installation finishes, quit the installation program.**

   That's all you have to do — the installer does everything for you.

To start up a Mac from an iPod that holds Mac OS 9, connect the iPod, hold down Option, and choose Restart from the Apple menu (or if your system is already hosed, use the Power button to reboot while holding down Option). Eventually, as the Mac resets and scans itself for any startup drives, all the startup drives appear as icons in a row, with a right-pointing arrow underneath the icons. Click the icon representing the iPod hard drive, and then click the right-pointing arrow to start the system from that drive.

Removing the system

Removing Mac OS 9 from an iPod is easy: Simply drag the System Folder from the iPod hard drive to the Trash when your iPod is connected as a hard drive.

Removing Mac OS X isn't as easy because OS X installs hidden files and directories, and there is no easy way to drag them to the Trash. (Perhaps that's why Apple doesn't support this feature.) The quickest and easiest way to remove OS X from an iPod is to restore the iPod, as we describe in Chapter 27. Restore erases and reformats the iPod to its original factory condition. Be sure to copy any important files stored on your iPod before doing this. Although all your music and files are erased in this one step, it's much easier to then add your music from iTunes, your calendars and contacts, and your files, than it is to try to delete files associated with OS X. Restore, and then copy everything back to your iPod as needed.

Chapter 24

Transferring and Viewing Photos

. . . .

. . . .

*T*aking photos has never been easier. Digital cameras and photo editing software have combined to turn computers into digital darkrooms — no need for a real darkroom with smelly chemicals and film processing equipment. In fact, you no longer need film. What a relief! You can take all the pictures you want without ever having to find a store to buy another roll of film.

Now maybe your vacation photos bore other people, but to you they're priceless, preserving special memories. Family pictures, vacations, weddings. . .these events don't happen every day. You want to take these pictures with you when you visit friends and relatives, who promised not to be bored. But you don't want to lug a slideshow projector and a carousel loaded with expensive slides, nor do you want to set up a computer. Why not use your iPod?

The color-display iPod models store photos that you can view on the iPod display, and it also connects easily with televisions and video equipment to display photos and slideshows to a larger audience. You can transfer your digital photo library on your computer directly to a color-display iPod in one easy step and keep your color-display iPod synchronized when you add more photos to your library.

This chapter tells you all you need to know about digital cameras to get your photos into your color-display iPod and make fabulous slideshows. It also describes accessories you can use to transfer photos directly from digital cameras and memory card readers to your iPod's hard drive for temporary storage, so that you never run out of memory for photos when shooting pictures on the run.

Importing Photos to Your Computer

Digital photography is truly instant gratification — you see the results immediately and can then take more pictures based on what happened an instant before. When you run out of exposures on your digital film card, connect your digital camera or card reader to your computer and offload the photos to a computerized photo library, and delete them from the memory card. Then go back and take more pictures!

Don't have a digital camera? You still like to use that old film camera your grandmother gave you? Don't worry. You can use a scanner to scan photographic prints, or send your film rolls to a photo service that can convert your film to digital images on a CD or the Web. (Odds are the photo service you already use offers this service. Next time you're there, ask about it.) For example, if your camera uses 35mm film, you can have your pictures developed by a digital imaging service, such as PhotoWorks (www.photoworks.com) or the "You've Got Pictures" service on America Online. Many services offer digital processing of film and choices on how to deliver the digital images — on CD, or posted on the Web for easy downloading to your Mac.

It makes sense to use a computer to organize and archive all your digital photos. You can organize even massive quantities of photos in the photo library in your computer. You can add keywords, titles, and film roll information to each photo automatically, to make locating a particular photo very easy. Keep the photos you like, and delete the ones you don't like. If you have a color printer, obtaining extra prints is as easy as using the Print command. You can even e-mail the photos to a service for high-quality prints.

Photo library software, such as iPhoto on the Mac or Adobe Photoshop Elements or Photoshop Album on a Windows PC, can organize any number of photos; the number is limited only by available hard drive space. At an average size of 2MB per photo (and many photos occupy less space), you can store 10,000 photos in a 20GB hard drive. And, of course, you can expand a photo library over multiple disks or create multiple libraries. The number of digital photos you can manage has no practical limit.

Connecting a digital camera or memory card reader

To import photos to your computer, connect your digital camera to the computer and use iPhoto on a Mac, or use the digital photo application supplied with your digital camera on a Windows PC. USB (Universal Serial Bus) is the connection of choice for connecting most digital cameras to a computer — the exceptions are very high quality cameras that offer FireWire. Fortunately, both types of connections work the same way.

Digital cameras typically come with a special USB or FireWire cable that has a very small connector on one end for the camera and a larger connector on the other end for the computer's USB or FireWire port. However, if both ends are the same on the cable you are using, it doesn't matter which end is plugged into the camera or the computer.

Be sure to power up your camera — most digital cameras have a power-on switch to save battery life. (Many smart people, including ourselves, have sat there waiting for the photos to appear, only to find that the camera was still asleep.) Connect your camera before you turn it on, because the computer may not recognize some camera models unless they are turned on while connected. If the computer doesn't recognize your camera, try turning the camera off and then turning it on again.

If your camera has an AC adapter, run the camera off the adapter when importing photos to save the camera's battery time. If your camera has a sleep mode, make sure that you disable or set it to a time increment long enough to allow your images to import. Importing 24 photos generally takes about one minute with most digital cameras.

A digital camera's memory cards are like extra rolls of film. A memory card reader is useful if you take lots of pictures and use additional cards. Rather than connecting your camera to your computer every time you want to transfer pictures, leave the card reader connected to the USB connection on your computer, and put the camera's memory card in the card reader. If you use multiple memory cards, this method is especially convenient.

iPhoto on a Mac can import photos from a card reader just as it does with a camera, using the same steps. Many Windows applications supplied with digital cameras can also import photos from memory card readers. For example, Preclick Silver Photo Organizer (www.preclick.com) can import photos from CDs, memory card readers and digital cameras that can connect by USB or FireWire and simulate a hard drive.

Using iPhoto on a Mac

To import pictures from a digital camera, connect the camera to your Mac. Click the iPhoto icon to start iPhoto (if it hasn't already started), and follow these steps:

1. **Click the Import mode button.**

   The tools pane changes to show the Import tools, as shown in Figure 24-1. iPhoto displays either a camera icon, a disk icon, or a memory card reader icon, depending on the type of camera or memory card reader you are using. Our Nikon CoolPix 4300 shows up with a disk icon.

2. **Choose whether or not to delete the photos in your camera after importing.**

   If you want to delete photos from your camera as soon as they are imported, click the "Erase camera contents after transfer" option in the tools pane (located at the bottom of the iPhoto window). Many cameras have a delete function, so you don't need to use this option. However, using this option enables you to import and delete photos in the camera all in one step. With the photos in the photo library, you no longer need to keep copies in your camera or memory card, and you can make room for new photos.

Figure 24-1: iPhoto is in import mode, ready to import photos from a digital camera.

3. **Click the Import button.**

   While the importing occurs, the Import button changes to a Stop button; to cancel the photo transfer at any time during your import, click the Stop button. When it finishes importing, iPhoto displays a small image for each photo in the photo library, as shown in Figure 24-2. The size of the images in the viewing area is controlled by the zoom slider in the lower right corner of the iPhoto window, just underneath the viewing area. These small versions of your images, which can be reduced to very small, are called *thumbnails*.

4. **Disconnect the camera (eject it first if necessary).**

   If ejecting is required, the camera's icon appears on the desktop. To eject the camera, click the camera's icon and hold down the mouse button. The Trash icon changes to the Eject icon. You can then drag the camera icon over the Eject icon to eject the camera properly. Although nothing really happens (nothing actually ejects from the machine, nor do any doors open), you may find that if you don't eject as required with some cameras, your images may not delete from the camera even if you have the delete option enabled.

Figure 24-2:
Imported photos appear as thumbnails in the photo library.

Using digital camera software on a PC

To import pictures from a digital camera, connect the camera to your computer and launch the Windows-based photo application supplied with your camera. While there are different applications for different cameras, they generally provide instructions for these four steps:

1. **Connect your camera and set your application into import mode.**

   After connecting your digital camera, your application offers a simple method of importing photos from the camera into your computer. Set up the application so that it is ready to import. For example, in Adobe Photoshop Album, click the Get Photos button, and then choose Digital Camera or Scanner.

2. **Choose whether or not to delete the photos in your camera after importing.**

   Most camera applications offer an option to delete photos from your camera as soon as they are imported. Many cameras have a delete function, so you don't need to use this option. However, using this option enables you to import and delete photos in the camera all in one step. With the photos in the photo library, you no longer need to keep copies in your camera or memory card, and you can make room for new photos.

3. **Start the importing process by choosing an import command or clicking an import button.**

4. **Disconnect the camera (eject it first if necessary).**

   To eject the camera, right-click the camera's icon, choose Eject from the pop-up menu, and then disconnect the camera. Another method is to click the Safely Remove Hardware icon in the bottom-right corner of the screen. The Safely Remove Hardware shortcut menu appears — select the IEEE 1394 (FireWire) device if you use FireWire, or the USB Mass Storage device if you use USB, from the shortcut menu. When the alert dialog appears, click OK and then disconnect the camera.

Organizing photos into albums or collections

You've probably seen photo albums with plastic sleeves for holding photographic prints. A *digital* photo album is similar in concept but holds digital photo files instead of prints. In both cases, an album is simply a way of organizing photos and placing them in a proper sequence. You select the photos from your photo library and arrange them in the order you want. iPhoto uses *album* as its term; Adobe Photoshop Elements and Photoshop Album call it a *collection*. We use the term album for both.

You can use photo albums to assemble photos from special events, such as a vacation, or to display a particular subject, such as your favorite nature photos. If you have many more photos in your library than you want to put on a color-display iPod, you may want to organize albums specifically for transfer to the color-display iPod and for automatic updating. The order that your photos appear in the album is important — it defines the order of photos in a slideshow on your color-display iPod. You can also use albums to organize photos for a slideshow, QuickTime movie, or Web page.

You can make as many albums as you like using any images from your photo library. Because the albums are *lists* of images, they don't use up disk space by copying the images — the actual image files remain in the photo library. Like an iTunes playlist, a photo album is a list of references to photos in your library. You can include the same photo in several albums without making multiple copies of the photo and wasting disk space.

To assign photos to an album in iPhoto, follow these steps:

1. **Click the Organize mode button.**

   The photos in your library appear as thumbnails in the viewer pane.

2. **Click the + button.**

   The + button is underneath the Source pane; refer to Figure 24-2. Alternatively choose File⇨New Album or ⌘+N.

   The New Album dialog box appears.

3. **Type the album name and click OK.**

   The default name appears highlighted in the New Album dialog box. Type a name for the album (other than "Album 01" — something descriptive.

4. **Select photos in your library and drag them into the album.**

   When you click on a photo, you know the photo is selected when an outline appears around it — drag the photo over the name of the album in the Source pane. You can select multiple photos for dragging by clicking the first one and holding down the Shift key while clicking the last one — the first, last, and all the photos between them are selected automatically. You can also add individual photos to a selection by ⌘-clicking or Ctrl-clicking each photo. You can then drag the selection over the name of the album in the Source pane, as shown in Figure 24-3. A number appears, showing the number of selected photos in the range.

Figure 24-3:
Add multiple
photos at
one time to
an album.

5. **Click the photo album name in the Source pane to rearrange the photos in the album.**

   When you click an album name in the Source pane, only the photos you dragged to the album appear in the viewer pane, not the entire library. You can reorder pictures within the album by simply dragging them to a different position.

iPhoto also lets you create *smart albums.* Smart albums add photos to themselves based on prearranged criteria. You can set up a smart album that decides which photos to include based on the ratings you assign to them. For example, you might want to set up a smart album with only the highest-rated photos taken during the last six months.

To create a smart album in iPhoto, follow these steps:

1. **Choose File⇨New Smart Album and type a name for the album in the name field.**

2. **Set the criteria for including photos in the smart album.**

   Make your criteria selections from the pop-up menus. Select a condition from the first pop-up menu and choose a comparison, such as the greater than or less than, from the second pop-up menu.

3. **Combine conditions for better results.**

   To add additional matching conditions, click the Add (+) button. Then decide whether to match *all* or *any* of these conditions by choosing either option from the pop-up menu next to Match.

4. **Click OK.**

   When finished adding conditions to establish the smart album criteria, click OK to save your smart album.

iPhoto automatically updates your smart album when any photo that matches the criteria is added or removed from the library.

Windows users can assign photos to a collection using Adobe Photoshop Album. Follow these steps:

1. **Click the Collections tab.**

2. **Click the "Create new collection" button.**

   The Create Collection dialog box appears.

3. **Type the collection name and click OK.**

4. **Select photos and drag them into the collection.**

   You can select multiple photos by clicking the first one and holding down the Ctrl key while clicking more photos. Drag the selected photos to the new collection tag to add them to the collection.

5. **Click the check box next to the collection name to view the collection and rearrange the photos in the collection.**

   You can reorder pictures within the album by simply dragging them to a different position.

With your photos organized into albums or collections, you are ready to set up automatic transfer to your color-display iPod.

Transferring Pictures to a Color-display iPod

You can take your pictures with you, safely tucked into your color-display iPod. On a Mac, you can use iPhoto (version 4.0.3 or newer) to import photos into your computer and organize them into albums. You can then use iTunes to transfer photos from your iPhoto library automatically.

On Windows, you can use Adobe Photoshop Album (version 1.0 or newer), or Photoshop Elements (version 3.0 or newer), to import photos into your computer and organize your photos into collections. You can then use iTunes to transfer photos from your photo library automatically.

On either Mac or Windows, you can use any other photo editing or organizing software and store your photos in a folder on your hard drive. You can then use iTunes to transfer photos from the folder.

Whether you transfer photos from a library or from a folder on your hard drive, you can keep your color-display iPod synchronized with the photo library and its albums, or with the subfolders and image files in the folder. Your color-display iPod can be kept up-to-date every time you connect it to your computer — not just with music, but also with photos.

If you connect your color-display iPod to another computer running iTunes, you might be in for a surprise. When you connect a color-display iPod previously linked to another computer, iTunes displays the message: `This iPod is linked to another photo library. Do you want to change the link to this photo library and replace all existing photos on this iPod with those from this library?` If you don't want to change your iPod to have this other photo library, click No. Otherwise, iTunes erases the photos on your iPod and updates your iPod with the other computer's photo library.

Transferring photos from a photo library

If you store photos in an iPhoto library on a Mac, or in a photo library managed by Adobe Photoshop Album or Photoshop Elements on a Windows PC, you can transfer photos to your color-display iPod automatically, and synchronize your iPod to your library so that any changes you make to the library are copied to your iPod. You can also limit the transfer and synchronization to albums or collections rather than the entire library.

To transfer all photos in a library to a color-display iPod and keep your iPod synchronized with your photo library, follow these steps:

1. **Connect the color-display iPod to your computer.**

   Your iPod must be connected for you to change the update preferences. iTunes starts automatically when you connect the iPod to your computer.

2. **Select the iPod in the iTunes Source pane.**

   Your iPod appears in the Source pane using the name you gave it when you installed the iPod software; see Chapter 2.

3. **Click the iPod Options button on the bottom-right side of the iTunes window, or click the iPod button in the iTunes Preferences dialog.**

   The iPod Options button appears only when an iPod is connected and selected in the Source pane. You can also choose iTunes⇨Preferences on a Mac or Edit⇨Preferences on a Windows PC, and click the iPod button — whether or not the iPod is selected in the Source pane (although it has to be connected). The iPod Preferences dialog appears.

4. **Click the Photos button to view the iPod Photos preferences.**

   The Photos button appears for color-display iPod models. The iPod photo preferences pane appears, as shown in Figure 24-4.

Figure 24-4: Set your color-display iPod to synchronize with your photo library.

5. **Click the "Synchronize photos from" option and select the library from the pop-up menu.**

   The pop-up menu lists iPhoto on a Mac; on a Windows PC, your choices are Photoshop Album or Photoshop Elements.

6. **Click the "Copy all photos and albums" option.**

7. **Click OK.**

From this point on, until you change these preferences, every time you connect your color-display iPod to this computer, iTunes automatically synchronizes your iPod with your entire photo library, keeping the iPod up-to-date with any new photos, improvements to photos, or deletions in your library. Your iPod also copies your photo album assignments, so that your photos are organized by album.

To transfer only photos in specific albums in a library to a color-display iPod and keep your iPod synchronized with these albums (not the entire library), follow these steps:

1. **Connect the color-display iPod to your computer.**

   Your iPod must be connected for you to change the update preferences. iTunes starts automatically when you connect the iPod to your computer.

2. **Select the iPod in the iTunes Source pane.**

3. **Click the iPod Options button on the bottom-right side of the iTunes window, or click the iPod button in the iTunes Preferences dialog.**

4. **Click the Photos button to view the iPod Photos preferences.**

5. **Click the "Synchronize photos from" option and select the library from the pop-up menu.**

6. **Click the "Copy selected albums only" option.**

7. **In the list box, select each album that you want to copy.**

   Select the check box next to each album to select it for the update, as shown in Figure 24-5.

8. **Click OK.**

From this point on, until you change these preferences, every time you connect your color-display iPod to this computer, iTunes automatically synchronizes your iPod with the selected albums in the photo library, keeping your iPod up-to-date with any new photos, improvements to photos, or deletions that occur in those albums.

Figure 24-5:
Set your color-display iPod to synchronize only with selected albums in your photo library.

Transferring image files from a hard drive folder

No matter what photo application you use, you can save photos as image files in a folder on your hard drive, and then bring them into your color-display iPod whenever you want. It's rare for a color-display iPod to meet an image file format it doesn't like. Use JPEG (JPG), GIF, TIFF (TIF), Pict, PNG, PSD (Photoshop), PDF, jpg 2000, SGI, and BMP on a Mac. On a Windows PC, use JPEG (JPG), GIF, TIFF (TIF), PNG, and BMP.

To transfer all photos in a folder on your hard drive to a color-display iPod, follow these steps:

1. **Connect the color-display iPod to your computer.**

   Your iPod must be connected for you to change the update preferences. iTunes starts automatically when you connect the color-display iPod to your computer.

2. **Select the iPod in the iTunes Source pane.**

   Your iPod appears in the Source pane using the name you gave it when you installed the iPod software; see Chapter 2.

3. **Click the iPod Options button on the bottom-right side of the iTunes window, or click the iPod button in the iTunes Preferences dialog.**

   The iPod Options button appears only when an iPod is connected and selected in the Source pane. You can also choose iTunes➪Preferences on a Mac or Edit➪Preferences on a Windows PC, and click the iPod button — whether or not the iPod is selected in the Source pane (although it has to be connected). The iPod Preferences dialog appears.

4. **Click the Photos button to view the iPod Photos preferences.**

   The Photos button appears for color-display iPod models. The iPod photo preferences pane appears; refer to Figure 24-4.

5. **Click the "Synchronize photos from" option and select "Choose Folder" from the pop-up menu.**

   The pop-up menu offers the "Choose Folder" item, as shown in Figure 24-6.

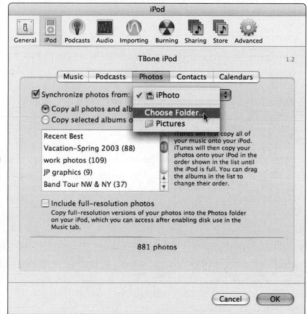

Figure 24-6: Set your color-display iPod to synchronize with a folder of image files.

6. **Browse your hard drive for the folder containing images, and click Choose on a Mac or OK on a Windows PC.**

   If you want your photos to appear in separate albums on your color-display iPod, create subfolders inside the folder and organize your image files inside these subfolders. iTunes copies the subfolder assignments as if they were album assignments.

7. **Click OK.**

From this point on, until you change these preferences, every time you connect your color-display iPod to this computer, iTunes automatically synchronizes your iPod with the folder on your hard drive, keeping your iPod up-to-date with any new photos, changed photos, or deletions.

Transferring full-resolution photos and images

Picture quality with a digital camera is measured by the number of pixels — specific points of information in a picture, also known as the image *resolution*. Digital cameras are often described by the image resolution in millions of pixels, or *megapixels*. Higher megapixel counts usually result in better images. A 2-megapixel camera produces good 4×6-inch prints and acceptable 8×10-inch prints. A 3-megapixel camera produces very good 4×6-inch prints and magazine-quality 8×10-inch prints. A 5-megapixel camera produces good quality 10×14-inch prints. And so on.

A color-display iPod, by default, doesn't need the full resolution of photos to display them well on televisions and use them with video projectors, which are far lower in resolution than prints; certainly the tiny iPod display doesn't need high resolution in the photos it displays. The more resolution you have, the more space the photo takes up, so during the transfer, the color-display iPod software optimizes photos for video display to save space.

If you intend to use your color-display iPod to transfer images to another computer or to make a backup of your photos in their original resolution, you can set an option to include full-resolution versions of the photos when transferring photos. You would do this to preserve the full quality of the photo so that you can use the version on the iPod for making prints.

To include full-resolution images, follow the steps outlined above to transfer your photos to a color-display iPod. In the color-display preferences (refer to Figure 24-6), click the "Include full-resolution photos" option. This option copies the full-resolution photos into the Photos folder of your color-display iPod, which you can access on your computer by enabling your iPod for hard drive use, as described in Chapter 23.

Transferring photos with the iPod Camera Connector

Don't you just hate it when you fill up your digital camera's memory card while on the road, away from your computer? No matter how many pictures you take, you can't run out of memory if you use a color-display iPod and Apple's iPod Camera Connector, available from the Apple Store — a compact storage solution that lets you shoot your photos, dump them into a color-display iPod for storage, preview them on the iPod, and continue shooting. Depending how much space you have on your iPod, you could continue shooting photos indefinitely without having to visit your computer or use more memory cards.

The iPod Camera Connector is a convenient adapter — about the size of a flash memory card and about twice as thick — that connects to a color-display iPod's dock connection and lets you plug in a USB cable connected to your digital camera. You can then temporarily store photos from digital camera memory cards at full resolution on the iPod, for later importing into your computer.

To transfer photos using the iPod Camera Connector, follow these steps:

1. **Connect your digital camera to the iPod Camera Connector.**

   Use the USB cable supplied with your camera.

2. **Connect the iPod Camera Connector to the dock connection of your color-display iPod.**

3. **Turn your digital camera on.**

   The Import menu appears on the iPod color display, showing the number of photos in the camera and the space occupied, along with the Import and Cancel menu functions.

4. **To import photos, highlight Import and press the Select button.**

   The Photo Import menu appears, showing the progress of the download to your iPod. During this process you can choose the Stop and Save function to save the pictures you've downloaded, or Cancel to cancel the download. When the download finishes, your color-display iPod gives you the option to erase the camera's memory card.

To preview your photos on the iPod, see the next section, "Viewing Photos with Your Color-display iPod" in this chapter.

Viewing Photos with Your Color-display iPod

You may remember the old days when slides were projected onto white walls or sheets, and the click-clack sound of the slide carousel on the projector drowned out everything else. Now you can throw away those old slide projectors, connect up your television, and present a slideshow with music and transitions between each photo. All you need is your color-display iPod and a television, video monitor, video projector, or similar video equipment.

Viewing photos on your iPod color display

To see photos on your iPod color display, follow these steps:

1. **On the iPod, select the Photos menu from the main menu.**

2. **Select either Photo Library or the album name in the Photos menu.**

   Photo Library displays thumbnail images of all the photos in your iPod. Selecting an album displays thumbnail images of only the photos assigned to that album.

3. **Use the scroll wheel to highlight the photo thumbnail you want, and press the Select button.**

   You may have several screens of thumbnails — use the scroll wheel to scroll through photo thumbnails in a screen and over several screens, or use the Next/Fast-forward and Previous/Rewind buttons to skip to the next or previous screen. When you select a photo thumbnail, your iPod color display fills up with the photo you selected.

If you previously connected the iPod Camera Connector to your color-display iPod, you can use the Photo Import function in the Photos menu. Select Photo Import to see the photos you've imported using the iPod Camera Connector — the photos are organized into albums named as film rolls (Roll#1, Roll#2, and so on). Select a roll and choose Browse in the Roll menu to view your imported photos.

Connecting to a television or to video equipment

You can connect your full-size color-display iPod (but not an iPod nano) to any television that offers standard RCA video and audio connections, or an S-video connection. Color-display iPods (except for the iPod nano) are supplied with the iPod AV Cable, a special cable you can plug into the headphone connection of the color-display iPod, or to the line-out connection on the dock supplied with the iPod. (You must use a color-display iPod dock; other docks do not support video out.) The cable offers RCA video (yellow) and stereo audio (red and white) connectors to plug into your television or video equipment. You must use the AV Cable supplied with your iPod — Apple warns that others won't work.

For even better picture quality, you can use a television monitor that supports S-video, and your color-display iPod dock. Plug a standard S-video cable into the dock's S-video connection, and plug the other end into your television's S-video connection. Plug the supplied AV Cable into the color-display iPod headphone or dock line-out connection, and the AV Cable stereo audio connectors (but *not* the yellow video connector) into the television. For better sound, plug the AV Cable stereo audio connectors into a stereo system with good speakers.

You can set your color-display iPod to play slideshows on your television. If you don't see a picture on your television, check to be sure your television is set to the correct input source — video in (RCA) or S-video in (if you use an S-video cable and a color-display iPod dock). You can also use other types of video equipment; for example, a video recorder that accepts RCA or S-video input can record the slideshow, and a video projector can display it on a large screen.

Setting up and playing a slideshow

Slideshows are a far more entertaining way of showing photos, because you can include music and transitions between each pair of photos. You can display your slideshow on the iPod color display or on a television. Your slideshow settings work with any photo album or with the entire photo library on your iPod.

To set up a slideshow, follow these steps:

1. **On your color-display iPod, select Photos from the main menu, and Slideshow Settings from the Photos menu.**

2. **Select Time Per Slide from the Slideshow Settings menu to set the duration of each slide.**

   You can select choices ranging from 2 to 20 seconds, or Manual to set the slideshow to advance to the next slide only when you click the iPod Next/Fast-forward button.

3. **Pick music to play by selecting Music from the Slideshow Settings menu, and selecting a playlist.**

   You can choose any playlist in your iPod, including the On-The-Go playlist, or the Now Playing choice, to play along with your slideshow. You can also choose to play the music set in iPhoto (if you're using a Mac) — iPhoto lets you assign an iTunes playlist to an iPhoto album, and that assignment is saved in your iPod — if the playlist has been copied to your iPod, it is automatically assigned to the slideshow.

4. **Select a transition to use between photos in the slideshow by choosing Transitions in the Slideshow Settings menu.**

   Wipe across is our favorite, but you can select versions of the standard Wipe and Push transitions including Push across, Push down, Wipe down, and Wipe center. Choose Random if you want to use a randomly different transition for each photo change. Choose Off for no transition.

5. **To TV or not TV? Set the color-display iPod to display the slideshow on a TV, or to ask first, by choosing TV Out from the Slideshow Settings menu.**

   You have three choices for TV Out: On, Ask, or Off.

   - On displays the slideshow on a television (through the video out connection). You can also see the slides in large thumbnail form on your iPod color display, along with the number of the photo within the album or library, and Next and Previous icons.

   - Ask displays a screen first, asking you to select TV Off or TV On, so that you can make the choice each time you play a slideshow.

   - Off displays the slideshow with full-sized images on the iPod color display.

6. **Select other options from the Slideshow Settings menu: Repeat, Shuffle Photos, and TV Signal.**

   Choose Repeat and select On to repeat the slideshow over and over, or Off to turn off repeating. Choose Shuffle Photos and select On to shuffle photos in the slideshow in a random order, or Off to turn off random shuffling. If traveling or living outside the U.S., choose TV Signal to change your television signal to PAL for European and other countries that use PAL as the video standard, or to NTSC for the U.S. standard.

To play a slideshow, follow these steps:

1. *Optional:* **If you want to display the slideshow on a television, connect the color-display iPod to the television first.**

2. **On your iPod, select Photos from the main menu.**

3. **Highlight an album name or Photo Library from the Photos menu, and press the Play/Pause button.**

   Highlighting Photo Library first includes the entire library in the slideshow; highlighting an album includes only the photos in that album.

   You can also start a slideshow by pressing the Select button when you are viewing a photo on the iPod color display.

4. **If you set TV Out to Ask, choose TV On or TV Off for your slideshow.**

   TV On displays the slideshow on a television (through the video out connection). You can also see the slides in large thumbnail form on the iPod color display. TV Off displays the slideshow with full-sized images on the iPod color display.

5. **Use the iPod buttons to navigate your slideshow.**

   If you set Time Per Slide to Manual, use the Next/Fast-forward and Previous/Rewind buttons to move through the slideshow. Next/Fast-forward moves to the next photo in the slideshow, and Previous/Rewind moves to the previous photo.

   If you set Timer Per Slide to a duration, use Play/Pause to pause and play the slideshow.

6. **Press the Menu button to stop the slideshow and return to the Photos menu.**

Transferring Photos from a Camera to an iPod Hard Drive

You can still make an iPod useful for photo work even if you don't have a color-display iPod. With full-size iPods that have a dock connector, including color-display iPods, you can use an accessory to temporarily store photos from digital camera memory cards at full resolution, so that you can later import the photos into your computer.

If you're traveling with just your digital camera and your iPod, you can shoot all the pictures you want without worrying about filling up your camera's memory card. Shoot all the pictures you want, and then connect the camera to your iPod with an accessory such as the Belkin Media Reader for iPod, and transfer the photos to your iPod hard drive. Then delete the pictures from your camera's memory card and go snap some more. You could travel for weeks on end, shooting thousands of photos in locations around the world without running out of space in your iPod.

The key to these capabilities is the fact that the iPod serves as an external hard drive. After you mount the iPod on your Mac or Windows desktop, you can use it as a hard drive.

The Belkin Media Reader for iPod connects to the iPod's dock connection transfers photos quickly to the Photos folder on your iPod hard drive. Your iPod can hold hundreds or even thousands of photos (depending on how much music is already stored on it). Available from the Apple Store, the Belkin accessory works only with full-size iPod models with dock connectors.

With the Belkin Media Reader and a color-display iPod (updated with iPod Software 1.1 or newer), you can browse photos you just imported without having to synchronize the iPod with your computer. It works just like the iPod Camera Connector. (See "Transferring photos with the iPod Camera Connector" in this chapter.)

To transfer the photos to the iPhoto library on a Mac, mount the iPod as a hard drive, as we describe in Chapter 23. Then import the photos by dragging the files directly from the iPod hard drive and dropping them over the iPhoto window. To transfer the photos to a Windows photo application such as Adobe Photo Album or Photo Elements, drag the files or the entire Photos folder directly from the iPod hard drive into a folder on your hard drive, and open them with the photo application.

Chapter 25

Getting Personal

*Y*our iPod is capable of helping you manage your activities on the road to the point where it competes in some respects with personal digital assistants (PDAs). You can manage your address book, calendar, and To-Do list for the road all on your computer, and then update or synchronize your iPod to have all the information that you need for viewing and playback. As a result, you might not ever need an additional PDA — especially if you prefer typing data into your computer before loading it into the device. Your iPod is a *player* — not just in the world of music, but also in the world of personal productivity.

The most likely bit of information that you might need on the road is a phone number, an address, or information related to an event or calendar appointment. Your iPod can store your personal information right alongside your music so that the information is available at your fingertips. After entering and managing your personal information on your computer, you can then copy the information to your iPod or synchronize with information already on your iPod.

The iPod accepts industry-standard iCalendar and vCalendar files for calendars and To-Do lists, which you can export from most applications that offer calendars and To-Do lists. It also accepts industry-standard *vCards,* or *virtual business cards,* which are records containing contact information for people, including physical addresses, e-mail addresses, phone numbers, and so on. Again, most applications that offer address books or contact lists can export vCards.

If you're a Mac user, you have it easy: You can use the free iCal and Address Book applications and automatically synchronize the information with your iPod calendar and contact list with iTunes; see Chapter 26. Mac users can also choose other applications and export (or drag) the information to your iPod.

If you're a Windows user, you have a variety of choices for managing contacts and calendar information, and you also have choices of third-party utilities for putting the information on an iPod, as well as the tried-and-true technique of exporting (or dragging) information to the iPod.

This chapter shows you how to enter your personal information into the computer by using Address Book and iCal (on a Mac) or Microsoft Outlook and Microsoft Address Book (on a Windows PC).

Keeping Appointments with iCal on the Mac

iCal, the free desktop calendar application that you can download from Apple's software download page (www.info.apple.com/support/downloads.html), creates calendars that you can copy to your iPod. iCal requires Mac OS X version 10.2.3 or newer. You can create custom calendars for different activities, such as home, office, road tours, exercise and diet schedules, mileage logs, and so on. You can view them separately or all together. After editing your calendars on the Mac, you can synchronize your iPod to have the same calendars as we describe in Chapter 26.

If you use another application to manage your personal calendar, you might still want to use iCal just to transfer your calendar information to the iPod painlessly. You can import calendars from other applications that support the iCal or vCal format, such as Microsoft Entourage, Microsoft Outlook, and Palm Desktop. When your information is in iCal, you can synchronize your entire calendar with your iPod using iTunes.

Launch iCal by double-clicking the iCal application or clicking its icon in the Mac OS X Dock. iCal displays a calendar, as shown in Figure 25-1, and you can switch the view from an entire month to just one week or one day by clicking the Day or Week buttons at the bottom of the window.

iCal starts you off with two calendars: Home and Work. Their names have check marks next to them in the upper-left corner of the iCal window, indicating that both are visible, and they're merged into the calendar view. To see only your Home calendar, deselect the Work option in the Calendars pane on the left, and vice versa. It's easy to set up appointments and events for either calendar.

Figure 25-1:
View your
personal
calendar
with iCal.

Setting up an appointment or event

Some appointments and events are a drag, and some are fun, but either way you can drag your mouse to create one. Click the Week button at the bottom of the window to see just an entire week, and then click and drag over a period of time to create an appointment. You can choose File⇨New Event to do the same thing.

To see the details of an event or appointment, do one of these things:

- ✔ Double-click the event or appointment.

- ✔ Click the event or appointment to select it, and then click the "i" button in the lower-right corner.

- ✔ Click the event or appointment to select it, and then choose Window⇨Show Info.

The detail for the event or appointment appears in the info drawer that sticks out on the right side of the iCal window, as shown in Figure 25-2.

Figure 25-2:
View the
details of a
new iCal
event or
appointment
in the info
drawer.

In the info drawer, you can type over the filler "New Event" and "location"
text, change the date and time, add attendees, specify the status and whether
the event or appointment should be repeated, and so on. You can type a note
in the Notes section at the bottom and assign the event to a specific calendar
(in this case, the Home calendar). If you have created custom calendars within
iCal (as we describe in "Creating a custom calendar"), select the calendar
that you want to add the event to from the Calendar pop-up menu. You can
set the event to automatically repeat every day, week, month, or year by
using the Repeat pop-up menu.

Need to be reminded? Set an alarm for an event in iCal by selecting an option
from the Alarm pop-up menu. If you select the Message with Sound option,
the alarm works with your iPod when you synchronize your calendar with
your iPod, as we describe in Chapter 26.

Adding a To-Do item

If you're petrified like the White Rabbit in Carroll's *Alice in Wonderland* with
so little time and so much to do, iCal can keep track of your To-Do list. Click
the thumbtack icon to view the To Do items pane of the iCal window (or
choose Window➪Show To Dos). Choose File➪New To Do to add an item to
the list.

You can set the priority of the To-Do item so that it sorts to the top (highest
priority) or bottom (no priority) of the To-Do list. You can also set its due
date in the Due Date pop-up menu — if you set a due date, the alarm pop-up
appears so that you can also set an alarm for the To-Do item. (The alarm also

works in your iPod when you synchronize your calendar with your iPod.) iCal lets you assign the To-Do item to a specific calendar and even add a Web address to the URL field to link the To-Do item to a Web page. To mark a To-Do item as finished, select the Completed option for the item.

Creating a custom calendar

You can create custom calendars in iCal that show only the events that are assigned to the custom calendar. For example, you might create one custom calendar for work events, another for family events, another for an exercise plan, and so on. Your custom calendars are maintained by iCal so that you can see them all at once or individually in the calendar view. The list of custom calendars appears in the top-left corner of the iCal window, with a check box next to each calendar. When you select the check box, the custom calendar's events show up in the calendar view. If you select more than one custom calendar, the events from all selected custom calendars are merged in the calendar view.

iPod as PDA: You can play, but you can't type

We could never get used to tiny portable computers and PDAs. We use computers for all our information needs, but we've never really gone smaller than a laptop because the keyboards on smaller devices are too small for touch-typists.

People who use the hunt-and-peck method of typing can quickly adapt to using forefingers and thumbs or a stylus to type reasonably well on a cell phone or PDA. However, PDAs can be hard to use for people who are trained to hold their hands a certain way and touch-type with all fingers.

There's true irony in this. The original reason for the QWERTY arrangement of keys on the keyboard, standard to this day, was to *slow down* the human typist and place commonly used letter combinations on opposite sides of the keyboard so that the mechanical arms of the typewriter wouldn't jam. Efforts to change this during the computer age were ignored even if they did allow for increased typing speed and higher productivity. People assimilated the original arrangement and learned to type quickly with it, and they simply refused to change.

Small keyboards and clumsy human interfaces hamper the use of PDAs for input, raising the question for the laptop users: "Why bother?" Laptops (and possibly the new tablet computers) are excellent for input and organizing information. Besides, if you use more than one device to enter input, you run the risk of being out of sync — most often you end up accidentally overwriting the new stuff put into the PDA with the stuff from your laptop.

A Mac laptop and iPod combo is our answer to this dilemma. We input and edit all information with a Mac laptop and update the iPod as necessary. We can then take the iPod into situations in which we need to view but not change the information. And we don't need PDAs — except to play with as gadget freaks.

To create a custom calendar, follow these steps:

1. **Choose File⇨New Calendar, or click the plus (+) button in the bottom-left corner of the iCal window.**

   An Untitled item appears in the list of calendars in the top-left corner.

2. **Type a new name for the Untitled item.**

   Click inside the Name text box and type a new name.

3. **Turn on or off the custom calendar.**

   Deselect the custom calendar if you don't want its events to be displayed. Select it to display the custom calendar along with other selected custom calendars (merged with the other custom calendar events).

Keeping Appointments with Microsoft Outlook

Microsoft Outlook is offered as part of Microsoft Office (Windows version), and Microsoft Outlook Express is offered free with Windows. In addition, a Mac version of Outlook is available from Microsoft. You can use any of these applications to create calendars and export the calendar information to your iPod.

Outlook provides extensive calendar and scheduling functions and task management. You need only a fraction of Outlook's features to keep a calendar and To-Do list that can be viewed on your iPod. Many of the more advanced functions, such as scheduling conferences and meetings to coincide with the schedules of other people on a network, have no meaning on an iPod. Nevertheless, the iPod is useful for viewing the results of Outlook activity. If you use those features, any event, appointment, or meeting that displays in your Outlook calendar is also copied to your iPod along with the calendar.

With your calendar and To-Do tasks set up in Outlook, you can export the information to your iPod, as we describe in Chapter 26.

Setting up an appointment or event

To set up an appointment or event in Microsoft Outlook, first launch Outlook, and then follow these steps:

1. **Click the Calendar icon and click any time slot to select it in the Outlook calendar.**

   The time slots in the Outlook calendar, as shown in Figure 25-3, appear when you click the Calendar icon.

Figure 25-3:
Select a
time slot in
the Outlook
calendar
for an
appointment.

2. **Choose File⇨New⇨Appointment to create an appointment or event, and then fill in the information.**

   Alternatively, you can right-click the selected time slot and choose New Appointment (or choose New Recurring Appointment for appointments that repeat often). Specify start and end times and a location, as shown in Figure 25-4.

Figure 25-4:
Type
information
for a
specific
event or
appointment
into the
Outlook
calendar.

3. **Click the Save and Close button to save the appointment or event.**

Adding a To-Do task

The outlook for your future plans might be bright, but you need more than a crystal ball to keep them that way. If you already use Outlook for your e-mail and calendar functions, you might also want to use it to keep track of your To-Do list.

To create a To-Do task in Outlook, choose New⇨Task, and type a subject name for the task. To make the task a recurring task, select the Recurrence option and choose a frequency (Daily, Weekly, Monthly, or Yearly) for the recurring task. Finally, click the Save and Close button to save the task.

Storing Contacts in the Mac OS X Address Book

Address Book, a free application that's provided with OS X for the Mac, has just about all the features you could ever want for storing names, addresses, phone numbers, e-mail addresses, and physical addresses. You can drag and drop addresses and phone numbers from incoming e-mails to avoid having to type the information, and you can wirelessly copy cards from your address book to cell phones, PDAs, and other Bluetooth-enabled devices. Keeping your iPod synchronized with your addresses and phone numbers is simple and automatic. You can then have your friends' addresses and phone numbers with you at all times, right on your iPod.

If you use some other application for storing contact information, you might want to use Address Book in addition to your other application so you can import contact information from other applications that support vCards or the LDIF format. (LDIF is the file format for *LDAP,* which stands for *Lightweight Directory Access Protocol.*) To do so, launch Address Book and choose File⇨Import, select the format that you used from the submenu, and select the file that contains the exported information. Once your information is in Address Book, you can synchronize the information with your iPod, eliminating the hassle of dragging vCards to the iPod individually.

Adding and editing contact information

Launch Address Book by double-clicking the Address Book application or by clicking its icon in the Mac OS X Dock. To add a new card, follow these steps:

1. **Choose File➪New Card or click the plus (+) button at the bottom of the Name pane.**

   A new blank card appears, ready for you to add information.

2. **Type the person's first and last name over the placeholder first and last name text boxes, and add contact information to the other text boxes.**

   You can type addresses, phone numbers, e-mail addresses, and so on, as shown in Figure 25-5. To add multiple addresses, phone numbers, or other text boxes, click the tiny plus (+) icon next to each type of information to add more. If some of the text boxes don't apply, skip them, and they won't show up in the edited card. You can even enter a two-line address by pressing Return to continue to the second line.

3. **To save your changes, click the Edit button, and Address Book saves the edits.**

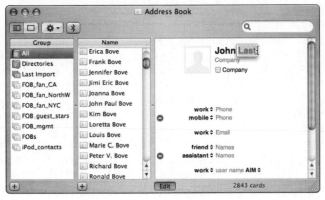

Figure 25-5:
Add
information
to a new
card in
Address
Book.

To edit a card, select the person in the Name pane and click the Edit button. To save your changes, click the Edit button again, and Address Book saves the edits.

You can also add new people to your address book from the Mail program by selecting an e-mail message and choosing Message➪Add Sender to Address Book. You can then open Address Book, click the name in the Name pane, and click the Edit button to edit the person's card. Choosing Add to Address Book in the Mail program From field's contextual menu adds the address and opens the card for editing in Address Book.

If you receive a vCard as an e-mail attachment (with the `.vcf` extension), you can simply drag the attachment to your Address Book window to add the vCard to your address book. Wouldn't it be nice if all your friends sent you vCards to keep you up to date, and you never had to retype the information?

Be careful with vCards from unknown persons — vCards can carry viruses.

Merging cards

One of the coolest features of Address Book is its ability to merge cards. You might occasionally end up with multiple cards for the same person in Address Book, typically by saving the sender's e-mail address from the Mail application while also dragging a vCard from the same person. To fix that, you can hold down Shift and click cards in the Name pane to select the ones that you want to combine. Then choose Card⇔Merge Cards. Address Book creates a new card that combines all the unique information. You can then delete the excess cards.

Searching in Address Book

Can't find the person you're looking for? Address Book lets you search for any text in any of the text boxes of any card. If you're searching for a person, and all you have is part of a phone number or even just part of the person's name, type the text in the Search text box at the top-right corner of the Address Book window. As you type, Address Book displays the names of the people who have the text fragment anywhere in their cards. Address Book searches all the information on the cards, including the Notes text box, and it searches *fast,* displaying names immediately. If more than one matching card is found, click the arrow buttons at the bottom of the window to switch between the cards. Or, choose View⇔Card And Columns to see a list of all the cards. To see all your cards again, delete the text from the Search text box.

Managing contacts in groups

You can combine address cards in Address Book into a *group* to make it easy to select all the addresses at once. For example, you might want to group together all your local friends or all your co-workers. You can then send an e-mail to all of them at once by choosing the group as the e-mail recipient.

You can also use a group to keep track of a subset of contacts. For example, you might want only a subset of your contact list on your iPod rather than the entire list. To do this, create a group for the subset of contacts and export the group as a single vCard file that you can then use on your iPod.

To create a group of contacts in Address Book

1. **Click the plus (+) sign at the bottom of the Group pane.**

   Address Book creates a new entry in the Group column with a high-lighted text box so that you can type a new name for the group.

2. **Type a name for the group.**

3. **Select the All item in the Group pane to see your entire list of names.**

4. **Drag and drop names over the group name to add them to your new group.**

After creating a new group, you can see the names in the group by clicking the group name in the Group pane. Select the All item in the Group pane to see all the names in the address book.

To put your addresses on the iPod, you can export a vCard file to the iPod Contacts folder or use iTunes, as we describe in Chapter 26.

Storing Contacts in Microsoft Address Book or Outlook

Microsoft Outlook, provided with the Windows version of Microsoft Office, provides extensive features for managing contacts with e-mail and address information. You can also import address books and contact information into Outlook from programs such as Eudora, Lotus Organizer, Netscape Messenger, Microsoft Mail, or Microsoft Schedule+.

Outlook actually uses another application, Microsoft Address Book, to store the contact information. Microsoft Address Book lets you gather address books from other sources, including Microsoft Exchange Server and Internet directory services (depending on how you've set up Outlook). It also includes all the contacts in your Outlook Contacts folder. When you update the information in your Outlook Contacts folder, the Microsoft Address Book is updated as well, so you can make all your changes in the Outlook Contacts folder.

To create a contact in Outlook, which saves the contact information in Microsoft Address Book, launch Outlook and then follow these steps:

1. **Click the Contacts icon to open the Contacts folder.**

   The Contacts icon appears in the Outlook Shortcuts pane on the left of the Outlook display; refer to Figure 25-3.

2. **Choose New⇨Contact, and then type a name for the contact.**

   The Contact window appears (Windows version). To enter multiple entries for a text box, such as more than one physical address or e-mail address, click the down-arrow next to the text box to display more lines for that text box. Enter all the information you want (or as little as you want).

3. **Click Save and Close to save the contact.**

   Your contacts are displayed in the Contact window of Outlook.

You can also create a new contact automatically for the sender of an e-mail message that you receive. Open the e-mail message, and in the From text box, right-click the name that you want to add to your Contacts folder, and then choose Add to Contacts.

You can export the contact information from Microsoft Outlook (and Microsoft Address Book) to your iPod, and for more on that, flip to Chapter 26.

Chapter 26

Synchronizing Information with Your iPod

*W*e chose the iPod for music, but we also find it useful while traveling for viewing the personal information — contacts, appointments, events, and To-Do tasks — that we manage on our computers.

If you've already read Chapter 25, you know how to manage your calendar activities and your contacts on your computer. In fact, you're probably knee-deep in vCards (virtual business cards) for your Address Book, and the calendars in your vCalendar files look like they were drawn up in the West Wing. Information changes often, and new information accumulates quickly, but you're well armed with an iPod that can be kept up to date. This chapter shows you how to *synchronize* your iPod to have all the information that you need for viewing and playback. We also show you how to simply copy the information to your iPod to update it.

Synchronizing with Mac Calendars and Contacts

Chances are that you make a lot of changes to addresses, phone numbers, calendar events, and To-Do lists on your Mac. Even though you can update your iPod with this information manually, remembering to copy each file you need is difficult. iTunes version 4.8 and newer versions can perform this function automatically and keep all your information updated on your iPod.

To synchronize your iPod with calendars in iCal on a Mac, follow these steps:

1. **Connect your iPod to the Mac.**

   iTunes launches automatically.

2. **Select the iPod name in the iTunes Source pane.**

3. **Click the iPod Options button on the bottom-right side of the iTunes window, or click the iPod button in the iTunes Preferences window.**

   The iPod Options button appears only when an iPod is connected and selected in the Source pane. You can also choose iTunes➪Preferences and click the iPod button — whether or not the iPod is selected in the Source pane (although it has to be connected). The iPod preferences pane appears.

4. **Click the Calendars button to view the iPod Calendars preferences.**

   The iPod Calendars preferences pane appears, as shown in Figure 26-1.

Figure 26-1:
Set your
iPod to
synchronize
with iCal
calendars
on a Mac.

5. **Select the "Synchronize iCal calendars" option.**

   A check mark appears next to the option after you select it.

6. **Select the "Synchronize all calendars" option, or select the "Synchronize selected calendars only" option and pick calendars to synchronize.**

   You can synchronize all calendars in iCal, or just those you click to add a check mark.

After setting the iPod Calendars preferences, every time you connect your iPod, iTunes goes to work synchronizing your iPod with your calendars automatically.

To synchronize your iPod with contacts in Address Book on a Mac, follow these steps:

1. **Connect your iPod to the Mac.**

   iTunes launches automatically.

2. **Select the iPod name in the iTunes Source pane.**

3. **Click the iPod Options button on the bottom-right side of the iTunes window, or click the iPod button in the iTunes Preferences window.**

4. **Click the Contacts button to view the iPod Contacts preferences.**

   The iPod Contacts preferences pane appears, as shown in Figure 26-2.

Figure 26-2:
Set your iPod to synchronize with a group of contacts in Address Book on a Mac.

5. **Select the "Synchronize Address Book contacts" option.**

   A check mark appears next to the option after you select it.

6. **Select the "Synchronize all contacts" option, or select the "Synchronize selected groups only" option and pick groups to synchronize.**

   You can synchronize all contacts in Address Book, or just groups of contacts by clicking to add a check mark to each group.

After setting the iPod Contacts preferences, every time you connect your iPod, iTunes synchronizes your iPod with your Address Book contacts automatically.

After you finish synchronizing and otherwise using your iPod with your Mac, be sure to eject the iPod (by dragging the iPod icon to the Trash, or in OS X 10.3 or newer, by clicking the Eject icon next to the iPod icon in the Finder Sidebar) before disconnecting it. If you forget this, your iPod's hard drive might freeze up, and you might need to reset your iPod — find out how in Chapter 1.

After updating and ejecting the iPod, you can view your addresses and phone numbers by choosing Extras⇨Contacts, and then choosing a name.

You can look at your calendars by choosing Extras⇨Calendars, and then choosing a calendar or All. Use the scroll wheel to scroll through the days of the calendar, and the Select button to select a day. You can then use the Select button to select an event to see the event's details. Use the Next and Previous buttons to skip to the next or previous month. To see your To-Do list, choose Extras⇨Calendars⇨To Do.

If your calendar events use alarms, you can turn on the iPod's calendar alarms. Choose Extras⇨Calendars and select Alarms in the Calendars menu once to set the alarm to Beep, or once again to set it to Silent (so that only the message for the alarm appears), or one more time to set it to Off. The Alarms choices cycle from Beep to Silent to Off and then back to Beep.

Synchronizing Microsoft Outlook (Windows)

Third-party programs are available for Windows iPod users that will automatically synchronize your iPod with contacts and calendar info from Microsoft Outlook.

For example, iPodSync (available at `http://www.ipod-sync.com/`) is a utility for Windows that lets you keep your Outlook calendar, contacts, and To-Do tasks synchronized between your PC and your iPod.

iPodSync displays a row of icons along the top of its window. The icons represent different types of information that you can synchronize with your iPod. These include contacts from the Outlook Contacts folder (Microsoft Address Book), calendar appointments and events from the Outlook Calendar, and To-Do tasks from Outlook Tasks. Click an icon to choose the type of information (such as Contacts), and then modify your choice with the options available (such as including birthdays in the notes field for contacts). When everything is set, click the Sync iPod button to automatically synchronize your iPod. iPodSync exports contacts into a single vCard file for your iPod Contacts folder and exports calendar information for the iPod Calendar folder.

Outlook can export contacts and calendar information, but it's a tedious process of exporting each contact and appointment individually. This failing of Outlook opens a window of opportunity for entrepreneurs, and several utilities and applications provide a way to export contacts and calendar data all at once. The following are samples of enterprising shareware utilities:

- ✔ **OutPod** at `http://outpod.stoer.de`. This utility lets you export contact and calendar information in bulk from Microsoft Outlook to vCard and vCalendar files, which you can then drag to the iPod, as we describe in "Adding Calendars Manually" and "Adding Contacts Manually" in this chapter.

- ✔ **EphPod** at `www.ephpod.com`. This utility lets you update your iPod with contacts from Outlook. EphPod is a full-featured Windows application that you can use in place of MusicMatch Jukebox. It supports standard WinAmp (`.m3u`) playlists and can synchronize the iPod with a library of music files. It imports Microsoft Outlook contacts and lets you create and edit your own contacts. EphPod can also download the latest news, weather, eBooks, and movie listings to an iPod. If you're using MusicMatch, a companion Web site is available at `www.dummies.com/go/ipod`.

Adding Calendars Manually

If you use your iPod as a hard drive, as we describe in Chapter 23, you can copy calendar files directly to the Calendars folder on your iPod. You can copy industry-standard iCalendar or vCalendar files, which can be exported by many applications including Microsoft Entourage, Microsoft Outlook, and Palm Desktop.

In most cases, you can drag an iCalendar file (with the filename extension .ics) or a vCalendar file (with the filename extension .vcs) to your iPod Calendars folder. For example, you can copy iCalendar files saved from Microsoft Outlook into the Calendars folder using Windows Explorer, as shown in Figure 26-3.

Figure 26-3:
Copy exported calendars in the iCalendar format to the Calendars folder on the iPod.

To save calendar information in the iCalendar format from Microsoft Outlook, you must save each appointment separately as an ICS (iCalendar) file. Select the appointment in the calendar view or open the appointment by double-clicking it. Use the Save As command and select iCalendar from the Save As Type pop-up menu, and then select a destination for the ICS file. The destination can be a folder on your hard drive, or it can be the iPod's Calendars folder. If you select a folder on your hard drive, be sure to copy the files to the iPod's Calendars folder.

Some applications, such as Microsoft Entourage for the Mac, don't offer a convenient way to export calendar information (except perhaps by dragging each appointment or event onto the desktop). However, iCal for the Mac can import Entourage calendars, so you can import into iCal (choose File⇨Import), and then use iTunes to synchronize your iPod, as we describe earlier in this chapter.

You can look at your calendars on the iPod by choosing Extras⇨Calendars⇨All. Select a calendar and then use the scroll wheel to scroll through the days of the calendar, or select an event to see the event's details. Press the Next and Previous buttons to skip to the next or previous month. To see your To-Do list, choose Extras⇨Calendars⇨To Do.

To remove a calendar from your iPod, connect the iPod to your computer and enable the iPod as a hard drive; see Chapter 23. You can then open the Calendars folder on the iPod and delete the calendar file. You can also copy calendar files from the iPod to your hard drive.

Adding Contacts Manually

If you use your iPod as a hard drive, as we describe in Chapter 23, you can copy contacts in vCard files directly to the Contacts folder on your iPod.

A vCard, or *virtual card,* is a standard format for exchanging personal information. The iPod sorts and displays contacts in the vCard format — you can use separate vCard files for each person or use a group vCard file that contains records for many people.

After enabling the iPod as a hard drive, simply export your contacts as vCards directly into the Contacts folder of your iPod. In most cases, you can drag vCard-formatted contacts from the application's address book to the iPod Contacts folder.

You can copy one card, a group of cards, or even the entire list as a vCard file (with a .vcf extension) by dragging the vCard file into the Contacts folder. Contacts must be in the vCard format to use with the iPod.

You can use applications to export vCard files directly to your iPod. For example, in Microsoft Outlook, you can export a vCard file for a contact directly into your iPod's Contacts folder by following these steps:

1. **Choose File⇨Export to vCard.**

2. **Use the Save In drop-down menu in the dialog to select the iPod as the destination drive.**

3. **Then select the Contacts folder to save the contacts file.**

As of this writing, the iPod supports only a portion of what you can put into a vCard. For example, you can include photos and sounds in vCards used by other applications, but you can't open up those portions of the vCard by using the iPod.

Using Utilities to Copy Files and Music

The iPod has spawned a thriving industry of third-party accessories and products. Some of the most useful products are utility programs that expand the capabilities of the iPod or your ability to update the iPod, and even full-featured programs that are designed as replacements for iTunes and MusicMatch Jukebox. With so many programs to check out, you might be overwhelmed. We've selected three of the best programs for the Mac and Windows (as of this writing). Again, if using MusicMatch, see this book's companion Web site at www.dummies.com/go/ipod.

Keep in mind, with programs that allow music copying functions, that copying copyrighted material to other computers without permission is illegal. Don't steal music — or anything else, for that matter.

Mac utilities

On the Mac, third-party offerings have focused on extending the capabilities of the iPod and its software to do things like copying music from the iPod to the computer and updating the iPod with contacts and calendar information. Take a glance at the following examples:

- ✔ **iPod It** at www.zapptek.com/ipod-it/. With this software, you can transfer personal information to your iPod from Entourage, Stickies, Mail, Address Book, and iCal. You can even download weather forecasts and news headlines directly to your iPod.

- ✔ **iPod Access** at www.findleydesigns.com/ipodaccess. This utility lets you transfer songs from an iPod to a Mac. iPod Access is available from Findley Designs, Inc.

- ✔ **iPodRip** at www.thelittleappfactory.com/software/ipodrip.php. This third-party utility, available from The Little App Factory, lets you transfer music from your iPod back to your iTunes library and listen to music on your iPod through your computer (saving hard drive space). It supports all iPod song formats including MP3, AAC, Protected AAC, and Audible.com books.

Windows utilities

On Windows, third-party offerings fill a void left by the lack of synchronization capabilities in iTunes that work with Microsoft Outlook. Lots more third-party programs exist for Windows, and they do everything from extending the capabilities of the iPod and updating contacts and calendar information to replacing the need for MusicMatch Jukebox and iTunes.

✔ **iPodSync** at `www.ipod-sync.com/`. Keep Microsoft Outlook calendars, contacts, tasks, and notes synchronized between a Windows PC and an iPod. iPodSync exports industry standard vCards for contacts, and uses the iCalendar format for appointment information. iPodSync can even synchronize Outlook notes and tasks. For more information, see the iPodSync Web site.

✔ **EphPod 2** at `www.ephpod.com`. This shareware utility lets you update your iPod with contacts from Outlook. It's a full-featured Windows application that can be used in place of MusicMatch Jukebox or iTunes. It supports standard WinAmp (`m3u`) playlists and can synchronize the iPod with a library of music files. It imports Microsoft Outlook contacts and also lets you create and edit your own contacts. EphPod can also download the latest news, weather, e-books, and movie listings to an iPod.

✔ **XPlay 2** at `www.mediafour.com/products/xplay`. This utility, from Mediafour Corp., provides read and write access to your iPod hard drive for documents and data files, plus the ability to organize your music from the Explorer-based XPlay interface or from Windows Media Player, as an alternative to MusicMatch Jukebox or iTunes. XPlay makes your iPod appear as a normal drive under Windows for the sharing of data files, and it makes your songs, playlists, artists, and albums appear in custom folders in Explorer, so they're easy to access and manipulate and organized similarly to how the iPod organizes them. XPlay is available from Mediafour Corp.

Chapter 27

Updating and Troubleshooting

· ·

In This Chapter

▶ Your first steps for troubleshooting iPod problems

▶ Updating the iPod system software and firmware for Mac or Windows

▶ Restoring an iPod to its original factory condition and settings

· ·

*T*his chapter describes some of the problems that you might encounter with your iPod and computer and how to fix them. If your iPod fails to turn on, or if your computer fails to recognize it, you can most likely find a solution here.

This chapter also covers updating the firmware and software on your iPod, and restoring your iPod to its factory default condition. (*Firmware* is software encoded in hardware.) That last option is a drastic measure that erases any music or information on the iPod, but it usually solves the problem if nothing else does.

First Troubleshooting Steps

Problems can arise with electronics and software that can prevent the iPod from turning on at all or from turning on properly with all its music and playlists. You can also have problems in the connection between your iPod and your computer.

When you turn on your iPod, built-in startup diagnostic software checks the iPod hard drive for damage and attempts to repair it if necessary. If the iPod finds an issue when it is turned on, it automatically uses internal diagnostics to check for and repair any damage. You might see a disk scan icon on your iPod screen after turning it on, indicating that a problem was fixed. If this happens, update your iPod firmware and software, as we describe in "Updating the iPod with the iPod Updater," later in this chapter.

Checking the Hold switch

If your iPod refuses to turn on, check the position of the Hold switch on top of the iPod. The Hold switch locks the iPod buttons so that you don't accidentally activate them. Slide the Hold switch away from the headphone connection, hiding the orange layer, to unlock the buttons. (If you see the orange layer underneath one end of the Hold switch, the switch is still in the locked position.)

Checking the power

Got power? The battery might not be charged enough. If the battery is too low for normal operation, the iPod doesn't turn on. Instead, a low battery screen appears for about three seconds, and then disappears. At that point, your only choice is to connect the iPod to an AC power source, wait for a moment, and then turn the power on by pushing any button on the iPod. If your source of AC power is your computer (using the FireWire connection), make sure that the computer is on and not set to go to sleep. The battery icon in the upper-right corner of the display indicates whether it's full or recharging. For more information about maintaining a healthy battery, see Chapter 1.

If your iPod shuffle doesn't turn on or respond, recharge its battery by connecting it to the USB connection on your computer.

Resetting the iPod

This operation resets the operating system of the iPod and restarts the system. Sometimes when your iPod gets confused or refuses to turn on, you can fix it by resetting it.

For current fourth-generation iPod models including iPod mini, iPod U2 Special Edition, and color-display iPod, follow these steps:

1. **Connect the iPod to a power outlet using the AC power adapter.**
2. **Toggle the Hold switch.**

   Push the Hold switch to hold (lock), and then set it back to unlock.
3. **Press the Menu and Select buttons simultaneously and hold for at least six seconds or until the Apple logo appears; then release the buttons when you see the Apple logo.**

   The appearance of the Apple logo signals that your iPod is resetting itself, so you no longer have to hold down the buttons.

It's important to release the Menu and Select buttons as soon as you see the Apple logo. If you continue to hold down the buttons after the logo appears, the iPod displays the low battery icon, and you must connect it to a power source before using your iPod again.

For first, second, and third generation iPod models, follow these steps:

1. **Connect the iPod to a power outlet using the AC power adapter.**

2. **Toggle the Hold switch.**

   Push the Hold switch to hold (lock), and then set it back to unlock.

3. **Press the Menu and Play/Pause buttons simultaneously and hold for at least five seconds until the Apple logo appears; then release the buttons when you see the Apple logo.**

   The appearance of the Apple logo signals that your iPod is resetting itself, so you no longer have to hold down the buttons.

It's important to release the Menu and Play/Pause buttons as soon as you see the Apple logo. If you continue to hold down the buttons after the logo appears, the iPod displays the low battery icon, and you must connect it to a power source before using your iPod again.

To reset your iPod shuffle, disconnect it from a computer, switch the slider on the back to the Off position — the green stripe under the switch should not visible. Wait five seconds, and then switch the slider back to the Shuffle songs or Play in order position.

After resetting, everything should be back to normal, including your music and data files.

Draining the iPod battery

Certain types of battery-powered devices sometimes run into problems if the battery hasn't drained in a while. In rare cases, the iPod might go dark and can't be reset until the battery is drained. If the above steps didn't resolve the issue, disconnect the iPod from any power source and leave it disconnected for approximately 24 hours. After this period, connect it to power and reset.

Try to keep the iPod at room temperature — generally near 68 degrees Fahrenheit (20 degrees Celsius), but you can use iPod anywhere between 50 to 95 degrees Fahrenheit (10 and 35 degrees Celsius). If you have left the iPod in the cold, let it warm up to room temperature before waking it from sleep. Otherwise, a low-battery icon might appear, and the iPod won't wake up properly. If the iPod doesn't wake from sleep after warming up, connect the power adapter and reset the iPod, as we describe in the previous section.

Hitting the panic button

Actually it's never a good idea to hit the panic button, even if there is one, but if you have tried the solutions above and your iPod still doesn't turn on, check the following:

- ✔ Make sure that the iPod is the only device in your FireWire or USB chain. Although you can connect a FireWire or USB device to another FireWire or USB device that has a connection, forming a chain, it isn't a good idea to do this with an iPod.

- ✔ Make sure that you use the FireWire or USB cable that came with your iPod and that the cable is in good condition.

- ✔ Try connecting the iPod to the built-in FireWire or USB connection of a different computer to see if the symptom persists.

If, after turning on the iPod, all you see on the display is the Apple logo and iPod name, and the device seems to be restarting over and over, try force-enabling your iPod as a hard drive. (This is also known as "putting your iPod into Disk Mode.")

For current fourth-generation iPod models including iPod mini, iPod U2 Special Edition, and color-display iPod, follow these steps:

1. **Be sure your iPod is charged with power.**

   If your iPod needs to be recharged, connect it to a power source as described in Chapter 1.

2. **Reset the iPod as described in "Resetting the iPod," earlier in this chapter.**

3. **When the Apple icon appears on the display, immediately press and hold the Select and Play/Pause buttons until** `Disk Mode` **appears on the iPod display.**

4. **If your iPod isn't connected to your computer, disconnect the iPod from the power adapter and connect it to your computer.**

   You can now use the iPod Updater to update or restore the iPod — see "Using iPod Updater" later in this chapter.

If the "Disk Mode" message doesn't appear, repeat Steps 2 and 3. (You might need to press the buttons more quickly.) If, after repeating these steps, the message still doesn't appear, the iPod might need to be repaired.

For first-, second-, and third-generation iPod models, follow these steps:

1. **Connect the iPod to your computer's FireWire or powered USB connection, or to an AC power adapter.**

   This procedure doesn't work with older USB connections that don't provide power. Make sure the computer is on and isn't set to go to sleep.

2. **Reset the iPod as described in "Resetting the iPod," earlier in this chapter.**

3. **When the Apple icon appears on the display, immediately press and hold the Previous and Next buttons until the** Do not disconnect **message or FireWire icon appears.**

4. **If your iPod isn't connected to your computer, disconnect the iPod from the power adapter and connect it to your computer.**

   Some iPods show the message OK to Disconnect before you connect it to the computer. This changes to the Do not disconnect message after connecting.

   You can now use the iPod Updater to update or restore the iPod — see "Using iPod Updater" later in this chapter.

If the Do not disconnect message or FireWire icon doesn't appear, repeat Steps 2 and 3. (You might need to press the buttons more quickly.) If, after repeating these steps, the message or FireWire icon still doesn't appear, the iPod might need to be repaired.

After using the iPod in Disk Mode, you need to reset the iPod (described in "Resetting the iPod" earlier in this chapter) to return your iPod to normal operation.

You can get more information, updated troubleshooting instructions, and links to the iPod repair site by visiting the Apple support site for the iPod (www.apple.com/support/ipod/).

Using iPod Updater

The iPod Updater can update the system software that controls the iPod and can also update the firmware for the iPod's hard drive, if necessary. The update doesn't affect the music or data stored on iPod's drive. iPod Updater is provided on the CD-ROM that comes with your iPod. To find out whether a new version is available for downloading, go to the Apple Web page for the iPod (www.apple.com/ipod).

If you use MusicMatch Jukebox rather than iTunes on your Windows PC, skip this and see this book's companion Web site at www.dummies.com/go/ipod.

If you use a Mac and you've turned on the Software Update option in your System Preferences, Apple automatically informs you of updates to your Apple software for the Mac, including iTunes, iCal, Address Book, and the iPod system software. All you need to do is select which updates to download and click the Install button to download them.

Before downloading the iPod Updater from the Apple Web site, make sure that you pick the appropriate version — Mac or Windows. The iPod Updater includes updates for all generations of iPods and can detect which iPod you have.

Updating the iPod with iPod Updater

Be sure that your iPod has the most recent iPod firmware update installed. To determine which version of the iPod software is installed on your iPod, press the Menu button until you see the iPod main menu, and then choose Settings➪About. (With first-generation and second-generation iPods, choose Settings➪Info.) You see information next to the word Version that describes the software version installed on the iPod.

You can also determine the software version on your iPod by using iPod Updater. Connect the iPod to your computer and launch iPod Updater. The iPod Updater window appears. The software version appears next to the Software Version heading. If this version of the iPod Updater application has a newer software version that it can install on the iPod, you see (needs update) next to the version number. If not, you see (up to date).

To update the iPod's firmware and software, follow these steps for both the Mac and Windows versions:

1. **Connect the iPod to your computer.**

    iTunes opens, and if you set your iPod for automatic update, iTunes synchronizes the iPod with music and playlists from its library. The iTunes display notifies you when the iTunes music update is complete.

2. **Quit iTunes.**

    On a Mac, quit by choosing iTunes➪Quit iTunes. On a Windows PC, choose File➪Exit.

3. **Launch the iPod Updater application.**

    On a Mac, this application is located in the Utilities folder, which is in your Applications folder. On a Windows PC, you can find it under iPod in the Start menu. The Updater dialog appears, as shown in Figure 27-1 (Windows version).

Figure 27-1:
The iPod
Updater
utility lets
you update
or restore
your iPod.

4. **Click the Update button.**

   (In Mac OS X, you might need to click the padlock and type an administrator account name and password first.) If the Update button is grayed out, the software on the iPod is the same version or a newer version than the iPod Updater application.

   Note: The Update button is grayed out if the iPod isn't properly formatted for Windows. It may be formatted for a Mac. You must use the Restore button and restore the iPod to its original factory condition, erasing all music and data, to reformat it for Windows.

5. **Follow the instructions to disconnect your iPod and connect it to an AC power adapter, if required.**

   Some iPod models need to be disconnected temporarily and connected to an AC power adapter during the process of updating the software; others do not. If you see a message asking you to disconnect the iPod, follow the instructions displayed with the message. Some iPod models also need to be reconnected to the computer after this process.

   The iPod Updater notifies you when the update is finished, and the Update button is grayed-out, indicating that your iPod no longer needs an update.

6. **When the update is finished, quit iPod Updater.**

   On a Mac, you can quit by choosing iPod Updater➪Quit iPod Updater. On a Windows PC, quit by clicking the dialog's Close button. Refer to Figure 27-1.

7. **Eject the iPod.**

   When you quit iPod Updater, iTunes might launch again because your iPod is still connected. You can eject the iPod by clicking the iPod Eject button in iTunes.

   If iTunes doesn't launch, you can eject the iPod on a Mac clicking the Eject button next to the iPod name in the Finder or by dragging the iPod icon to the Trash. On a Windows PC, right-click the iPod name or icon and choose Eject from the shortcut menu.

After ejecting the iPod, wait for its display to show the main menu or the OK to disconnect message. You can then disconnect the iPod from its dock or disconnect the dock from the computer. Don't ever disconnect an iPod before ejecting it. You might have to reset your iPod, which we describe earlier in this chapter.

Restoring an iPod with iPod Updater

Restoring the iPod erases the iPod's hard drive and restores the device to its original factory settings, so make sure that you back up any important data that you keep stored on your iPod. To replace music that was erased by the restore operation, synchronize or update your iPod from your computer's music library, as we describe in Chapter 10.

To restore an iPod, follow these steps for both the Mac and Windows versions:

1. **Connect the iPod to your computer.**

   If your iPod is working, iTunes opens, and if you set your iPod for automatic update, iTunes synchronizes the iPod with music and playlists from its library. The iTunes display notifies you when the iTunes music update is complete. If your iPod isn't working, skip to Step 3.

2. **Quit iTunes.**

   On a Mac, quit by choosing iTunes⇨Quit iTunes. On a Windows PC, choose File⇨Exit.

3. **Launch the iPod Updater application.**

   On a Mac, this application is located in the Utilities folder, which is in your Applications folder. On a Windows PC, you can find it under iPod on the Start menu. The Updater dialog appears; refer to Figure 27-1.

4. **Click the Restore button.**

   (In Mac OS X, you might need to click the padlock and type an administrator account name and password first.) An alert dialog appears to confirm you want to restore iPod.

5. **Click the Restore button to confirm the restore operation.**

   A progress bar appears, indicating the progress of the restore operation.

6. **Follow the instructions to disconnect your iPod and connect it to an AC power adapter, if required.**

   Some iPod models need to be disconnected temporarily and connected to an AC power adapter after the restore operation and during the process of updating the software; others do not. If you see a message asking you to disconnect the iPod, follow the instructions displayed with the message. Some iPod models also need to be reconnected to the computer after this process.

The iPod Updater notifies you when the restore is finished, and the Update button is grayed out, indicating that your iPod no longer needs an update.

7. When the restore operation is finished, quit iPod Updater.

On a Mac, you can quit by choosing iPod Updater⇨Quit iPod Updater. On a Windows PC, quit by clicking the dialog's Close button. Refer to Figure 27-1.

8. Set up your iPod by using the iTunes Setup Assistant.

In the iTunes Setup Assistant dialog, type a name for iPod in the space provided, and then proceed with setting up iTunes with your iPod, as we describe in Chapter 2.

9. Quit iTunes Setup Assistant, and update your iPod from your music library.

When you quit iTunes Setup Assistant, iTunes might launch again because your iPod is still connected. You can use this opportunity to update your iPod with the music in your library, as we describe in Chapter 10. You can also copy data to the iPod while it's mounted as a hard drive; see Chapter 23.

10. When you're finished updating the iPod with music and data, eject the iPod.

You can eject the iPod by using the iPod Eject button in iTunes.

If iTunes doesn't launch, you can eject the iPod on a Mac by clicking the Eject button next to the iPod name in a Finder window Sidebar or by dragging the iPod icon to the Trash icon (which turns into an Eject icon). On a Windows PC, right-click the iPod name or icon and choose Eject from the shortcut menu.

Part VI
The Part of Tens

The 5th Wave   By Rich Tennant

"He stepped outside, said he wanted to listen to his iPod on the way home, but then accidentally pulled out his iLightning Rod instead."

In this part . . .

In this part, you find two chapters chock full of information.

- ✔ Chapter 28 offers 10 common iPod problems and their solutions.
- ✔ Chapter 29 provides 11 tips on using the equalizer.

Chapter 28

Ten iPod Solutions

*U*nfortunately, humans and the machines they make are not perfect. Even though we think the iPod comes as close to perfection as possible, at some point your iPod isn't going to work as you expect it to. When that happens, turn to this chapter. Here we show you how to fix the most common problems.

How Do I Get My iPod to Wake Up?

If your iPod doesn't turn on, don't panic — at least not yet. Try the following suggestions to get your iPod to respond:

- ✔ **Check the Hold switch's position on top of the iPod.** The Hold switch locks the iPod buttons so you don't accidentally activate them. Slide the Hold switch away from the headphone connection, hiding the orange layer, to unlock the buttons.

- ✔ **See whether the iPod has enough juice.** Is the battery charged up? Connect the iPod to a power source and see whether it works.

- ✔ **Reset your iPod if the iPod still doesn't turn on.** See Chapter 27 for resetting instructions.

If your iPod shuffle doesn't turn on or respond, recharge its battery by connecting it to the USB connection on your computer. If the iPod shuffle status light blinks orange when you press a button, it means the buttons are disabled. Press and hold the Play/Pause button for at least three seconds or until the status light blinks green.

How Do I Get My Battery to Last Longer?

You can do a lot to keep your battery going longer (much to the envy of your friends), including the following:

- **Press the Play/Pause button to pause (stop) playback.** Don't just turn off your car or home stereo or take out your headphones — if you don't also pause playback, your iPod continues playing until the playlist or album ends. When playback is paused, the power-save feature turns off the iPod after two minutes of inactivity.

- **Hold down the Play/Pause button to turn off the iPod when not using it.** Rather than wait for two minutes of inactivity for the power-save feature to turn off the iPod, you can turn it off yourself and save battery time.

- **Turn off the backlighting.** If you don't need to use backlighting, turn it off. It can drain the power.

- **Avoid changing tracks by pressing the Previous/Rewind or Next/Fast-Forward buttons.** The iPod uses a memory cache to load and play songs. If you frequently change tracks by pressing the Previous or Next buttons, the cache has to turn on the hard drive to load and play the songs, which drains the battery.

- **Use compressed AAC or MP3 files.** Playing larger uncompressed AIFF or WAV files takes more power because the hard drive inside the iPod has to refresh its memory buffers more frequently to process more information as the song plays. Apple Lossless files, though compressed, also deplete battery power a bit more than AAC or MP3 files.

How Do I Keep My Scroll Wheel from Going Crazy?

Second-generation and third-generation iPods use a nonmoving scroll wheel that works like the *trackpad* (also sometimes called a *touchpad*) of a laptop computer. Although the trackpad-style scroll wheel is far better than the first-generation moving wheel (which could be hampered by sand or dirt and had moving parts that could be damaged), it has problems of its own: it goes crazy sometimes, and it can be very sensitive — not sensitive to criticism, but to the touch of your finger.

The trackpad-style scroll wheel translates the electrical charge from your finger into movement on the iPod display. If you use more than one finger or have another finger nearby, the scroll wheel might detect the signal and skip over selections or go backwards while scrolling forwards, and so on. If the scroll wheel has excessive moisture on it, from humidity or a wet hand, wipe the wheel with a soft, dry cloth.

Don't use lotion or moisturizer on your hand right before touching the scroll wheel. Don't use pencil erasers, pen caps, or other types of pointers to scroll the scroll wheel. (They won't work with trackpad-style scroll wheels and may damage other types of scroll wheels.) Don't use your ring finger or the hand that sports a heavy bracelet or similar jewelry — these can throw off the sensors in the scroll wheel.

How Do I Get My Computer to Recognize My iPod?

Follow the first troubleshooting steps outlined in Chapter 27. If iTunes or MusicMatch Jukebox still does not recognize the iPod, you can use the iPod Updater to restore the iPod. (If you're using MusicMatch, a companion Web site is available at www.dummies.com/go/ipod.)

Also, make sure that your FireWire or USB cable is in good condition. For iPods that work with either FireWire or USB, try one type of connection or the other; if one connection type works, but not the other, the problem is probably not in your iPod. Try connecting your iPod to another computer by using the same type of connection to see whether the same problem occurs. (Your computer might be to blame.) If the same type of connection (FireWire or USB) to the other computer works, the problem is most likely your computer's connection or software. If it doesn't work, the problem is most likely your cable or connection. You can try a new cable to see whether that works.

What Do I Do if a Strange Icon Appears on My iPod?

When you turn on your iPod, built-in diagnostic software checks the iPod hard drive. If the iPod finds a problem when it's turned on, it automatically uses internal diagnostics to check for and repair any damage. You might see a disk scan icon on your iPod screen after turning it on, indicating that a problem was fixed. If this happens, restore your iPod to its original factory condition (see Chapter 27), and load it again with music.

If the iPod displays any other strange icon, such as a backwards Apple logo, a disk icon with a flashing question mark, or the dreaded disk-with-magnifying glass icon, it might need to be repaired. You can arrange for repair by visiting the Apple support site for the iPod (www.apple.com/support/ipod).

How Do I Restore My iPod to its Original Condition from the Factory?

Restoring the iPod erases your iPod's hard drive and returns the device to its original factory condition. Restore erases all of the data on the hard drive, so make sure that you back up any important data that you have stored on your iPod. You can use the iPod Updater utility to restore your iPod, as we describe in Chapter 27. When finished, add music back to your iPod from the iTunes library or from your MusicMatch Jukebox library, and then resynchronize your iPod with calendar and contact information. (If you're using MusicMatch, a companion Web site is available at www.dummies.com/go/ipod.)

How Do I Update My iPod to Have the Newest Software?

To determine which version of the iPod software is installed on your iPod, press the Menu button until you see the iPod main menu, and then choose Settings⇨About (in earlier versions, choose Settings⇨Info). Look at the version number that describes the software version installed on your iPod. You can use the iPod Updater application to update or restore your iPod; see Chapter 27.

How Do I Update My iPod with Music When My Library Is Larger Than My iPod's Capacity?

If you have less space on your iPod than music in your iTunes library, you can update manually (by album, artist, or songs), update automatically by selected songs only, or update automatically by playlist.

When you update by playlist automatically, you can create playlists exclusively for your iPod. A smart playlist can be limited to, for example, 18GB (for a 20GB iPod).

By combining the features of smart playlists (in Chapter 9) and updating automatically by playlist (in Chapter 10), you can control the updating process while also automatically limiting the amount of music you copy to your iPod.

You can also update automatically and keep your iPod synchronized to a subset of your library. iTunes creates a new playlist specially designed for updating your iPod automatically — a smart playlist named "*your iPod name* Selection." iTunes decides which songs and albums to include in this playlist by using the ratings that you can set for each song in the iTunes song information, as we describe in Chapter 10.

How Do I Cross-Fade Music Playback with My iPod?

You can fade the ending of one song into the beginning of the next one to slightly overlap songs, just like a radio DJ, when you use iTunes. The *cross-fade setting* is the amount of time between the end of the fade-out from the first song and the start of the fade-in to the second song.

To cross-fade songs on your iPod, you have to play your iPod songs through iTunes on your computer. Connect your iPod to your computer and connect your computer to a stereo or connect speakers (or headphones) to your computer. Hold down ⌘-Option (on a Mac) or Ctrl-Alt (on a PC) as you launch iTunes and you can then select iPod in the iTunes Source pane.

By default, iTunes is set to have a short cross-fade of one second.

If you're playing songs on an iPod that's connected to your computer and also playing songs from your iTunes library (or even on a second iPod, both connected to your computer), your songs cross-fade automatically.

You can change this cross-fade setting by choosing iTunes⇨Preferences (on a Mac) or Edit⇨Preferences (on a PC), and then clicking the Audio button. You can then increase or decrease the amount of the cross-fade with the Crossfade Playback option.

How Do I Get Less Distortion with Car and Portable Speakers?

iPod models designed for the Unites States have a powerful 60-milliwatt amplifier to deliver audio signals through the headphone connection. It has a frequency response of 20 Hz to 20 kHz, which provides distortion-free music at the lowest or highest pitches, but it might cause distortion at maximum volume depending on the recorded material.

For optimal sound quality, set the iPod volume at no more than three-quarters of the maximum volume and adjust your listening volume by using the volume control or equivalent on your car stereo or portable speaker system. (If no volume control exists, you have no choice but to control the volume from the iPod.) By lowering the iPod from maximum volume, you prevent over-amplification, which can cause distortion and reduce audio quality.

Chapter 29

Eleven Tips for the Equalizer

In This Chapter

▶ Adjusting the equalizer on your home stereo

▶ Taking advantage of the iPod's equalizer preset

▶ Getting rid of unwanted noise

*Y*ou play your iPod in many environments. The same song that sounds like music to your ears in your car might sound like screeching hyenas on a plane. In this chapter, we show you how to fix most sound problems that occur with iPods. Soon you'll be cruising to the beat all the time — no matter where you are.

Setting the Volume to the Right Level

Before using the iPod equalizer (EQ) to refine the sound, make sure the volume of the iPod is set to about half or three-quarters (not more) so that you don't introduce distortion. Then set your speaker system or home stereo volume before trying to refine the sound with equalizers.

Adjusting Another Equalizer

When you have the iPod connected to another system with an equalizer, try adjusting that equalizer:

▸ **Home stereo system:** Refine the sound with your home stereo's equalizer because it might offer more flexibility and can be set precisely for the listening environment.

▸ **Car stereos:** The same rule applies as your home stereo — adjust the car stereo's equalizer as you begin to listen to music on your iPod, before adjusting the iPod's equalizer.

Setting Booster Presets

When playing music with your iPod through a home stereo or speakers (without a built-in equalizer) in a heavily draped and furnished room, try the iPod's Treble Booster EQ preset or create your own EQ preset (see Chapter 19) that raises the frequencies above 1 kHz. Boosting these higher frequencies makes the music sound naturally alive.

Reducing High Frequencies

When using your iPod to play music through a home stereo (without a built-in equalizer) in a basement with smooth, hard walls and concrete floors, you might want to use the iPod's Treble Reducer EQ preset, which reduces the high frequencies to make the sound less brittle.

Increasing Low Frequencies

If you use high-quality acoustic-suspension compact speakers, you might need to add a boost to the low frequencies (bass) with the Bass Booster EQ preset so that you can boogie with the beat a little better. The Small Speakers EQ preset also boosts the low frequencies and lowers the high frequencies to give you a fuller sound.

Setting Presets for Trucks and SUVs

We use our iPods in different types of cars — one is a sedan; the other a 4-wheel drive truck. Trucks need more bass and treble, and the Rock EQ preset sounds good for most of the music that we listen to. We also recommend the Bass Booster EQ preset when using your iPod in a truck if the Rock preset doesn't boost the bass enough. In the sedan, the iPod sounds fine without any equalizer adjustment.

Setting Presets When You're Eight Miles High

When using your iPod on an airplane where jet noise is a factor, try using the Bass Booster EQ preset to hear the lower frequencies in your headphones and compensate for the deficiencies of headphones in loud environments. You might want to use the Classical EQ preset, which boosts both the high and low frequencies for extra treble and bass. Try the Bose QuietComfort 2 Acoustic Noise Canceling headphones (www.bose.com) for plane travel — they work great!

Reducing Tape Noise and Scratch Sounds

To reduce the hiss of an old tape recording (or the scratchy sound of songs recorded from an old vinyl record), reduce the highest frequencies with the Treble Reducer EQ preset.

Reducing Turntable Rumble and Hum

To reduce the low-frequency rumble in songs recorded from a turntable (for vinyl records) or recorded with a hum pickup, choose the Bass Reducer EQ preset.

Reducing Off-Frequency Harshness and Nasal Vocals

To reduce a particularly nasal vocal sound reminiscent of Donald Duck (caused by off-frequency recording of the song source, making the song more harsh-sounding), try the R&B EQ preset, which reduces the midrange frequencies while boosting all the other frequencies.

Cranking Up the Volume to Eleven

If you want that larger-than-life sound, use the Loudness preset, and then jack up the Preamp slider to the max, turn up your stereo all the way, and put your fingers in your ears to protect them. Then consult the DVD *This is Spinal Tap* or the Spinal Tap fan site at http://spinaltapfan.com/.

Index